Eighteen Sermons

by the Late Rev. George Whitefield

George Whitefield

APPLEWOOD BOOKS
Bedford, Massachusetts

Eighteen Sermons
was originally published in
1771

ISBN: 978-1-4290-1985-9

APPLEWOOD'S
American
Philosophy AND *Religion*
SERIES

Thank you for purchasing an Applewood book. Applewood reprints America's lively classics—books from the past that are still of interest to modern readers. This facsimile was printed using many new technologies together to bring our tradition-bound mission to you. Applewood's facsimile edition of this work may include library stamps, scribbles, and margin notes as they exist in the original book. These interesting historical artifacts celebrate the place the book was read or the person who read the book. In addition to these artifacts, the work may have additional errors that were either in the original, in the digital scans, or introduced as we prepared the book for printing. If you believe the work has such errors, please let us know by writing to us at the address below.

For a free copy of our current print catalog featuring our bestselling books, write to:

APPLEWOOD BOOKS
P.O. Box 365
Bedford, MA 01730

For more complete listings, visit us on the web at:
awb.com

Prepared for publishing by HP

EIGHTEEN
SERMONS

Preached by the late

Rev. GEORGE WHITEFIELD, A.M.

On the following SUBJECTS:

Taken verbatim in Short-Hand, and faithfully Transcribed
by JOSEPH GURNEY.

Revised by ANDREW GIFFORD, D.D.

LONDON:

Printed for and sold by JOSEPH GURNEY, Bookseller, Nº 54,
in Holborn, opposite Hatton-Street.

M.DCC.LXXI.

[Price Five Shillings in Boards.]

TO THE

RIGHT HONOURABLE

SELINA

COUNTESS DOWAGER OF

HUNTINGDON.

THESE SERMONS

ARE MOST HUMBLY INSCRIBED

BY HER LADYSHIP's

MOST DEVOTED

AND OBEDIENT

HUMBLE SERVANT

JOSEPH GURNEY.

TO THE
READER.

POfthumous publications generally need an apology. This poor Orphan's plea is, that it attempts to preferve the genuine remains of One who has inconteftibly proved himfelf the deftitute helplefs Orphan's friend yet fpeaking to a ferious auditory hanging on his lips for inftruction, and comfort, though in a fainter light, as the glorious luminary of the heavens, the ruler of the day, feems vifible, even after it is fet, by the refraction of its refplendent rays. As to its fpots, if fuch there are, let them be put down to the account of the editor.

A. G.

ERRATA.

Page 51, line 24, for *to* read *for*

  - 82, - 11 and 16, for *needy* read *naughty*

  - 220, - 10 and 11, for *ſtars* read *palms*

THE
CONTENTS.

SERMON I.

A Faithful Minifter's parting Blefling.
A Farewell Sermon, February 23, 1763.

REVEL. xxii. 21.

THE grace of our Lord Jefus Chrift be with you all. Amen. page 1

SERMON II.

CHRIST, the Believer's Refuge.
On the Death of Mr. BECKMAN.

PSALM xlvi. 1—6.

GOD *is our refuge and ftrength, a very prefent help in trouble; therefore will we not fear, though the earth be removed, and the mountains be carried into the midft of the fea, though the waters thereof roar, and be troubled, though the mountains fhake with the fwelling thereof, Selah. There is a river, the ftreams whereof fhall make glad the city of God, the holy place of the tabernacles of the Moft-High: God is in the midft of her, fhe fhall not be moved;*

b

The CONTENTS.

SER-

The CONTENTS.

The CONTENTS.

The CONTENTS.

The CONTENTS.

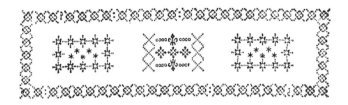

SERMON I.

A Faithful Minifter's Parting Bleffing.

REVELATIONS xxii. 21.

The grace of our Lord Jefus Chrift be with you all. Amen.

T is very remarkable that the old teftament ends with the word curfe ; whereby we are taught, that the law made nothing perfect : but bleffed be God, the new teftament ends otherwife, even a precious bleffing, that glorious grace put into the heart, and dropt by the pen of the difciple whom Jefus loved.

My brethren, as the providence of God calls us now to bid each other a long farewel, can I part from you better than in enlarging a little upon this fhort but glorious prayer ; can I wifh you,

you, or you me, better in time and eternity, than that the words of our text may be fulfilled in our hearts, *the grace of our Lord Jefus Chrift be with you all, Amen.* In opening which,

Firft, it will be proper to explain what we are to underftand by the word grace.

Secondly, what by the grace of our Lord Jefus Chrift, and its being with us all; and then to obferve upon the word Amen: fhewing you why it is that every one of us may wifh, that the grace of our Lord Jefus Chrift may be with us all.

Perhaps, there is not a word in the book of God that has a greater variety of interpretations put upon it than this little, this great word grace: I don't intend to fpin out, or wafte the time by giving you all. It will be enough in general to obferve, that the word grace fignifies favour, or may imply the general kindnefs that God bears to the world; but it fignifies that here which I pray God we may all experience, I mean the grace, the fpecial grace of the blefled God communicated to his people; not only his favour difplayed to us outwardly, but the work of the blefled Spirit imparted and conveyed inwardly and moft powerfully to our fouls, and this is what our

church

church in the catechism calls special grace;
for though Jesus Christ in one respect is the
Saviour of all, and we are to offer * Jesus
Christ universally to all, yet he is said in a
special manner to be the saviour of them that
believe; so that the word grace is a very complex word, and takes in all that the blessed
Spirit of God does for a poor sinner, from the
moment he first draws his breath, and brings
him to Jesus Christ, till he is pleased to call
him by death; and as it is begun in grace, it
will be swallowed up in an endless eternity of
glory hereafter; this is called the grace of our
Lord Jesus Christ: why so? because it is pur-
chased † for us by the Lord Jesus Christ: the
law was given by Moses, but grace and truth,
in the most emphatical manner, came by Jesus
Christ the Son of God, If it was not for the
purchase of a Mediator's blood, if it was not
that Jesus Christ had bought us with a price,
even with the price of his own blood, you and
I should never have had, you and I could never
have had the grace of God manifested at all to
our souls. The covenant of works being broken, our first parents stood convicted before
God: they were criminals, though they did

B 2   not

* Preach.   † Procured.

not care to own it; condemn'd before God,
and in themfelves, fo that like their children
they made excufes for their fin. Man by nature had but one neck, and if God had pleafed
to have done it, he might juftly have cut it off
at one blow ; but no fooner had man incurred
the curfe of the law, but behold a Mediator is
provided under the character of the feed of the
woman, which fhould bruife the ferpent's
head; implying what the Redeemer was firft
to do without, and afterwards to do in the
hearts of all his people : well therefore are we
taught in our church collects to end all our
prayers with the words, *through Jefus Chrift
our Lord.*

Moreover, brethren, this grace may be called the grace of our Lord Jefus Chrift, becaufe it is not only purchafed * by him, but
it is conveyed into our hearts through Chrift;
the federal head of his glorious body, is a head
of influence to thofe for whom he fhed his
blood : thus his difciples faid, he was full of
grace and truth, and out of his fulnefs we,
all that are true believers, receive grace for
grace ; grace upon grace, fays Mr. Blackwall,
in his Sacred Claſſicks : grace for grace, that

is,

* Procured.

is, says Luther, every grace that is in Christ
Jesus, will be by his blessed Spirit transcribed
into every believer's heart, even as the warm
wax receives the impress of the seal upon it;
as there is line upon line upon the seal left
upon the wax, so in a degree, though we come
greatly short of what the law requires, the
grace that is in Jesus Christ is, in a measure,
implanted in our souls; but the Lord Jesus
Christ, blessed be God, has our stock in his
hands. God trusted man once, but never will
more; he set Adam up, gave him a blessed
stock, placed him in a paradise of love, and he
soon became a bankrupt, some think in twenty-
four hours, however, all agree it was in six or
seven days, and that he never had but one sabbath; but now, blessed be God, we are un--
der a better dispensation, our stock is put into
Christ's hands, he knows how to keep it, and
us too; so this grace may be said to be the
grace of our Lord Jesus Christ, secured by
his blood, and conveyed to our souls by his
being the head of his church and people.

This grace has a variety of epithets put to it,
and I question whether there is any kind of
grace but what the Lord Jesus Christ exercises
towards his people some way or other, every
hour, every moment of the day.   First,

Firft, His reftraining grace; why, if it was not for this, God's people would be juft as weak and wicked as other folks are: remember what David faid when Abigail came to him; he was going to kill a neighbour for affronting him, forgot that he was a Pfalmift, and was only acting as a creature: bleffed be God, fays he, that has fent thee to meet and keep me: My brethren, we may talk what we pleafe, and build upon our own ftock; we are juft like little children that will walk by themfelves; well, fays the father, walk alone then, they tumble down, get a broken brow, and then are glad to take hold of the father: thus Jefus Chrift is always acting in a reftraining way to his people; if it was not fo, by the blindnefs of their underftandings, the corruptions of their hearts and affections, together with the perverfenefs of their will, alas! alas! there is not a child of God that would not run away every day, if Chrift did not reftrain him!

Secondly, There is convicting grace, which from the Lord Jefus Chrift acts every day and hour. Oh! it is a bleffed thing to be under the Redeemer's convicting grace! a man may fpeak to the ear, but it is the Spirit of God alone

alone can fpeak to the heart : I am not fpeaking of convicting grace that wounds before converfion, and gives us a fenfe of our fin and mifery; no, I mean convicting grace that follows the believer from time to time. If a heathen Socrates could fay, that he had always a monitor with him to check him when he did amifs, and direct him when he went right, furely the Chriftian may fay, and bleffed be God for it, that he has got a Jefus that kindly fhews him when he goes aftray, and by his grace puts him into the way of righteoufnefs, that his feet may not flip; this is what the fhepherd does to his fheep when they have wandered; what does the fhepherd do, but fends fome little cur, his dog, after them, to bring them to the fold again? what does Jefus Chrift do in temptations, trials, and afflictions? he fetches his people home, and convinces them that they have done amifs.

Then, thirdly, There is the converting grace of our Lord Jefus Chrift. Oh! what poor unhappy creatures are they, that think they can turn to God when they pleafe, to which abominable principle it is owing, that they leave it till they cannot turn in their beds : Satan tells them then, it is too late, their consciences are filled with horror, and they go off in a whirlwind; may this be the case of none here! That is a most excellent prayer in our Communion Office, *Turn us, O good Lord, and we shall be turned*; we can no more turn our hearts than we can turn the world upside down; it is the Redeemer, by his Spirit, must take away the heart of stone, and by the influence of the holy Spirit give us a heart of flesh. I might as well attempt to reach the heavens with my hand; I might as well go to some church-yard and command the dead to rise; I might as soon shake my handkerchief and bid the streams divide, and they give way, as to expect a soul to turn to God without the grace of the Mediator. Come, my dear hearers, I am of a good man's opinion, that prayed he might be converted every day. In the divine life, not to go forwards is to go backwards; and it is one great part of the work of the Spirit of God, to convert the soul from something that is wrong to something that is right, every day, hour, and moment of the believer's life, so that in short his life is one continued act of converting grace: there is not a day but there is something wrong; there is something we want to have taken away; we

want

want to get rid of the old man, and to get more
of the new man, and so the Spirit of God works
every day: O! my brethren, God give us
more of this converting grace!

Then there is establishing grace. David
prays, *Create in me a new heart, and renew a
right spirit within me*; in the margin, it is constant spirit; and you hear of some that are
rooted and grounded in the love of God, and
the apostle prays, that they may always abound
in the work of the Lord: again, it is good to
have the heart established with grace: there is
a good many people have some religion in
them, but they are not established; hence they
are mere weather-cocks, turned about by every
wind of doctrine; and you may as soon measure the moon for a suit of clothes, as some
people that are always changing; this is for
want of more grace, more of the Spirit of God;
and as children grow that are got stronger and
riper, so as people grow in grace, and in the
knowledge of the Lord Jesus Christ, they will
be more settled, more confirmed: on first set-
ting out they prattle, but they will be more
manly, more firm, more steady: young Christians are like little rivulets that make a large
noise, and have shallow water; old Chris-

C   tians

tians are like deep water that makes little noife,
carries a good load, and gives not way.

What think you, my brethren, of the Redeemer's comforting grace? O! what can you
do without it? *In the multitude of my thoughts
within me,* fays the Pfalmift, *thy comforts have
refrefhed my foul.* I believe you will all find
what lord Bolinbrooke, in fpite of all his fine
learning, and deiftical principles, found when
under affliction; he fent a letter which I faw
and heard read to me, at leaft that part of it in
which he fays: *Now I am under this affliction, I find my philofophy fails me.* With all
our philofophy and ftriving, it is too hard to
work ourfelves into a paffive ftate: alas! it is
commendable to ftrive, but we fhall never be
content, we fhall never be chearful under fufferings, but through the affiftance of the Redeemer. Even now, in refpect of parting from
one another, what can comfort friends when
feparated but the Spirit of God. Paul, when
going away for Jerufalem, faid, *What mean ye
to weep and to break my heart?* he alfo fays, *I
am ready not to be bound only, but alfo to die at
Jerufalem, for the name of the Lord Jefus,*
which he could not have faid, had he not
felt the comforting grace of Jefus Chrift.

Our

Our Lord, when going away, fays, *I will fend the Comforter*; I will not leave you comfortlefs, and helplefs, I will come again : the Lord helps the believer from time to time. We can eafily, my brethren, talk when not under the rod ourfelves ; there is not a phyfician or apothecary in London but can give good advice, but when they are fick themfelves, poor fouls! they are juft like their patients, and many times are more impatient than thofe they ufed to preach patience to; fo it is with the greateft Chriftian, we are all men of like paffions, there is not one of us when under the rod, if left to ourfelves, but would curfe God, and, Ephraim like, *be as a bullock unaccuftomed to the yoke* ; and there are many here, I do not doubt, that have faid to the Redeemer, *What doft thou?* or, perhaps, with Jonah, *We do well to be angry* ; if the Lord does but take away his goard from us, if he is pleafed to baulk us in regard to the creatures, how uncomfortable are we ? and, there are fo many afflictions and trials, that if it was not for the Lord Jefus Chrift's comfortings, no flefh could bear them.

In a word, what think you, my brethren, of the quickning grace of our Lord Jefus

Chrift ?

Chrift? Remember David fays, *Quicken me according to thy word, quicken me in thy way, quicken me in thy righteoufnefs :* God's people want quickening every day; this is trimming our lamps, girding up the loins of our minds, ftirring up the gift of God that is in us. It is juft with a foul as it is with the plants and trees; how would it be with them if the Lord did not command quickening life to them after the winter? the believer has his frofty and win-ter days, and wo be to them that think they have always a fummer; the believer at times can fay, *The winter is paft, the rain is over and gone, the flowers appear on the earth, the time of the finging of birds is come, and the voice of the turtle is heard in our land, the fig-tree putteth forth her green figs, and the vines with the tender grapes give a good fmell,* Cant. ii. 12. What is all this but God's quickening grace, reftoring the believer to his bleffed joy. Oh! my bre-thren, I have not time to fhow you in how many ways the Redeemer's grace is difplayed; but wherever this grace is, what reafon have you that are partakers of it, and I, to pray that it may be with us all; *the grace of our Lord Jefus Chrift,* fays John here, *be with you all :* it is not faid all minifters, it is not faid all of

this

this or that particular people, but with all believers. O! my friends, remember what Mr.
Henry said, he desired to be a Catholic, but
not a Roman Catholic. I have often thought
since I went to see the water-works, that it
was an emblem of Christ; there is a great
reservoir of water from which this great city
is supplied; but how is it supplied from that
reservoir? why by hundreds and hundreds of
pipes: but where does this water go, does it
go only to the dissenters or to the church people, only to this or that people? no, the pipes
convey the water to all; and I remember when
I saw it, it put me in mind of the great reservoir of grace, that living water that is in Christ
Jesus, and the pipes are the ordinances by
which his grace is conveyed to all believing
souls, God grant we may be of that happy
number. O what a mercy it is that Christ has
said, *I will be with you always even to the end of
the world*, Matt. xxviii. 20. and therefore we
must look upon this prayer to be as efficacious
now, as it was the moment the words dropt
from the apostle's pen. I believe the most
minute philosophers, and those that have the
greatest skill in astronomy, cannot perceive
there has been any abatement in the heat of the
sun

fun, fince God firft commanded it to rule the
day, then furely, if my God can make a fun
that for fo many thoufands of years fhall irradi-
ate, enlighten, and warm the world, without
lofing any of its light and heat, fo does the fun
of righteoufnefs, the Son of God, arife upon
the children of God with healing under his
wings; he raifes, warms, nourifhes, and comforts his people, and we have the gofpel on
the ends of the earth, as well as thofe who had
the honour of converfing with him in the days
of his flefh. I mention this in anfwer to all
thofe who have wrote againft the Methodifts,
and reprefented them as fanatics; there is no
other way of talking againft the divine influence,
but by allowing it was fo formerly, but that it
is not fo now; they fay the primitive Chriftians had it, but it is not to be fo with us now,
as it was formerly. O my brethren, what fools
thefe great men are when they talk about things
they know nothing of; give them a polyglot,
give them a lexicon, give them a geographical
text, or the chronological part of the fcripture,
they have fomething to fay; but when they
come to talk of the Spirit of God, they fee the
word Spirit, and they read the word grace, but
while they read it their hearts cry, becaufe
                                        their

their knowledge puffs them up, furely if it was fo, we great men that have been in the univerfity fhould have it, God would give it us; and becaufe they find it not in themfelves, their abominable pride will not own it may be in any. Pray what was Peter, James, and John, I don't mean to fpeak difrefpectfully of them, they were as weak, as blind, as obfti-nate, and worldly-minded as others, till Jefus Chrift changed their hearts; and that fame grace that changed their hearts, changes now the hearts of God's people; and bleffed be God, that fame grace is with all his people.

It is fo in his ordinances. Here is the dif-ference between a Formalift and a Chriftian; the Formalift goes to ordinances, but then he does not feel the God of ordinances, and that is the reafon moft formal people don't care to go to church very often: who cares to go to the houfe of a perfon he does not love? they will only juft knock at the door, and afk if fuch a perfon is at home, and are very glad to hear the fervants fay their mafter or miftrefs is not at home; the vifit is paid; fo it is with many people that go to church and meeting; and I do not doubt but there are many Metho-difts, hundreds and hundreds, that have been

at

at the ordinances, who never felt the God of ordinances converting them to this day.

The grace of our Lord Jefus Chrift is with his people in prayer. Who can pray without grace? they may laugh at it as will, but God give you and I a fpirit of prayer; let them laugh as they pleafe; what profit will it be to us to read this book without the grace of God. What a horrid blunder has the bifhop of G——r been guilty of? What do you think his lord-fhip fays, in order to expofe the fanaticifm of the Methodifts? Why, fays he, they fay they cannot underftand the fcriptures without the Spirit of God. Can any man underftand the fcriptures without the Spirit of God helps him? Jefus Chrift muft open our underftanding to underftand the fcriptures, and the Spirit of God muft take of the things of Chrift and fhow them unto us; as we are taught to pray, *O Lord, thou haft caufed thy holy fcriptures to be written,* &c. as in the fecond Sunday in Advent; and here the b——p pretends to tell us, there is no need of it; here our colle&t and b——p difagree very much. So with refpe&t to all ordinances it is the fame: what fignifies my preaching, and your hearing, if the Spirit of God does not enlighten? Formal minifters can fteal a fer-

mon,

mon, and add a little out of their own heads, but
a minister of the gospel cannot preach to purpose
without the assistance of the Spirit of God, no
more than a ship can sail without wind.   As
for a carnal man he may take his sermon in
his pocket, and you will find his sermons always the same ; but spiritual preachers are
seldom so ; sometimes they are in dark-
ness, so as to speak to those that are in dark-
ness ; sometimes they are tempted, so as to
speak to those that are tempted ; sometimes
they have a full gale, and go before the wind,
and this is all by the assistance of the Spirit of
God, and without this a man may preach like
an angel, and do no good at all.   So in respect
to hearing the word of God, I declare I would
not preach again, if I did not think that God
would accompany the word by his Spirit : what
are we but *sounding brass and tinkling cymbals?*
If the word is preached in the strength of the
Spirit, it will be attended with convictions,
and conversions, and the grace of God will be
both with preacher and hearer.

The grace of God is with his people in *his*
providence.   Oh ! says bishop Hall, a little aid
is not enough for me. My going on the
waters puts me in mind of what I have seen

many times: if the failors perceive a ftorm a coming, they do not chufe to fpeak to the paffengers for fear of frightening them, they will go quietly on deck, and give orders for proper care to be taken ; and if a failor can tell of ftorms approaching by the clouds, why can't God's people tell why God does fo and fo with them? The people of God eye him in his providence ; the very hairs of their heads are all numbered, and the grace of God is with them in the common bufinefs of life. Some people think that the Methodifts preach fo and fo to make them neglect their bufinefs, and we preach at unfeafonable times : we would not preach at this time, but that we are going to part from one another ; no, we preach that the grace of God may attend them in their counting-houfes, and wo be to thofe perfons that do not take the grace of God with them into their counting-houfes, and in their common bufinefs. O what bleffed times would it be if every one made the grace of God their employ, that when the Lord comes he may fay, Lord, here I am waiting for thee.

The grace of the Lord Jefus Chrift is with his people when *fick* and when *dying*. O my dear fouls, what fhall we do when death comes?

What

What a mercy it is that we have got a good maſter to carry us through that time ! As a poor converted Negro that ſaw a believer who was dying in comfort, ſaid, Maſter don't fear, Jeſus Chriſt will carry you ſafe through the dark valley of the ſhadow of death.—But the time would fail, if I was to ſhow you in how many reſpects *the grace of the Lord Jeſus Chriſt* helps us; but what I have ſaid will ſhow, that we need all join in a hearty Amen ; Amen, I pray God it may be ſo, ſo it is, ſo may it be ! May be what ? why that *the grace of the Lord Jeſus Chriſt, convicting, reſtraining, converting, eſtabliſhing* and *comforting grace,* may be with us in his ordinances, in his providences, in ſickneſs, and when dying : then, bleſſed be God, we ſhall carry it with us after time. And now, my dear hearers, by the help of my God, in whoſe ſtrength I deſire once more to go upon the waters, I ſhall pray wherever I am, that this *grace of the Lord Jeſus Chriſt may be with you all.*

To whom ſhall I ſpeak firſt by way of improvement ? Are there any of you here unconverted ? no doubt too many. Are there any of you here this morning come out of curioſity to hear what the babler has to ſay ? Many, per-

haps

haps, are glad it is my laft fermon, and that
London is to be rid of fuch a monfter: I
don't doubt but it has been a pleafant para-
graph for many to read; but whoever there
are of you that are unconverted, or whatever
you may think, fure you cannot be angry for
my wifhing that the *grace of God may be with
you.* O that it may be with every unconverted
foul. O pray for me, my dear friends, that
the Lord may blefs me to fome unconverted
foul; what wilt thou do if the grace of God is
not with thee? what wilt thou do with the
favour of man if thou haft not got the grace of
God? you will find, my brethren, it will not
do, you cannot do without the grace of God
when you come to die. There was a nobleman that kept a deiftical chaplain, and his
lady a chriftian one; when he was dying, he
fays to his chaplain, I liked you very well when
I was in health, but it is my lady's chaplain I
muft have when I am fick. Do you know
that you are nothing but devils incarnate? Do
you know that every moment you are liable to
eternal pains? The Lord help thee to awake O
finner, awake, awake thou ftupid foul, if the
grace of God was never with thee before, God
grant it may now, Don't fay I part with you in

an

an ill humour; don't say that a madman left you
with a curse. Blessed be God that when first I entered into the field, (and blessed be God that honoured me with being a field-preacher) I proclaimed the grace of God to the worst of sinners, and I proclaim it now to the vilest sinner
under heaven; could I speak so loud as that
the whole world might hear me, I would declare
that the grace of God is free for all poor souls
that are willing to accept of it by Christ;
God make you all willing this day.

There are many of you, I doubt not, but
have got this grace, and I believe there are
many of you that can say that this poor despised place was that which God honoured first
with giving it you: but whether you were
converted here, or elsewhere, if you have got
the grace of God, the Lord grant you more
grace; *grace, mercy and peace be multiplied unto
you all.* My brethren, they that have got
Christ never have enough of him; you want
more grace every day, and hour, and moment:
I see for my part more of my want of grace than
I did ten or twenty years ago; may be that is
because I don't grow in grace; but those that
grow in grace will grow every day more sensi-
ble of their want of grace, they will feel their
weak-

weaknefs more and more every day. Some who are called Chriftians are a moft foul-mouth people, they abufe their neighbours, but real believers abufe themfelves moft, and call themfelves, *i. e.* what is in themfelves, the worft of neighbours. O my brethren, may the Lord Jefus Chrift's grace be with you more and more, that you may be transformed into the divine likenefs, and pafs from glory to glory by the Spirit of the Lord. May God grant that this grace may be with you all, particularly thofe young men that have given up their fouls to Chrift. It delights my foul when I go round the communion table, to fee how many young fouls have given themfelves to Chrift, the Lord grant that you may not return again to folly. O young men, flee youthful lufts; O young women, the Lord Jefus Chrift grant that grace may be with you all, that you may ftudy the beauties of the mind, fhine in the beauties of holinefs, and be wife to everlafting falvation.

May the grace of the Lord Jefus Chrift be with you all that are in the marriage ftate. It needs much grace to bear with heavy trials, much grace to deal with fervants, children, and under difappointments in trade; to walk with God with a pure heart. Some people
think

think it clever to have wives and children, but they want a thousand times more grace than they had when they were single; you have need of much grace to honor God in your houses, much grace to teach you to be prophets, much grace to teach you to be kings in the family; to know, when to be pleased; to know, when to be silent; to know, when to be angry: but the greatest grace is to be angry when called to it, to be angry without sin. O! may the grace of God be with you all in your closets, every time you pray, every time you come to an ordinance; O! may the grace of God be with you all when you frequent this despised place! blessed be God some may say, that ever it was built; though as soon as it was built I was called away. As soon also as the chapel was built I was then called away, and so am now; and when I came out of my chamber, I could hardly support it. I would as lieve go to an execution, if my way was not very clear; what is dying? that is but for a moment. O may the grace of God be with all, that preach the gospel here. Blessed be God his grace has been with them; don't let the world say, he is gone, and all the people are gone now:

don't

don't weaken the hands of thofe that fhall
labour here; I fhould not mention fuch a
word if I was not going away. The Lord
Jefus Chrift grant that you may keep fteady,
and honor the preachers more and more; there
will be good Mr. Adams, bleffed be God,
from time to time, with Mr. Beridge, and fo
there will be a bleffed change: may the Spirit
of God be with them, and you, more and
more! and O my dear friends, if the Lord
God has vouchfafed to own thefe labours to
any of you, do remember me in a particular
manner, when gone; for though my body
has been weak, yet I thank God that he
has enabled me to fpeak when called to it.

And fo I muft go, whether well or ill;
pray, that if it fhould pleafe God to fpare me,
that I may fpeak more effectually to you,
when I come back again; pray, that the grace
of the Lord Jefus Chrift may be with me
in a reftraining, comforting, fupporting, and
transforming way, that it may be with me
when I am fick, and when I die. O my
brethren, I fee I want the grace of the Lord
Jefus Chrift, in every one of thefe refpects,
every moment; O may the Lord God blefs
you all that have been kind to me, and for-
                                    give

give every thing that I have done amifs.
I am afhamed of myfelf, fo much of the man
comes up with me, though I humbly hope,
and dare to fay, that at the bottom my heart
is upright towards God; I would employ it
to his praife, but there is fo much fin mixed
with all I do, that was not the blood of Chrift
conftantly applied to my foul, and the grace
of God continually manifefted to me, I could
not preach any more. You may fee a thoufand
things wrong in me, but I fee ten thoufand
more, O may *the Grace of God be with you
all.* Now, dear friends, farewel! dear tabernacle, farewel! if I never preach here any
more; O that we may meet in a better tabernacle, when thefe tabernacles are taken
down, when thefe bodies fhall drop, when we
fhall be for ever with the Lord. I muft have
done, I can't bear it; *the Lord blefs you, the
Lord God caufe his face to fhine upon you.* I
cannot fay more, I dare not: *The Grace of
our Lord Jefus be with you all, Amen.*

✤✤✤✤✤✤✤✤✤✤✤✤✤✤✤✤✤✤✤✤✤✤✤✤✤

SERMON II.

CHRIST the Believer's Refuge.

PSALM xlvi. 1—6.

God is our refuge and ftrength, a very prefent help in trouble; therefore will we not fear, though the earth be removed, and the mountains be carried into the midft of the fea, though the waters thereof roar, and be troubled, though the mountains fhake with the fwelling thereof, Selah. There is a river, the ftreams whereof fhall make glad the city of God, the holy place of the tabernacles of the Moft High: God is in the midft of her, fhe fhall not be moved; God fhall help her, and that right early.

THERE was a tradition among the ancient Jews, that the manna which came down from heaven, though it was a little grain like coriander-feed, yet fuited every tafte; as milk unto babes, and
ftrong

ſtrong meat to grown perſons. Whether this ſuppoſition be founded on fact or not, the ob- ſervation will hold good in a great meaſure reſpecting the ſayings of David; for if we have eyes to ſee, and ears to hear, if God has been pleaſed to take away the veil from our hearts, we ſhall find, by happy experience, that let our circumſtances be what they will, the book of Pſalms may ſerve as a ſpiritual magazine, out of which we may draw ſpiri- tual weapons in the time of the hotteſt fight, eſpecially thoſe that are under trouble, *when the hand of the Lord is gone* ſeemingly *forth againſt them*; when unbelief is apt to make them ſay, *all theſe things are againſt me!* if we can have the preſence of mind to turn to the book of Pſalms, we may find ſomething there ſuitable to our caſe, a word to refreſh us in purſuing our ſpiritual enemy. This is true of the 46th Pſalm in particular, part of which I have juſt now read to you, and which I pray the bleſſed Spirit of God to apply to every one of our hearts. It is uncertain at what time, or upon what occaſion, David wrote it; probably under ſome ſharp afflic- tion, which made him eloquent; or when the affliction was over, when his heart was ſwim-

ing

ing with gratitude and love, and when out of the fulnefs of it his pen was made *the pen of a ready writer.* It was a favourite Pfalm with Luther; for whenever Melancthon, who was of a melancholy turn, or any other of his friends, told him fome fad news, he ufed to fay, come, come, let us fing the 46th Pfalm; and when he had fung that, his heart was quiet. May every true mourner here, and afflicted perfon, experience the fame! I know not when I read it which to admire moft, the piety, or the poetry; the matter, or the manner; and I believe I may venture to defy all the criticks on earth to fhew me any compofition of Pindar, or Horace, that any way comes up to the diction of this Pfalm confidered only as human : he that hath an ear to hear, let him hear, *God is our refuge and ftrength, a very prefent help in trouble.* Stop here, my friends, let us paufe a while, and before we go further, may the Lord help us to draw fome comfort from this very firft verfe: for obferve, it is not faid, *God is* my *refuge*; David fays fo in another Pfalm; but he fays here, *God is* our *refuge* : he fpeaks in the plural number, implying, that this Pfalm was of no private interpretation, but was in-

tended

tended for the comfort and encouragement of all believers, till time fhall be no more. Obferve the climax, *God is our refuge,* is one degree ; *God is our ftrength,* another; *God is our help,* and not only fo, but is a *prefent help,* yea, *is a very prefent help,* and at a time when we want it moft, *in the time of trouble.* It is here fuppofed, that all God's people will have their troubles, *man is born to trouble, as the fparks fly upward* ; and if we are born to trouble as men, we are much more fo as chriftians. We forget ourfelves, and the ftation in which God has placed us, when we fo much as begin to dream of having much refpite from trouble while we are here below. The decree is gone forth like the laws of the Medes and Perfians, it alters not; through tribulation, through much tribulation, we muft all go ; but bleffed be God we are to be carried through it ; and bleffed be God, glory is to be the end of it : may God give us to know this by happy experience ! *in the world,* fays our bleffed Lord, *ye fhall have tribulation,* tribulation and trouble of different kinds ; and in another place, *if any man will come after me,* fays he, *let him take up his crofs daily, and follow me* ; fo that the day, when we take up no crofs, we may fay as Titus did,

when

when he reflected that he had done no good that day, I have loft a day! But then what fhall we do, my dear hearers, when trouble comes, when one trouble comes after another, and afflictions feem to purfue us wherever we go, feem to arife up out of the ground, meet us as we are walking along? why blefled be God, if we have an intereft in Chrift, mind that, if we have an intereft in Chrift, God is our help, God is our afylum, our city of refuge, a place appointed by God himfelf, to which the purfued faints may fly by faith, and be fafe. The wicked have no notion of this; when they are in trouble, what is their refuge? let a foul be under fpiritual trouble, and cry out *what fhall I do to be faved?* let him go to a carnal minifter, an unconverted wretch that knows nothing about the matter, he fhall be told, oh! go, and play an innocent game at cards, and divert yourfelf; that is to fay, the devil muft be your refuge. Wordly people have worldly refuges; and Cain would feem as if he was in earneft when he faid, *my punifhment is greater than I can bear:* what does he do, he goes and diverts himfelf by building a city, goes and amufes himfelf by building. The devil, my brethren, will give

you

you leave to amuſe yourſelves; you may have your choice of diverſions, only take care to be diverted from God, and the devil is ſure of you; but the believer has ſomething better: faith *ſweeps away the refuge of lies,* and the believer turns to his God, and ſays *O my God, thou ſhalt be my refuge.* The devil purſues me, my falſe friends have deſigns againſt me, my own wicked heart itſelf moleſts me, *my foes are thoſe of my own houſe;* but do thou, O God, be my refuge I will fly there; by theſe it may be ſaid, *God is our refuge.* The queſtion is, what ſhall I do to make him my refuge? how ſhall I be helped to do ſo? you bid me fly; you ſay, I may fly there, but where ſhall I get wings? how ſhall I be ſupported? Here is a bleſſed word, *God ſhall not only be our refuge,* but *God ſhall be our ſtrength* alſo. Strength, what is ſtrength? why, my brethren, to make every day of trouble ſo eaſy to us by his power, as to carry us through it; God has ſaid, and will ſtand to it, *as thy day is, ſo ſhall thy ſtrength be.* Afflictions even at a diſtance will appear very formidable, when viewed by unbelief. Our fears ſay, O my God, if I come to be tried this or that way, how ſhall I bear it? but we don't know what

we

we can bear till the trial comes, and we do not
know what ftrength God can give us, or what
a ftrong God he will be, till he is pleafed to
put us into a furnace of affliction; and therefore it is faid, not only that *God is our refuge
and our ftrength,* but that *God is our help* alfo.
What help? why, my dear friends, help to
fupport us under the trouble; help fo as to
comfort us as long as the trouble lafts; and
bleffed be God, that the help will never leave
us, till we are helped quite over and quite
through it. But what kind of an help is it?
O bleffed be God, *he is a very prefent help.*
We may have an helper, but he may be afar
off; I may be fick, I may want a phyfician,
and may be obliged to fend miles for one; he
might be a help if he was here, but what
fhall I do now he is at a diftance. This cannot be faid of God, he is not only a help, but
he is a *prefent help: the gates of the new Jerufalem are open night and day.* We need not
be afraid to cry unto God; we cannot fay
of our God as Elijah does of Baal, *perhaps he
is afleep, or talking, or gone a journey:* it is
not fo with our God, *he is a prefent help;* he
is likewife a fufficient help, that is, *a very
prefent help,* and that too *in the time of trouble.*

It

It is but to fend a fhort letter, I mean a fhort prayer, upon the wings of faith and love, and God, my brethren, will come down and help us. Now to this David affixes his *probatum eft*, David proves it by his own experience, and therefore if *God is our refuge*, therefore if *God is our ftrength*, if *God is our help*, if *God is a prefent help*, if *God is a very prefent help*, and that too *in a time of trouble*, what then? *therefore will we not fear.*—Therefore, is an inference, and it is a very natural one, a conclufion naturally drawn from the foregoing premiffes; for Paul fays, *if God be for us, who can be againft us?* There is not a greater enemy to faith than fervile fear and unbelief. My brethren, the devil has got an advantage over us when he has brought us into a ftate of fear; indeed in one fenfe we fhould always fear, I mean with a filial fear; *bleffed is the man,* in this fenfe, *that feareth always:* but, my brethren, have we ftrong faith in a God of refuge? this forbids us to fear; fays Nehemiah, *fhall fuch a man as I flee?* and the Chriftian may fay, fhall a believer in Jefus Chrift fear? fhall I fear that my God will leave me? fhall I fear that my God will not fuccour me? no, fays David, *we will not fear;* how fo? why *though*

F *the*

the mountains be carried into the midſt of the ſea,
though the waters thereof roar and be troubled,
though the mountains ſhake with the ſwelling
thereof. Where is Horace, where is Pindar,
now ? let them come here and throw their
palms down before the ſweet ſinger of Iſrael.
There is not ſuch a bold piece of imagery in
any human compoſition in the world. Can
any thing appear more great, more conſider-
able than this ? Imagine how it was with us
ſome years ago, when an enthuſiaſtic fool
threatened us with a third earthquake ; imagine
how it was with us when God ſent us the
ſame year two dreadful earthquakes ; had the
earth been at that time not only ſhook, but
removed, had the fountains of the ſea been
permitted to break in upon us, and carry all
the mountains of England before it, what a
dreadful tremor muſt we all unavoidably have
been in ? David ſuppoſes that this may be the
caſe, and I believe at the great day it will be
ſomething like it : the earth and all things
therein, are to be burnt up ; and, my brethren,
what ſhall we do then if God is not our refuge,
if God is not our ſtrength ?

We may apply it to civil commotions :
David had lately been beſet with the Philiſ-
tines,

tines, and other enemies, that threatened to deprive him of his life; and there are certain times when we fhall be left alone. This alfo, my brethren, may be applied to creature-comforts: fometimes the earth feems to be removed, what then? why all the friends we take delight in, our moft familiar friends, our foul-friends, friends by nature, and friends by grace, may be removed from us by the ftroke of death; we know not how foon that ftroke may come, it may come at an hour we thought not of; the mountains themfelves, all the things that feem to furround and promife us a lafting fcene of comfort, they themfelves may foon be removed out of our fight, what then fhall we do? *they may be carried into the midft of the fea;* what is that? our friends may be laid in the filent grave, and *the places that knew them may know them no more.* It is eafy talking, but it is not fo eafy to bear up under thefe things: but faith, my brethren, teaches us to fay, though all friends are gone, bleffed be God, God is not gone. As a noble lady's daughter told her mother, when fhe was weeping for the death of one of her little children, a daughter four years old faid, Dear mamma, is God Almighty dead, that you cry

fo

fo long after my fifter? No, he is not dead,
neither does he fleep. But here the imagery
grows bolder, the painting ftronger, and the
refemblance more ftriking, *though the waters
thereof roar and be troubled, though the mountains ſhake with the ſwelling thereof*; what
won't this make us fearful? will not this ſhake
us off our bottom, our foundation, and take
up the roots? No, no, even then the believer
need not fear; why, *God is in the midſt of her.*
Don't you remember God fpoke to Mofes out
of the bufh? did he ftand at a diftance, and
call to him at a diftance from the bufh? no,
the voice came out of the bufh, *Mofes! Mofes!* as Mr. Ainfworth, who was a fpiritual
critic, fays.

    Learn from hence, *that in all our afflictions
God is afflicted; he is in the midſt of the buſh;*
and oh! it is a fweet time with the foul when
God fpeaks to him out of the bufh, when he
is under affliction, and talks to him all the
while. Though it was threatened by the fire
which furrounded it with immediate and total
defolation; *yet the buſh burned, and was not
confumed.* I do not know whether I told you,
but I believe I told them at Tottenham-court,
and perhaps here, that every chriftian has got

a

a coat of arms, and I will give it you out of Chrift's heraldry, that is the *burning bufh*; every chriftian is burned, but not confumed. But how is it the faint is held up, whence does he get this ftrength; or how is this ftrength, this fupporting, comforting ftrength, conveyed to his heart? read a little further, you fhall find David fay, *there is a river,* mind that, *there is a river the ftreams where-of make glad the city of God, the holy place of the tabernacles of the Moft High*; need I tell you, that probably here is an allufion to the fituation of Jerufalem, and the waters of Shiloah, that flowed gently through the city of Jerufalem, which the people found fweet and refrefhing in the time of its being befieged. So the rivers run through moft of the cities in Holland, and bring their commodities even to the doors of the inhabitants. Pray, what do you think this river is? why, I believe it means the covenant of grace; O that is a river, the fprings of which firft burft out in Paradife, when God faid, *the feed of the woman fhall bruife the ferpent's head*; then God made this river vifit the habitation of man, as the firft opening of his everlafting covenant.

No

No fooner had the devil betrayed man, and thought he was fure to get him into the pit, even when he was laughing at man's mifery, and thinking he was revenged of God for driving him out of heaven; at that very time did the great God open this river, and made it flow down in that bleffed ftream to man-kind, implyed in thofe words, *it fhall bruife thy head.* O this is a ftream which, I pray, may this night *make glad* this part of *the city of God.* If by the river we underftand the covenant of grace, then, my brethren, the *promifes* of God are the ftreams that flow from it. There is no promife in the Bible made to an unbeliever, but to a believer; all the promifes of God are his, and no one knows, but the poor believer that experiences it, how glad it makes his heart. God only fpeaks one fingle word, or applies one fingle promife; for if when one's heart is overwhelmed with forrow, we find relief by unfolding ourfelves to a faithful difinterefted friend; if a word of comfort fometimes gives us fuch fupport from a minifter of Chrift, O! my friends, what fupport muft a promife from God applied to the foul give? and this made a good woman fay, I have oft had a bleffed meal on the pro-

mifes

mifes, when I have had no bread to make a meal for my body.

But by the river we may likewife under-ftand, the *Spirit* of the living God. If you remember, Jefus Chrift declared at the great day of the feaft, *if any man believe on me, out of his belly fhall flow rivers of living water;* *this,* faith the beloved difciple, *fpake he of the Spirit, which they that believe on him fhould receive.* My brethren, the divine influences are not only a conduit, but a deep river, a river of broad waters. Here is room for the babes to walk, and for the man of God to bathe and fwim in from time to time; and fuppofing that the river means the Spirit of God, as I believe really it does, why then the ftreams that flow from this river are the means of grace, the ordinances of God, which God makes ufe of as channels, whereby to convey his bleffed Spirit to the foul. Nay, by the river we may underftand, *God himfelf* who is the believer's river, the Three-one, Father, Son, and Holy Ghoft. This river is in the midft of the city, not at the court-end of the town only, or one corner, or end, but quite through, in a variety of ftreams, fo that high and low may come to it for fupply; and not only be

fupported,

supported, but have their hearts made glad daily thereby; God help us to drink afresh of this river. If this be the case, well may David triumph and say, *glorious things are spoken of the city of God*; are spoken of *her*, in the feminine gender. The church is spoken of in that sense, because Eve, the first woman, was the mother of all believers; we may apply this to a single saint, as well as to a community, under trouble, *she shall not be moved*; not moved? pray, would you have them stupid? do you love when you strike a child, to see it hardened and regardless? do you not like the child should smart under it and cry, and when it is a little penitent, you almost wish you had not struck it at all. God expects, when he strikes, that we should be moved; and there is not a greater sign in a reprobate heart of a soul given over by God, to have affliction upon affliction, and yet *come out like a fool brayed in a mortar*, unmoved and hardened. My brethren, this is the worst sign of a man or woman's being given over by God. Jesus was moved, when he was under the rod; he cries, *father! if it be possible, let this cup pass from me!* he was moved so as to shed tears, tears of blood, falling to the ground.

Wo

Woe, woe, woe be to us, if when God knocks
at the door by ſome ſhocking domeſtic or foreign trial, we don't ſay, *my God ! my God !*
wherefore doſt thou ſtrike? When we are
ſick we allow phyſicians to feel our pulſe,
whether it be high or languid ; and when we
are ſick, and tried with afflićtion, it is time to
feel our pulſe, to ſee if we were not going into
a high fever, and do not want ſome ſalutary
purge. It is expećted therefore that we ſhould
be moved ; we may ſpeak, but not in a murmuring way : Job was moved, and God knows
when we are under the rod, we are all moved
more than we ought to be in a wrong way ;
but when it is ſaid here, *ſhe ſhall not be moved,*
it implies, not totally removed; *perplexed,*
ſays the apoſtle, *but not in deſpair* ; *perſecuted,*
but not forſaken ; *caſt down, but not deſtroyed* ;
therefore removal means deſtrućtion : *when the*
earth is moved, the mountains ſhake, and the
waters roar, where can we flee ? what can we
ſee but deſtrućtion all round us? But, my
brethren, ſincé *there is a river the ſtreams*
whereof make glad the city of God, ſince *God*
is our refuge, ſince *God is our ſtrength,* ſince
God is our help, ſince *God is a preſent help,*
ſince *God is a very preſent help in the time of*

trouble, ſince *God is in the midſt of her,* ſince
God cauſes the ſtreams to make her glad, bleſſed
be God, we ſhall not, my brethren, be totally
moved; nay, though death itſelf does remove
our bodies, though the king of terrors, that
griſly king, ſhould come armed with all his
ſhafts, yet *in the midſt of death we are in life,*
even then *we ſhall not be moved,* even though
the body is removed in ſleep, the ſoul is gone
where it ſhall be ſorrowful no more. One
would have imagined that David had ſaid
enough, but pray obſerve how he goes on,
he repeats it again, for when we are in an un-
believing frame we have need of *line upon line,*
words upon words, God ſhall help her ; ah !
but when ? when ? when will he help her ?
when will he help her ? why, *right early ;*
God ſhall help her, and that right early. Why
ſometimes we knock for a friend, but he will
not get up early in the morning, but *God ſhall*
help us, and that right early, in the morning.
Ah ! but, ſay you, I have been under trouble
a long while ; why God's morning is not come :
'you ſaid right early ; yes, but you are not yet
prepared for it, you muſt wait till the precious
right moment comes, and you may be aſſured
of it. God never gives you one doubt more
than

than you want, or even defers help one moment longer than it ought to be.

Now, my dear hearers, if theſe things are
ſo, who dares call the Chriſtian a madman?
If theſe things are ſo, who would but be a
believer? who would not be a faithful fol-
lower of the ſon of God? My brethren, did
you ever hear any of the devil's children com-
poſe an ode, that the devil is our refuge; the
God of this world, whom we have ſerved ſo
heartily, we have found to be a preſent help
in time of trouble? ah! a preſent help to help
us after the devil: or did you ever hear, ſince
the creation, of one ſingle man that dared to
ſay, that all the forty-fixth pſalm was founded
on a lie? No, it is founded on matters of fact,
and therefore believer, believer, I wiſh you
joy, although it is a tautology. I pray God,
that from this time forth till we die, you and
I, when under trouble, may ſay with Luther,
come let us ſing the forty-fixth pſalm.

As for you that are wicked, what ſhall I ſay
to you? are you in high ſpirits to night; has
curioſity brought you here to hear what the
babler has to ſay on a funeral occaſion? well,
I am glad to ſee you here, though I have
ſcarce ſtrength to ſpeak for the violence of

the

the heat, yet I pray God to magnify his
ſtrength in my weakneſs; and may the God
of all mercy over-rule curioſity for good to
you. I intend to ſpeak about this death to
the ſurviving friends; but, my dear hearers,
the grand intention of having the funeral ſermon to night, is to teach the living how to die.
Give me leave to tell you, that however briſk
you may be now, there will a time come when
you will want God to be your help. Some
pulpit may e'er long be hung in mourning for
you; the black, the dreary appendages of
death may e'er long be brought to your
home; and if you move in a high ſphere, ſome
ſuch eſcutcheon as this, ſome atchievement
may be placed at your door, and woe, woe,
woe be to thoſe who in an hour of death cannot ſay, *God is my refuge.* You may form
ſchemes as you pleaſe; after you have been
driven out of one fool's paradiſe, you may re-
treat into another; you may ſay, now I will
ſing a requiem to my heart, and now I ſhall
have ſome pleaſant ſeaſon; but if God loves
you he will knock off your hands from that,
you ſhall have thorns even in roſes, and it will
imbitter your comforts. O what will you do
when the elements ſhall melt with fervent
heat;

heat; when this earth, with all its fine furniture, ſhall be burnt up; when the archangel
ſhall cry, *time ſhall be no more!* whither then,
ye wicked ones, ye unconverted ones, will ye
flee for refuge? O, ſays one, I will fly to the
mountains: O ſilly fool, O ſilly fool, fly to the
mountains, that are themſelves to be burnt up
and moved. O, ſays you, I will flee to the
ſea; O you fool, that will be boiling like a
pot: O then I will flee to the elements; they
will be melting with fervent heat. I can ſcarce
bear this hot day, and how can you bear a hot
element? there is no fan there, not a drop of
water to cool your tongue. Will you fly to
the moon? that will be turned into blood: will
you ſtand by one of the ſtars? they will fall
away: I know but of one place you can go
to, that is to the devil; God keep you from
that! Happy they that draw this inference;
ſince every thing elſe will be a refuge of lies,
God help me from this moment, God help
me to make God my refuge! here you can
never fail; your expectations here can never
be raiſed too high; but if you ſtop ſhort of
this, *as the Lord liveth,* in whoſe name I
ſpeak, you will only be a ſport for devils; a
day of judgment will be no day of refuge to
you,

you, you will only be fummoned like a criminal that has been caft already, to the bar to
receive the dreadful fentence, *Depart, ye
curfed, into everlafting fire, prepared for the
devil and his angels.* There is no river to make
glad the inhabitants of hell, no ftreams to
cool them in that fcorching element: were
thofe who are in hell to have fuch an offer of
mercy as you have, how would their chains
rattle! how would they come with the flames
of hell about their ears! how would they rejoice even there, if a minifter was to tell them,
Come, come, after you have been here millions and millions of years, there fhall come a
river here to make you glad. But the day is
over; God help us to take warning: and oh!
with what gratitude fhould we approach him
to night, for bearing with, and for for-bear-
ing us fo long; let each fay to night, why am
I out of hell? how came I not to be damned,
when I have made every thing elfe my God,
my refuge, for fo many years? May goodnefs
lead every unconverted foul to repentance, and
may love conftrain us to obedience: fly, fly,
God help thee to fly, finner; hark! hear the
word of the Lord, fee the world confumed, the
avenger of blood, this grim death, is juft at thy
heels,

heels, and if thou doft not this moment take refuge in God, to-night before to-morrow, you may be damned for ever; the arms of Jefus yet lie open, his loving heart yet ftreams with love, and bids a hearty welcome to every poor foul that is feeking happinefs in God. May God grant that every unconverted foul may be of the happy number.

But, my brethren, the moft heavy tafk of this night yet lies unperformed; indeed, if my friendfhip for the deceafed did not lead me to it, I fhould pray to be excufed; my body is fo weak, my nerves fo unftrung, and the heat beats too intenfely on this tottering frame, for me to give fuch a vent to my affections as I am fure I fhould give if I was in vigorous health; you may eafily fee, though I have not made that application, with what defign I have chofe this Pfalm; you may eafily fee by the turn, I hope no unnatural one, that has been given to the text as we have paffed along, that I have had in my view a mournful widow here before me. Did I think when this black furniture was taken from the pulpit when two branches were lopt off within about a year one after another, both lopt off from on earth, I hope and believe to be planted for ever in

hea-

heaven, little did I think that the axe was in a few months time to be laid to the root of the father; little did I think that this pulpit was then to be hung in mourning for the dear, the generous, the valuable, the univerfally bene-volent, Mr. Beckman; a benefactor to every body, a benefactor to the Tabernacle; he has largely contributed both to the Chapel and Ta-bernacle, and, my dear hearers, now his works follow him, for he is gone beyond the grave. Such a fingular circumftance I believe rarely happens, that though I was laft night at near eleven o'clock dead almoft with heat, I thought if death was the confequence, I would go to the grave and have the laft look at my dear departed friend; to fee a new vault opened; to fee a place of which he has been, in a great meafure, the founder; to fee a place which he was enlarging at the very time he died; to fee a new vault there firft inhabited by the father, and two only fons, and all put there in the fpace of two years time, Oh! it was almoft too much for me, it weighed me down, it kept me in my bed all this day; and now I have rifen, God grant it may be to give a feafonable word to your fouls. Oh! my friends, put yourfelves in the ftate of a furvi-

ving

ving widow, and then ſee who is ſecure from cutting providences. The very children when they are young are a trial; but the young man for whom a handſome fortune awaited; for a tender loving father to have his ſon taken away; for the widow to have the huſband taken away ſoon after; indeed, dear madam, you had need read the forty-ſixth Pſalm; you may well ſay, *call me no more Naomi*, that ſignifies pleaſant, but *call me Marah, for the Lord hath dealt bitterly with me.* Theſe are ſtrokes that are not always given to the greateſt ſaints. Such ſudden ſtrokes, ſuch blow upon blow, Oh! if God is not a ſtrength and refuge, how can the believer ſupport under it? but bleſſed be the living God, I am a witneſs God has been your ſtrength, I am witneſs that God has been your refuge; you have found, I know you have, already, that *there is a river*, a river in which you have ſwam now for ſome years, *the ſtreams whereof make glad* your waiting heart. Surely I ſhall never forget the moment in which I viſited your deceaſed huſband, when the hiccoughs came, and death was ſuppoſed to be really come, to ſee the diſconſolate widow flying out of the room, unable to bear the ſight of a departing

H   h uſband :

huſband : I know that God was then your refuge, and God will continue to be your refuge. You are now God's peculiar care, and as a proof that you will make God your refuge, you have choſen to make your firſt appearance in the houſe of God, in the Tabernacle, where I hope God delights to dwell, and where you met with God, and which I hope you will never leave till God removes you hence. Whatever trials may yet await you, remember you are now become God's peculiar care. You had before a huſband to plead for you ; he is gone, but your pleader is not dead, he lives, and will plead your cauſe ; may you find him better to you than ten thouſand huſbands ; may he make up the awful chaſm that death has made, and may the Lord God be your refuge in time, and your portion to all eternity ; and then you will have a bleſſed change. You are properly a *Naomi* ; I would humbly hope that your daughter-in-law, which ſo lately met with a ſtroke of the ſame nature, will prove a *Ruth* to you, and though young, and having a fortune, ſhe may be tempted to take a walk in the world, yet I hope ſhe will ſay, *where thou goeſt, I will go ; where thou lodgeſt, I will lodge ; thy peo-*

ple

ple fhall be my people, and thy God my God; where thou dieft, will I die, and there will I be buried; the Lord do fo to me, and more alfo, if ought but death part thee and me. It is to your honour, madam, and I think it right to fpeak of it, you had the fmiles of your departing father-in-law, you had behaved with deference and love; he was very fond of you; God make you a comfort to your furviving mother, who has adopted you, and may the Lord Jefus Chrift enable you to take God to be your portion.

As for you that are the relations of the deceafed, there is one of you that has been honourably called to the fervice of the miniftry: you, fir, was fent for over by an endearing uncle, you have been a ftranger in a ftrange land: the Palatines will blefs your miniftry; God has, I hope, bleffed it, and provided you a place to preach in. May God grant that that church may be filled with his prefence and his glory; and you, madam, be made the inftrument of fending the news to heaven to your hufband, that *this and that man was born of God there.* As for you, the other friends of the deceafed, may God grant that when you die, and when you are buried, the

H 2

people may follow you with tears as they did dear Mr. Beckman laft night. I was told by one this morning that walked along with the funeral, that it was delightful to hear what the people faid when the coffin paffed by; they bleffed the perfon contained therein, Oh! he was a father to the poor. The poor have indeed loft a friend; and I believe there has not been a man, a tradefman in London, for thefe many years, that has been more lamented than the dear man who now, I hope, is at reft. You well know how mindful he has been of you, and that foon after the deceafe of his dif-confolate widow, his fubftance will be divi-ded among fome of you. Give me leave to charge and intreat you, by the mercies of God in Jefus Chrift, to be kind to the honoured widow. Don't fay, Mr. Beckman my uncle is dead, come pluck up, let us plague her now fhe is living, we fhall have all when fhe is dead. The plague of God will follow you if you do: if you valued your dear uncle, do all you can to make her life eafy; pay her that refpect which you would pay the deceafed was he now living; this will fhew your love is genuine, and not counterfeit, and do not *lay up wrath againft the day of wrath.* Follow the

ex-

example of your dear deceafed uncle; the gentleman was vifible in him as well as the chriftian; he would be in his warehoufe early in the morning, that he might come foon to his country-houfe, and there employ himfelf in his friendly life, and open the door to the difciples of Jefus. It is time to draw to an end, but I will fpeak a word to the fervants of the family, who have loft a good and a dear maf-ter. May the Lord Jefus Chrift be your mafter for ever, that you may be the Lord's fervants, however you may be difpofed of in this world; that you may meet your mafter, your miftrefs, and all the family, in the king-dom of the living God, then we fhall have a whole eternity to reflect upon the goodnefs of a gracious God. O may God help us to fing the forty-fixth Pfalm; may we find him to be *our ftrength and our refuge, a very prefent help in the time of trouble*; may the river of the living God make glad your hearts, and may you be with God to all eternity; even fo, Lord Jefus, Amen and Amen.

SERMON

⁂⁂⁂⁂⁂⁂⁂⁂⁂⁂⁂⁂⁂⁂⁂⁂⁂

SERMON III.

Soul Prosperity.

3 Epistle JOHN ii.

Beloved, I wish above all things that thou mayst prosper, and be in health, even as thy soul prospereth.

WHAT a horrid blunder has one of the famous, or rather infamous, deistical writers made, when he says, that the gospel cannot be of God, because there is no such thing as friendship mentioned in it. Surely if he ever read the gospel, *having eyes he saw not, having ears he heard not*; but I believe the chief reason is, his heart being waxen gross, he could not understand; for this is so far from being the case, that the world never yet saw such a specimen of steady and disinterested friendship, as was displayed in the life, example, and conduct of Jesus of Nazareth.

John,

John, the writer of this epistle, had the honour of leaning on his bosom, and of being called, by way of emphasis, *the disciple whom Jesus loved*; and that very disciple, which is very remarkable concerning him, though he was one of those whom the Lord himself named Sons of Thunder, *Mark* iv. 17. and was so suddenly, as bishop Hall observes, turned into a son of lightning, that he would have called down fire from heaven to consume his Master's enemies; consequently, though he was of a natural fiery temper, yet the change in his heart was so remarkable, that if a judgment may be formed by his writings, he seems as full of love, if not fuller, than any of his fellow apostles. He learned pity and benevolence of the father of mercies; and to show how christian friendship is to be cultivated, he not only wrote letters to churches in general, even to those he never saw in the flesh, but private letters to particular saints, friends to whom he was attached, and wealthy rich friends, whom God had, by his Spirit, raised up to be helpers of the distressed. Happy would it be for us, if we could all learn that simplicity of heart which is displayed in these particular words; happy if we could learn this

one

one rule, never to write a letter without something of Jesus Christ in it; for, as Mr. Henry
observes, if we are to answer for idle words,
much more for idle letters; and if God has
given us our pens, especially if he has given us
the pen of a ready writer, it will be happy if
we can improve our literary correspondence
for his glory and one another's good. But
what an unfashionable stile, if compared to
our modern ones, is that of the apostle to
Gaius. The superscription *from the elder to
the well-beloved Gaius, whom I love in the
truth*; there is fine language for you! Many
who call themselves Christ's disciples, would
be ashamed to write so now. *I send this, and
that, and the other; I send my compliments.*
Observe what he stiles himself, not as the
pope;* but he stiles himself the elder. A judicious expositor is of opinion, that all the
other apostles were dead, and only poor John
left behind. I remember a remark of his,
" the taller we grow, the lower we shall
" stoop." The apostle puts himself upon a
level with the common elders of a church,
that

---

* Whether Universal Bishop, or Vicar of Christ, Supreme
Head, Lord or Governor of the World, or a more blasphe-
mous title, is uncertain, the writer not hearing distinctly the
Latin words in which it was expressed.

that he might not seem to take state upon him, not to rule as a lion, but with a rod of love; *the elder to the well-beloved Gaius, whom I love in the truth.* This Gaius seems to be in our modern language, what we call a gentleman, particularly remarkable for his hospitality, *Gaius mine host*; and this Gaius was well-beloved, not only beloved, but well-beloved; that is, one who I greatly esteem and am fond of; but then he shows us likewise upon what this fondness is founded, *whom I love in the truth.* There are a great many people in writing say, *dear sir*, or *good sir*, and subscribe *your humble servant, sir*; and not one word of truth either in the beginning or end; but John and Gaius's love was in truth, not only in words, *but in deed and in truth*; as if he had said, my heart goes along with my hand while I am writing, and it gives me pleasure in such a correspondence as this, or *whom I love for the truth's sake*, that is, whom I love for being particularly attached to the truth; and then our friendship has a proper foundation, when the love of God, and the Spirit of the Lord Jesus, is the basis and bond of it. One would think this was enough now; the epistles originally were not divided into verses as now that peo-

I   ple

ple may the better find out particular places, though perhaps not altogether fo properly as they might. The apoftle's faying *beloved* is not needlefs tautology, but proves the ftrength of his affection; *I wifh that thou mayft profper, and be in health, even as thy foul profpereth.* Gaius, it feems, at this time felt a weak conftitution, or a bad habit of body; this may fhow, that the moft ufeful perfons, the choiceft favourites of heaven, muft not expect to be without the common infirmities of the human frame; fo far from this, that it is often found that a thoufand ufeful Chriftians have weakly conftitutions. That great and fweet finger of Ifrael, Dr. Watts, I remember about two and thirty years ago told me that he had got no fleep for three months, but what was procured by the moft exquifite art of the moft eminent phyficians; and, my dear hearers, none but thofe that have fuch habits of body can fympathize with thofe that are under them. When we are in high fpirits we think people might do if they would, but when brought down ourfelves we cannot; but notwithftanding his body was in this condition, his foul profpered fo eminently, fo very eminently, that the apoftle could not think it a greater mercy,

or

or the church a greater blessing, than that his bodily health might be as vigorous as the health of his soul. I remember the great colonel Gardiner, who had the honour of being killed in his country's cause, closes one of his last letters to me, with wishing I might enjoy a thriving soul in a healthy body; but this is peculiar to the followers of Jesus, they find the soul prospers most when the body is worst; and observe, he wishes him a prospering body above all things, that he might have joy and health with a prosperous soul; for if we have a good heart, and good health at the same time, and our hearts are alive to God, we go on with a fresh gale. I observe, that the soul of man in general must be made a partaker of a divine life before it can be said to prosper at all. The words of our text are particularly applicable to a renewed heart, to one that is really alive to God. When a tree is dead we don't so much as expect leaves from it, nor to see any beauty at all in a plant or flower that we know is absolutely dead; and therefore the foundation of the apostle's wish lies here, that the soul of Gaius, and consequently the souls of all true believers, have life communicated to them from the Spirit of the living God.

Such

Such a life may God of his infinite mercy impart to each of us! and I think, if I am not mistaken, and I believe I may venture to say that I am not, that where the divine life is implanted by the Spirit of the living God, that life admits of decrease and increase, admits of dreadful decays, and also of some blessed revivings. The rays of the divine life being once implanted, it will grow up to eternal life; the new creation is just like the old when God said *let there be light, there was light*, which never ceased since the universe was made, and the favourite creature man was born. Upon a survey of his own works, God pronounced *every thing good, and entered into his rest*; so it will be with all those who are made partakers of the divine nature. *The water that I shall give him, shall be a well of water springing up into everlasting life.*

My brethren, from our first coming into the world, till our passing out of it to *the spirits of just men made perfect*, all the Lord's Children have found, some more, and others less, that they have had dreadful as well as blessed times, and all has been over-ruled to bring them nearer unto God: but I believe, I am sure, I speak to some this night, that if it

was

was put to their choice, had rather know that their souls prospered, than to have ten thousand pounds left them : and it is supposed that we may not only know it ourselves, but that others may know it, *that their profiting,* as Paul says, *may appear to all.* Because John says, *I wish above all things, that thy body may be in health, as thy soul prospers.* O may all that converse with us see it in us! We may frequently sit under the gospel, but if we don't take a great deal of care, however orthodox we are, we shall fall into practical Antinomianism, and be contented that we were converted twenty or thirty years ago, and learn, as some Antinomians, *to live by faith.* Thank God, say some, we met with God so many months ago, but are not at all solicitous whether they meet with him any more ; and there is not a single individual here that is savingly acquainted with Jesus Christ, but wishes his soul prospered more than his body.

The great question is, how shall I know that my soul prospers? I have been told that there is such a thing as knowing this, and that I can be conscious of it myself, and others too. It may not be mispending an hour, to lay down some marks whereby we may know

whe-

whether our fouls profper or no. If there be
any of you of an Antinomian turn of mind,
(I don't know there are any of you) I don't
know but you will be of the fame mind of the
man that came to me in Leadenhall twenty-
five years ago: Sir, fays he, you preached
upon the marks of the new birth. Marks,
fays I, yes, fir: O thank God, fays he, I am
above marks, I don't mind marks at all: and
you may be affured perfons are upon the brink
of Antinomianifm, that fay away with your
legal preaching. I wonder they don't fay as
they go along the ftreets, away with your
dials, away with your dials, we don't want
marks, we know what it is o'clock without
any. If the marks upon the foul of a believer
are like the fun-dial, there are marks to prove
that we are upon the right foundation: if the
fun does not fhine on the fun-dial, there is
no knowing what o'clock it is; but let it
fhine, and inftantaneoufly you know the time
of the day; this is not known when it is
cloudy; and who dare to fay but that a child
of God, for want of the fun of righteoufnefs
fhining upon his heart, may write bitter things
againft himfelf. A good man may have the
vapours, as one Mr. Brown had, that wrote
a book

a book of good hymns, who was so vapour-
ish, that no body could make him believe he
had a soul at all. Let the sun shine, the believer can see whether the sun is in the meridian at the sixth, ninth, or twelfth hour. O
that there might be great searching of heart.
I have been looking up to God for direction;
I hope the preaching of this may be to awaken some, to call back some backsliders, to
awaken some sinners that don't care whether
their souls prosper or no. I don't mean the
Tabernacle comers, or the Foundery comers,
or the church, or dissenters, but I speak to all
of you, of whatever denomination you are;
God of his infinite mercy give you his Spirit.
You that are believers, come, let us have that
common name among us all; if we have got
it, we go off well. If you want to know
whether your souls prosper, that is, whether
they are healthy; you know what a person
means when he wishes your body to prosper;
let me ask you how it is between you and
God, with respect to secret prayer? Good Mr.
Bunyan says, if we are prayerless, we are
Christless. None of God's people, says he,
come into the world still-born. Good Mr.
Birket (whose commentary has gone through
five

five or fix-and-twenty editions; and yet I think
if he was now alive, and to preach once or
twice a day, they would cry, Away with his
commentary, and preaching and all) fpeaks
to the fame purpofe. *Come into the world ftill-
born !* what language is that in a preacher's
mouth ? but it will do for thofe that like to
ufe marks and figns. *I will pour out a Spirit of
grace and fupplication,* fays the Lord ; and I
will venture to fay, if the Spirit of grace re-
fides in the heart, the Spirit of fupplication will
not be wanting. Perfons under their firft love
dare not go without God; they go to God,
not as the formalift does, not for fear of going
to hell, or being damned. It is a mercy any
thing drives to prayer; and a perfon under the
fpirit of bondage, that has been juft brought
to the liberty of the fons of God, goes freely to
his heavenly father, under the difcoveries and
conftraints of divine love. Come, I will appeal to yourfelves; did not you, like a dear
fond mother, if the child, the beloved child,
made but the leaft noife in the world, O, fays
the mother, the dear child crys, I muft go and
hufh it: fo time was, when many hearkened
to the call of God, and could no more keep
from the prefence of God in fecret, than a

fond

fond mother from the presence of her dear
child. Now. if your souls do prosper, this
connection between you and God will be kept
up; I don't say that you will always have
the same fervour as when you first set out; I
don't say you will always be carried up into
the third heavens; the animal spirits possibly
will not admit of such solace; but you should
enquire with yourselves, whether you would
be easy to be out of God's company? Steal
from behind your counter, and go and converse with God. Sir Thomas Abney, who
was observable for keeping up constant prayer
in his family, being asked how he kept up
prayer that night he was sworn in Lord-
Mayor? Very well, says he, I got the company into my room, and entertained them,
and when the time came, I told them I must
leave them a little, while I went and prayed
with my family, and returned again. God
grant we may have many such Lord-Mayors.
If our souls prosper, the same principle will
reign in us, and make us conscientiously attend
on the means of grace. It is a most dreadful
mark of an enthusiastic turn of mind, when
persons think they are so high in grace, that
they thank God they have no need of ordi-

nances.

nances. Our being the children of God, is so
far from being the cause of our wanting no
ordinances, that, properly speaking, the ordinances are intended for the nourishing of the
children of God ; not only for the awaking the
soul at first, but for the feeding the soul afterwards. If the same nourishment the child receives before, feeds it after it is born ; and as
the manna never failed, but the children of
Israel partook of it daily while in the wilder-
ness, till they came to Canaan, so we shall
want our daily bread, we shall want the God
of grace and mercy to convey his divine life
into our hearts, till we get into the heavenly
Canaan. There faith will be turned into vision,
and then we shall not want ordinances ; and
let people say what they will, if our souls
prosper we shall be glad of ordinances, we
shall love the place where God dwells; we
shall not say, *such a one preaches and I will not
go,* but if we are among them we shall be glad
of a good plain country dish, as well as a fine
garnished desert; and if our souls prosper, we
shall be fond of the messengers as well as the
message: we shall admire as much to hear a
good ram's-horn, such as blowed down the
walls of Jericho, as a fine silver trumpet. So

in

in all the ordinances of the Lord, that of the
Lord's-supper for example; if the soul does
not attend thereon, it is an evidence that it
does not prosper. It is a wonder if that soul
has not done something to make it afraid to
meet God at his table. *Adam, where art
thou?* says the eternal Logos to his fallen creature; and every time we miss, whether we
think of it or no, the Redeemer puts it down;
but if our souls prosper, how shall we run to
the table of the Lord, and be glad to come
often to the commemoration of his death.

I will venture to affirm farther, that if your
souls prosper, you will grow downwards.
What is that? why you will grow in the
knowledge of yourselves. I heard, when I
was at Lisbon, that some people there began
at the top of the house first. It is odd kind of
preaching that will do for the Papists, resting
merely in externals. The knowledge of ourselves is the first thing God implants. *Lord,
let me know myself,* was a prayer that one of
the Fathers put up for sixteen years together;
and if you have high thoughts of yourselves,
you may know you are light-headed, you forget what poor silly creatures you are. As our
souls prosper we shall be more and more sensi-

ble,

ble, not only of the outside, but of the inside;
we first battle with the outward man, but as
we advance in the divine life, we have nearer
views of the chambers of imagery that are in
our hearts ; and one day after another we shall
find more and more abominations there, and
confequently we shall fee more of the glory of
Jefus Chrift, the wonders of that Immanuel,
who daily delivers us from this body of fin and
death; and I mention this, becaufe there is
nothing more common, efpecially with young
Chriftians. I ufed formerly to have at leaft a
hundred or two hundred in a day, who would
come and fay, O dear, I am fo and fo, I met
with God ; ah! that is quite well: a week
after they would come and fay, O, fir, it is all
delufion, there was nothing in it ; what is the
matter? O never was fuch a wretch as I am,
I never thought I had fuch a wicked heart.
Oh! God cannot love me ; now, fir, all my
fervour, and all that I felt is gone ; and what
then? does a tree never grow but when it
grows upward? fome trees I fancy grow
downward; and the deeper you grow in the
knowledge of yourfelf, the deeper you grow
in the knowledge of God and his grace, that
difcovers the corruptions of your hearts. Do
not

not you find that aged men look back upon
some former states. I know some people
can't look back to see how many sins they have
been guilty of; but if grace helps us to a sight
of our inherent corruptions, it will make us
weary of it, and lead us to the blood of Christ
to cleanse us from it; consequently, if your
souls prosper, the more you will fall in love
with the glorious Redeemer, and with his
righteousness. I never knew a person in my
life that diligently used the word, and other
means, but as they improved in grace, saw
more and more the necessity of depending
upon a better righteousness than their own.
Generally when we first set out, we have got
better hearts than heads; but if we grow in
the divine life, our heads will grow as well as
our hearts, and the Spirit of God leads out of
abominable self, and causes us to flee more
and more to that glorious and compleat righteousness that Jesus Christ wrought out.

The more your souls prosper, the more you
will see of the freeness and distinguishing nature of God's grace, that all is of grace. We
are all naturally free-willers, and generally
young ones say, O we have found the Messiah,
of whom Moses and the prophets spoke;
which

which is right, except that word *we* have found; for the believer a little after learns, that the *Meffiah* had found him. I mention this, becaufe we ought not to make perfons offenders for a word; we fhould bear with young Chriftians, and not knock a young child's brains out, becaufe he cannot fpeak in blank verfe.

Let it not be forgotton alfo, that the more your fouls profper, the more you will get above the world. You cannot think that I mean you fhould be negligent about the things of this life. Nothing tries my temper more, than to fee any about me idle; an idle perfon tempts the devil to tempt him. In the ftate of paradife Adam and Eve were to drefs the garden, and not to be idle there; after the fall they were to till the ground: but if any body fays that the Methodifts think to be idle, they injure them. We tell people to rife and be at their work early and late, that they may redeem time to attend the word. If all that fpeak againft the Methodifts were as diligent, it would be better for their wives and families. What do you think a true Me-thodift will be idle? no, he will be bufy with his hands, he knows time is precious, and
there-

therefore he will work hard that he may have
to give to them that need, and at the same
time he will live above the world; and you
know the earth is under your feet, so is the
world. When he goes to sleep he will say,
I care not whether I wake more. I can look
back, and tell you of hundreds and hundreds
that once seemed alive to God, and have been
drawn away with a little filthy, nasty dirt.
How many places are there empty here, that
have been filled with persons that once were
zealous in their attendance? As a person the
other day, to whose having a place it was
objected, that he was a Methodist; no, says
he, I have not been a Methodist these two
years. I do not, for my part, wish people
joy when they get money; only take care it
does not get into, and put your eyes out; if
your money increases, let your zeal for good
works increase. Perhaps some stranger will
say, I thought you was against good works.
I tell you the truth, I am against good works,
don't run away before I have finished my sen-
tence; we are against good works being put
in the room of Christ, as the ground of our
acceptance; but we look upon it, if we have
a right faith, our faith will work by love.

Ever

Ever since I was a boy, I remember to have heard a story of a poor indigent beggar, who asked a clergyman to give him his alms, which being refused, he said, will you please, sir, to give me your blessing; says he, God bless you : O, replied the beggar, you would not give me that if it was worth any thing. There are many who will talk very friend- ly to you, but if they suppose you are come for any thing, they will run away as from a pick-pocket; whereas, if our souls prospered, we should *count it more blessed to give than to receive.* When we rise from our beds this would be our question to ourselves, what can I do for God to day? what can I do for the poor? have I two, or five, or ten talents? God help me to do for the poor as much as if I knew I was to live only this day.

In a word, if your souls prosper, my dear hearers, you will grow in love. There are some good souls, but very narrow souls; they are so afraid of loving people that differ from them, that it makes me uneasy to see it. Party spirits creep in among Christians, and whereas it was formerly said, *see how these Christians love one another!* now it may be said, *see how these Christians hate one another!*

I de-

I declare from the bottom of my heart, that I am more and more convinced that the principles I have preached are the word of God. Pray what do you do at Change; is there fuch a thing as a Prefbyterian, or Independent, or Church-walk there? is there any chambers there for the Prefbyterians, and Independents, and Churchmen to deal in? People may boaft of their wildfire-zeal for God, till they can't bear the fight of a perfon that differs from them. The apoftle commends Gaius for his catholic love, for his love to ftrangers. That was a glorious faying of a good woman in Scotland, *Come in*, fays fhe, *ye bleffed of the Lord*; I have a houfe that will hold a hundred, and a heart that will hold ten thoufand. God give us fuch a heart; *he that dwelleth in love, dwelleth in God.* I could mention twenty marks, and fo go on wire-drawing till nine or ten o'clock; but it is beft to deal with our fouls as with our bodies, to eat but little at a time. It is fo with preaching; though I don't proceed any farther in my difcourfe, God blefs what has been faid.

But is there a child of God here that can go away without a drooping heart? I don't fpeak that you may think me humble: I love fin-

L   cerity,

cerity, inward and outward, and hate guile.
When I think what God has done to me,
how often he has pruned me, and dug and
dung'd about me, and when I think how little
I have done for God, it makes me weep if
possible tears of blood; it makes me cry, *O
my leanness, my leanness*, as I expressed myself
with my friend to day. This makes me long,
if my strength of body would permit, to begin to be in earnest for my Lord. What say
you, my dear friends, have all of you got the
same temper? have you made the progress you
ought to have done? O London! London!
highly favoured London! what would some
people give for thy privileges? what would
the people I was called to preach to but this
day se'ennight? A good, a right honourable
lady, about three-and-twenty miles off, has
brought the gospel there. The people that I
preached to longed and thirsted after the same
message; they said, they thought they never
heard the truth before. You have the manna
poured out round the camp, and I am afraid
you are calling it *light bread*; at least, I am
afraid you have had a bad digestion. Consider
of it, and for Jesus Christ's sake tremble for
fear *God should remove his candlestick from
among*

among you. Labourers are fick; thofe that did once labour are almoft worn out, and others they only bring themfelves into a narrow fphere, and fo confine their ufefulnefs. There are few that like to go out in the fields; broken heads and dead cats are no more the ornaments of a Methodift, but filk fcarves. Thofe honourable badges are now no more: the langour has got from the minifters to the people, and if you don't take care, we fhall all fall dead together. The Lord Jefus roufe us, the Son of God roufe us all. Ye fhould fhow the world the way, and ye that have been Methodifts of many years ftanding, fhow the young ones that have not the crofs to bear as we once had, what ancient Methodifm was.

As for you who are quite negligent about the profperity of your fouls, who only mind your bodies, who are more afraid of a pimple in your faces, than of the rottennefs of your hearts; that will fay, O give me a good bottle and a fowl, and keep the profperity of your fouls to yourfelves. You had better take care what you fay, for fear God fhould take you at your word. I knew fome tradefmen and farmers, and one had got a wife perhaps with a fortune too, who prayed they might be

excufed,

excufed, they never came to the fupper, and God fent them to hell for it too; this may be your cafe. I was told to-day of a young woman, that was very well on Sunday when fhe left her friends, when fhe came home was racked with pain, had an inflammation in her bowels, and is now a breathlefs corpfe. Another that I heard of, a Chriftlefs preacher, that always minded his body, when he was near death he faid to his wife, I fee hell opened for me, I fee the damned tormented, I fee fuch a one in hell that I debauched; in the midft of his agony he faid, I am coming to thee, I am coming, I muft be damned, God will damn my foul, and died. Take care of jefting with God; there is room enough in hell, and if you neglect the profperity of your fouls what will become of you? what will you give for a grain of hope when God requires your fouls? *awake thou that fleepeft*; hark! hark! hark! hear the word of the Lord, the living God. Help me, O ye children of God: I am come with a warrant from Jefus of Nazareth to night. Ye minifters of Chrift that are here, help me with your prayers: ye fervants of the living God, help me with your prayers. O with what fuccefs did I preach in Moorfields when I had

ten

ten thoufand of God's people praying for me;
pray to God to ftrengthen my body: don't be
afraid I fhall hurt myfelf to-night: I don't
care what hurt I do myfelf if God may blefs
it; I can preach but little, but may God blefs
that little. I weep and cry and humble myfelf
before God daily for being laid afide; I would
not give others the trouble if I could preach
myfelf. You have had the firft of me, and
you will have the laft of me: the angels of
God waited for your converfion, and are now
ready to take care of the foul when it leaves
the rotten carcafe. The worft creature under
heaven, that has not a penny in the world,
may be welcome unto God. However it has
been with us in times paft, may our fouls profper in time to come; which God grant of his
infinite mercy, Amen.

✤✤✤✤✤✤✤✤✤✤✤✤✤✤✤✤✤✤✤✤✤✤✤✤

SERMON IV.

The Gofpel a dying Saint's Triumph.

A FUNERAL SERMON.

MARK xvi. ver. 15, 16.

And he faid unto them, Go ye into all the world, and preach the gofpel to every creature. He that believeth and is baptized fhall be faved, but he that believeth not fhall be damned.

I AM perfuaded I need not inform this auditory, that when ambaffadors are fent to a prince, or when judges go their refpective circuits, it is always cuftomary for them to fhow their credentials, to open and read their commiffions, by which they act in his Majefty's name. The fame is abfolutely neceffary for thofe who are ambaffadors of the Son of God, as they would be faithful to their Lord; fince they are to fit with him on the

throne,

throne, when he shall come the second time
to judge both evil angels and men. If any
should ask me, where is their commission? it
has been just now read unto you. Here it is
in my hand, it is written with the King's own
hand, by the finger of the ever-blessed God,
and sealed with the signet of his eternal Spirit,
with his broad seal annexed to it. The commission is short, but very extensive; and it is
remarkable, it was given out just before the
Redeemer went to heaven; he reserved it in
infinite wisdom for his last blessing, to appoint
and employ vicegerents to carry on his work
on earth. *He that hath an ear to hear, let
him hear* what the Son of God says to a company of poor fishermen. There was not one
scholar among them all. What does he say;
*Go ye into all the world, and preach the gospel
to every creature.* Let us pause a while, and
before we go further let us see what mercy,
what love, and yet withal, what equal majesty are blended in this expression or commission. *Go ye,* ye poor fishermen, ye that
the letter-learned doctors will look upon as
illiterate men; *Go ye,* that have hitherto been
dreaming of temporal preferments, quarrelling
*who should sit on my right hand and on my left
hand*

hand in my kingdom ; *Go ye,* not ſtay till the
people come to you, but imitate the conduct
of your Maſter ; *Go ye,* remembring that the
devil will not permit ſouls to be fond of hearing you : Go therefore ; where ? *into all the*
world ; there is a commiſſion for you ; there
never was ſuch a commiſſion on the earth ;
there never was any like this ; *Go into all the*
world, that is, into the Gentile as well as the
Jewiſh world. Hitherto my goſpel has been
confined to the Jews ; I once told you, you
muſt not go to the Gentiles ; I once told a
poor woman that came to me, *it is not meet*
to take the childrens bread, and give it unto
dogs : but the partition wall being now broke
down, the veil of the temple being now rent
in twain, he gave them a univerſal commiſſion ; *Go ye, therefore, into all the world* ;
how ! what go into other miniſters pariſhes ?
for there was not a diſtrict then but what was
ſettled with ſhepherds, ſuch as they were ;
yes, yes, *Go into all the world* ; and though
I will not pretend to ſay, that this enjoins miniſters to go into every part of the world ; yet
I inſiſt upon it, and by the grace of God, if I
was to die for it, I will ſay, that no power on
earth has power to reſtrain miniſters from

preach-

preaching where a company of people are willing to hear; and if minifters were of a right temper, they would fay as a minifter did at Oxford, that ufed to vifit the prifoners there; I remember once I went to afk him whether I might go and vifit fome of his parifh, whether he was offended at our going to vifit the prifoners? No, no, fays he, I am glad I have any fuch young curates as you. And if minifters were of fuch a temper now, O dear the devil would fly before us. As good Mr. Philip Henry faid to the minifter of Broad Oaks, from whence he was ejected, but preached afterwards in a barn, and meeting the minifter after fermon was over; *Sir*, fays Mr. Henry, *I have been making bold to throw a handful of feed into your ground.* Thank you, fir, fays he, God blefs it, there is work enough for us both. We may talk of what we will, fearch into the bottom, it is not for want of light, but of more zeal and love to the Son of God: if we were as warm, and full of the love of God as we ought to be, thefe pretty excufes we urge to fave our bones, would not be fo much as mentioned; we fhould go out and leave thefe carcafes to the grace of God. I don't fee how we can act as priefts

of the church of England without doing it.
Be fo kind as read the Ordination Service as
foon as you go home ; for the office of ordination and confecration of bifhops, priefts,
and deacons, is left out of moft of the common prayer books, fo that people are as ignorant of it as if it was not. The office of a
prieft is this : he is not to confine himfelf to
his place, no; what then? why he is *to go
forth, and feek after the children of God that
are difperfed in this needy world*; thefe are the
very words that the bifhop fpeaks to us when
we are ordained ; but if we are confined to one
particular place, and are to be fhut up in one
corner, pray how do we feek the children of
God that are difperfed in this needy world?
Parifhes and fettled minifters there muft be,
but we are not, I infift on it, to be hindered
from preaching Chrift any where, becaufe he
bids us *go into all the world*; here is our licence. I acknowledge the Chapel is licenfed ;
here is my licence, and wherever I go I will
produce my licence ; where? why out of the
16th of Mark; *Go ye, and preach the gospel
to all the world :* there is the licence, and the
Spirit of Chrift helping us to preach by that
licence, will make all the devil's children
cowards

cowards before us. We have tried them thefe thirty years, would to God we fet about it now; if I had ftrength I would fet about it to-morrow; I only grieve that my body will not hold out for field-preaching, elfe Kennington-Common fhould be my pulpit, for any place is confecrated where Chrift is prefent. Well, what muft we go forth to do? *Go ye into all the world, and preach;* preach! what is that? why the original word for preach is to fpeak out, as a crier does that cries goods that are loft; proclaim it. And Ifaiah would be reckoned a dreadful enthufiaft if now alive. How does he preach? he preaches in the King's chapels fuch language and eloquence as would carry all before it; and yet how does he preach? *Ho, every one that thirfteth.* O, *he lifts up his voice like a trumpet.* And the word preach fignifies to proclaim; *to cry aloud, and fpare not.* How do you like one that cries your loft goods if he only whifpers? would you chufe to employ a man that you could not hear two yards? O, fay you, I fhall never find my goods: and if perfons have what qualifications they may, if they cannot be heard at all; they need not preach at all. I know a prebend in the cathe-

dral

dral of York, who spoke so very low nobody heard him; somebody said, they never heard such a *moving* sermon in all their lives in that cathedral, for it made all the people *move out*, because they could not hear. The matter of the ministry of the gospel is of infinite importance: unless, my brethren, we could be heard, what do we preach for? It implies earnestness in the preaching, and the preacher. You expect a person, like one that is crying your goods, to be in earnest; and if we preach, and make the King's proclamation, we should be in earnest. It is said, *Christ opened his mouth and taught.* Now a modern critic would laugh at that; open his mouth, say they, how could he speak without opening his mouth? Would it not be better to say, *he taught them?* No, no, there is no idle word in God's book. It is said, *the Lord Jesus opened his mouth:* what for? why, to get in breath that he might speak loud to the people, when the heavens were his sounding board; then did he open his mouth, and taught them in earnest, powerfully; and therefore the people make this observation when he had done speaking, *that he spoke as one having authority, and not as the Scribes.* There is no dispensa-

tion

tion from preaching, but ficknefs or want of abilities, to thofe that are ordained to preach; and therefore it was a proverb in the primitive church, *that it becomes a bifhop to die preaching.* Bifhop Jewell, that bleffed minifter of the church of England, gave that anfwer to a perfon that met his lordfhip walking on foot in the dirt, going to preach to a few people. Why does your lordfhip, weak as you are, expofe yourfelf thus? fays he, it becomes a bifhop to die preaching. Lord fend all the world that have bifhops fuch jewels as he was! Pray what are they to preach? not themfelves. What are they to preach? why they are to preach not morality: not morality! come, don't be frightened, any of you that are afraid of good works don't be frightened this morning: I fay not morality; that is, morality is not to be the grand point of their preaching; they are not to preach as an heathen philofopher would. A late bifhop of Lincoln, who has not been dead a long while, faid to his chaplain, You are not a minifter of Cicero, or any of the heathen philofophers; you are not to entertain your people with dry morality, but remember you are a minifter of Chrift; you are, therefore, to preach the gofpel; and if

you

you will not preach the gospel in the church, you must not be angry for the poor people's going out into the fields where they hear the gospel; that is to be your grand theme, *Go into all the world and preach the gospel.*

Now the gospel signifies good news, glad tidings: *Behold I bring you*, said the angel, *glad tidings of great joy.* Mean and contemptible as the office of a preacher may be thought now, the angels were glad of the commission to preach this gospel: and Dr. Goodwin, that learned pious soul, says in his familiar way, and that is the best way of writing, God had but one Son, and he made a minister of him ; and I add, he made an itinerant minister of him too. Well, and some say, you must not preach the law; you cannot preach the gospel without preaching the law; for you shall find by and by, we are to preach something that the people must be saved by: it is impossible to tell them how they are to be saved, unless we tell them what they are to be saved from. The way the Spirit of God takes, is like that we take in preparing the ground : do you think any farmer would have a crop of corn next year unless they plow now; and you may as well expect a crop of corn on

un-

unplowed ground, as a crop of grace, until the foul is convinced of its being undone without a Saviour. That is the reafon we have fo many mufhroom converts, fo many perfons that are always happy! happy! happy! and never were miferable; why? becaufe their ftony ground is not plowed up; they have not got a conviction of the law; they are ftony-ground hearers; *they hear the word with joy, and in a time of temptation,* which will foon come after a feeming or real converfion, *they fall away,* They ferve Chrift as the young man ferved the Jews that laid hold of him, who, when he found he was like to be a prifoner for following Chrift, left his garments; and fo fome people leave their profeffion. That makes me fo cautious now, which I was not thirty years ago, of dubbing people converts fo foon. I love now to wait a little, and fee if people bring forth fruit; for there are fo many bloffoms which March winds you know blow away, that I cannot believe they are converts till I fee fruit brought forth. It will do converts no harm to keep them a little back; it will never do a fincere foul any harm.

We are to preach the gofpel: to whom? *to every creature:* here is the commiffion, *every crea-*

creature. I ſuppoſe the apoſtles were not to
ſee every creature; they did not go into all
nations; they had particular diſtricts; but
wherever they did go, they preached. Did
you ever hear Paul, or any of the apoſtles,
ſent away a congregation without a ſermon?
No, no : when turned out of the temple they
preached in the highways, hedges, ſtreets, and
lanes of the city : they went to the water-ſide;
there Lydia was catched. My brethren, we
have got a commiſſion here from Chriſt; and
not only a commiſſion, but we have a command *to preach to every creature*; all that are
willing to hear. *He that hath an ear to hear,*
let him hear; and if ſome ſhall ſay, they will
not come if we do preach, would to God we
tried them: *where the carcaſe is there will the*
eagles be gathered together. We are to preach
glad tidings of ſalvation; to tell a poor be-
nighted world, lying in the wicked one the
devil, their ſtate and condition : we are to tell
them, *God is love*; to tell them, that God
loves them better than they do themſelves.
We muſt preach the law, but not leave the
people there. We muſt tell them how Moſes
brings them to the borders of Canaan, and then
tell them of a glorious Joſhua that will carry
them

them over Jordan; firſt, to ſhew them their
wants; and then point out to them a Jeſus that
can ſupply, and more than ſupply, all their
wants. This we are *to tell every creature*;
and it is for this that people ſtone goſpel preachers. I don't think the priſoners would be
angry with us if we were to tell them, the
king commiſſions us to declare to them that
they might come out of their priſon, that their
chains may be knocked off. If you was to go
to one of them and ſay, Here you have your
chains; and he was to ſay, I have no chains
on at all; you would think that man's brains
turned; and ſo are every man's that does not
ſee himſelf to be in the chains of ſin and de-
ceit. We are *to preach liberty to the captives,
to proclaim the acceptable year of the Lord;
found the jubilee trumpet, and tell them the year
of releaſe is come*; that Jeſus can make them
happy.

But, pray, if we are to preach, what are
the creatures to do that ſee their need of this
ſalvation? I will tell you; they are to believe.
He that believeth, and is baptized, &c. The
grand topics Chriſt's miniſters are to preach,
are *repentance towards God, and faith in our
Lord Jeſus Chriſt.* The men of the world

fancy

fancy they have believed already, and some of them lift up their heads and say, Thank God, we have believed ever since we were born; and in one sense many people believe, but in what sense? just as the devil believes; they believe, and still continue devils in their carnal state; that is, they assent to the gospel, they assent to it as a thing that is credible. This is our school definition of faith; and I believe there are thousands that call themselves Christians, that don't believe a thousandth part of what the devil does. The devil believes more than an Arian, for he does not believe Christ to be God; the devil says, *I know whom thou art, the Holy One of God.* The devil will rise up in judgment against him. He believes more than a Socinian, who believes Jesus Christ to be no more than an extraordinary man; and he believes more of Jesus Christ than thousands of professors do, who are neither Arians or Socinians. There are a thousand things in this book * that many people, if you come to close-quarters with them, will say they do not believe, though they are ashamed to own it. The furthest that they go, is to assent to the Creed, to the Lord's-prayer,

* Holding out his bible.

prayer, and Ten Commandments; and if a person can fay thefe in their mother tongue, and have been baptized by the prieft, and confirmed by the bifhop, and go to church once a week, and now and then on holidays, they think they are not only believers, but ftrong believers. I am not againft going to church, nor againft the Creed, the Lord's-prayer, and the Commandments; I love and honour them, and I pray God we may always have them; and I would not have our liturgy or articles departed from for ten thoufand worlds. Many would have them altered, be-caufe there are fome faults in them; but if our modern people were to alter them, they would make them ten thoufand times worfe than they are. But believing is fomething more; it is a coming to Jefus Chrift, receiving Jefus, rolling ourfelves on Jefus; it is a trufting in the Lord Jefus. I do not know any one fingle thing more varioufly expreffed in the fcriptures than believing; why? becaufe it is the marrow of the gofpel. Without faith we cannot be juf-tified, either in our perfons or performances; and therefore the Holy Ghoft has varioufly expreffed it, to let us fee the importance of the point. It is expreffed by a coming, truft-

ing,

ing, receiving, and relying, (all which amounts
to the fame thing) under a felt conviction that
we are loft, undone, condemned without him:
for, as a good old Puritan obferves, Chrift is
beholden to none of us for our hearts; we
never fhould come to Jefus Chrift, the
finner's laft fhift, till we feel we cannot do
without him. We are like the woman with
the bloody iffue; fhe fpent a great deal of money upon phyficians; if fhe had had the fum
of one half-guinea more, till that was gone
fhe never would have come to Chrift; but
having fpent all, and then hearing that Jefus
was to come that way, a fenfe of her need, a
feeling fenfe of her impotence, and infufficiency
of all other applications, made her come to
Chrift; faying in her heart, *If I could but
touch the hem of his garment I fhould be whole;
Jefus, the fon of David, would have mercy on
me*; or words to that purpofe. She did not
go about and fay, pray lend me a common-
prayer book; it was not in print then. Where
muft fhe borrow one? her heart, touched by
God, was the beft common-prayer; and a few
words, uttered from a fenfe of her weaknefs
and mifery, was more rhetoric, was more
mufic in the ears of God, than an extempore

prayer

prayer by a gifted man, admiring himſelf for an hour and half,) As a perſon told me but yeſterday, of a poor outlandiſh Papiſt that was condemned to die, held out for a long while; he would not ſpeak to a Proteſtant miniſter, but a night or two before he ſuffered, comes out to him, and ſays, *Me now ſee the ne-ceſſity of a greater abſolution than a prieſt can give me*; and then, in his broken language, cries out, *Dear Lord Jeſus, ſhow thy charity to thy poor ſinner!* There is language! there is rhe-toric for you! and we ourſelves like ſuch language. You don't like fawning people that come into your room, and by their very man-ner of coming prove they are not ſincere; but a poor creature that comes to pour out two or three words you ſee is honeſt, you will not ſay to ſuch a one, Why do you come to me, and not ſpeak blank verſe? why do you come to me, and not ſpeak fine language? No; ſince-rity is the thing; ſincerity is all in all. When we are once convinced of our need and help-leſsneſs, and of Jeſus's being a Redeemer, that is mighty and willing to ſave, a poor ſoul then throws himſelf upon this Jeſus, receives this Jeſus, ventures upon this Jeſus, believes the word, and by thus venturing on the promiſe,

mife, receives from Jefus the thing promifed. *Faith comes by hearing, and hearing by the word of God.* But then where there is true faith, that will, my dear hearers, be attended with what? why, with falvation. *He that believeth, and is baptized,* faith our Lord, *fhall be faved:* faved from what? why, from every thing that he wants to be faved from, and receives every thing that God can give to compleat his whole falvation. What is it a poor finner wants to be faved from? O, fin, fin, the guilt of fin. The firft conviction brings the creatures to God by force; there are very few that are drawn by love intirely: and I feldom find any of thofe that have been drawn by love, but have had dreadful conflicts afterwards: for either before or after converfion, our hearts muft be plowed up, or we fhall never be prepared for the kingdom of heaven.

Ye fhall be faved from the painful guilt of fin: what is that? why, the common-prayer book will tell you, in the communion office; *the remembrance of our fins is grievous unto us, and the burden of them is intolerable.* There is methodiftical language. Cranmer, Latimer, or Hooper, were, my brethren, what? why, they were Methodift preachers; and they ufed

to

to preach in Paul's-Crofs, a pulpit faid to be
made in the fhape of a crofs, near St. Paul's
church ; and a falary given for that very purpofe, I believe, to this day. No matter where
we preach, fo that finners feel Chrift's power
in delivering them from this, which certainly
implies a confcioufnefs of pardon. I don't
think the poor creature that was refpited the
other day, would have believed it, had he not
feen the king's warrant juft before the others
were carried out. Why, fay they, here is his
majefty's pardon ; he takes and receives it with
joy, and is now freed from the gallows. And
if perfons can give this credence to an earthly
king, why cannot a believer have a fenfe of the
pardon of his fins from God ? If a perfon's
reading this to me, telling me the king has
pardoned me, has fuch an effect, why may
not God's word, backed by his Spirit, be
brought home with fuch power on my heart,
that I may be affured God has pardoned me,
as well as a criminal that his king has faved ?
If this is gofpel away with it, fay fome, who
think we are not to be juftified till we come to
judgment. O bleffed creatures ! this is modern
divinity ! our reformers knew nothing about it.
We are to be declared, if you pleafe, juftified,

in

in the day of Jesus Christ, who will pronounce it before all mankind. But, my brethren, we are to be married to Jesus Christ in this world, and the marriage is to be declared in another; and I will insist upon it, though I will not pretend to say that all that have not full assurance are not Christians, yet I will say, that assurance is necessary for the well-being of a Christian; the comfortable being, though not for his very existence: and I will venture to say, that a soul was never brought to Christ, but what had some ground of assurance of pardon; tho', for want of knowing better, he put it by, and did not know the gift of God when it came. But, my brethren, *we shall be saved from all our sins.* Here is *glad tidings of great joy* now come: satan may hear that; and any of you here that are coming into the Chapel as you pass along. I am glad to see poor creatures come, that I may tell them, *God is love.* Believers, you shall be saved from all your sins, every one of them; they shall all be blotted out. Generally, when persons are convinced, the devil preaches despair; some great sin lies upon them; and, says the poor sinner, I shall be saved from all but that; had I not been guilty of such a crime I might have hope, but

I am

I am guilty of fuch a fin, which is fo awful, with fuch dreadful aggravations, I am afraid I fhall never be pardoned. But, my dear fouls, Chrift is love; and when he loves to forgive, he forgives like a God; *I will blot out your iniquities, tranfgreffions, and fins. Come now,* faith the Lord, *let us reafon together; though your fins are as fcarlet, yet they fhall be as white as fnow.* I am fo far from being unwilling to fave or pardon, that the angels, every time the gofpel is preached, are ready to tune their harps, and long to fing an anthem to fome poor finner's converfion.

They fhall be faved from the power of fin. Don't you remember that when Jofhua was going on with his conquefts, that there were fome kings in a cave; and when he returned, he ordered them to bring the kings out for God's people to tread upon them. When I read that paffage, I ufed to think thefe kings were like our corruptions hid in the cave of our hearts, and the ftone of unbelief rolled to keep them in: but when we receive Chrift by faith, and have pardon in him, our great Jofhua takes away the ftone, and fays, *bring out thefe kings,* thefe corruptions, *that have reigned over my people, and by faith let*

O   *them*

them tread on the necks of them. Our great
Mafter, when he gave the command in the
text, fays, *thefe figns fhall follow them that
believe, in my name they fhall caft out devils,
they fhall fpeak with new tongues, they fhall
take up ferpents, and if they drink any deadly
thing it fhall not hurt them.* Thefe were
things peculiar, in one fenfe, to the apoftles;
but in the power of faith, and as brought home
to every believer, he cafts out devilifh lufts;
and if they had drank any deadly thing, as God
knows we have, they may do by them as Paul
did by the viper, through the power of faith
caft them off, and by this means prove that
Chrift is God.

This is, my dear hearers, a prefent falvation. The wickedeft wretch in the world
will cry, I hope to be faved, though they
have no notion of being faved but after their
death; as a woman in Virginia told me once,
when I faid fhe muft be born again; I believe
you, fir, but that muft be after I am dead.
And by peoples living as they do, one would
fuppofe that they think they are not to be
faved till they die, becaufe they live fo. But
as I have told you, I tell you again, Chrift's
falvation is a great falvation; and all that

Chrift

Chrift does for his people on earth, is but an earneft of good things to come, an anticipation of what he is to do for them in heaven. Our Lord fays, *the kingdom of God is within you; the kingdom is come nigh unto you.* You muft not only believe on Chrift, but believe in him: we are not only to be baptized in the name of the Father, Son, and Holy Ghoft, but we are to be baptized into the nature of the Father, Son, and Holy Ghoft; this is the baptifm of the Spirit, and this is that falvation which God grant we may all partake of.

We are to be faved, my brethren, from what? why, from the fear of death. *He came to deliver them who, through the fear of death, were all their life time fubject to bondage.* What are there no children of God but thofe that have full affurance? you never heard me fay fo; yet I am apt to fpeak a little faft, but at the fame time I would chufe not to fpeak fo faft as to fpeak contrary to the word of God. There are a great many good fouls, that at times may doubt of the reality of this work upon their fouls: a relaxed habit of body, a nervous diforder, you may fay what you pleafe, will make a weak child of God doubt of what God has done in them, and that hurts the

O 2   mind

mind as it has fuch a clofe connection with
the body; but then a believer is low : God's
people are low perfons : as the greateft ge-
nuiffes are moft liable to lownefs of fpirit, for
the fcabbard is not ftrong enough for the fword,
and perfons that talk much muft wear out in
time; but this I ftand to, it is our privilege to
live above the fears of death. We do not live
up to our dignity till every day we are waiting for the coming of our Lord from heaven;
and I am perfuaded of this, though I believe
there may be fome exceptions, that the reafon
why we do not live more above the fear of
death is, becaufe we keep in fo much with
thefe nafty earthly things. You may have the
beft eyes in the world, and only put your
hands before them, you will find the fun hid
from you; and fo you may have a large fire,
but throw fome earth upon the fire that is in
your parlour, or drawing rooms, and you will
find the fire damped. And how can people
have much of God or heaven, when they have
fo much of the earth in their hearts? It is our
privilege to live above the fear of death, though
we are not to be faved from dying; and I am
fure a believer would not be faved from dying
for a million of worlds; it would be death to

him

him not to die; but a foul touched with the
love of God, even in ficknefs, in the midft of
a burning fever, in the midft of a fire that
will burn a thoufand bodies up, convulfed
with tortures and pains in every limb ; a believer is enabled fometimes to fay, *O my God,*
O my God, thou art love ; *I am ready to come*
to thee in the midft of all. Bleffed be God, I
need not go far for example; yonder, under
the gallery, lies the remains, the carcafe of a
dear faint, who was for twenty-five days together burned with a fever, enough to fcorch
any creature up; yet, one filled with love
and power divine, bleffed the Lord Jefus;
though fhe cried out, If I was not fupported,
the agony of my body would make me impatient; yet never faid a murmuring word, but
in the midft of all cried out to thofe about her,
God is love ! O my joys ! O the comforts that I
feel ! and in her very laft moments cried out,
I am a coming ; *dear Lord, I am a coming* ;
and fo fweetly flept in Jefus.   If this is enthufiafm, God give us a good fhare of it when we
come to die! Thefe are dying and yet living
witneffes that *God is love !* She was in raptures
when Mr. Sheppard went to vifit her: fhe
defired me to tell you, that *God is love :* de-
                                                                fired

fired me to tell you in the Chapel pulpit, that
she was called about four years ago. I think
Mr. Lee was the instrument of her conversion.
Now her body is to be put to bed at noon;
but her soul is crying, O the joys! the joys!
the joys! of being saved by a blessed Emanuel!
Now will any one dare to deny this evidence?
Do you see worldly people work themselves
up into that frame when they die? Visit them
when they are near death: ah dear! they are
in the vapours; they are so afraid of dying,
that the doctor will not suffer us to come near
them; no, not common clergymen, for fear
we should damp their spirits: till they find they
are just gone, and then they give us leave to
say the farewel prayer to them: but they that
are born from above, that are made new creatures in Christ, feel something that smiles upon
them in death. She told them, *she believed
God would let her go over Jordan dry shod*;
that was her expression. If this is salvation on
earth, what must it be in heaven? If in the
midst of the tortures of a burning fever a rap-
tured soul can cry, O the joys! O the comforts! Lord, I am coming! I am coming!
what must that be when enclosed in a Redeemer's arms? in order to which, the glorious
angels

angels ſtand at the top of the ladder to take a
poor wearied pilgrim home. Lord, give us
not only ſuch a frame when we are dying, but
while we are living; for if it is comfortable to
die in ſuch a frame, why not to live in it?
to live in heaven on earth. O, ſay you, I
thank God I walk by faith; I have got the
promiſe. Well, thank God you have the promiſe; but with the promiſe, learn to walk by
that *faith which is the evidence of things not ſeen,*
which brings God down, brings heaven near,
and gives the ſoul a heart-felt experience, that
God is love. Here is a ſalvation worthy of a
God! here is a ſalvation worthy of the Mediator's blood! for this he groaned, for this he
bled, for this he died, for this he aroſe, for this
he aſcended, for this he ſent the Holy Ghoſt,
and for this purpoſe he now ſends him into the
hearts of his people.

My brethren, what ſay you to this? I hope
it is enough to make you cry out, *Lord, let
my latter end be like hers.* This may comfort
you that are mourners about her corpſe, this
may comfort a fond huſband, whoſe beloved
is now taken away by a ſtroke. What a
mercy is it, ſir, that you was inſtrumental to
bring her under the word? ſhe was once averſe

to

to coming here : *what, leave my parish church !*
said she ; *what, go to a conventicle, to a tabernacle of Methodists !* he advised her again and
again to come : at last, one day as they were going to St. Giles's, she says, Well, come put up
your walking-stick, if it falls towards St. Giles's I
will go there ; if to the Chapel, I will go there ;
the stick fell towards the Chapel, she came,
and was converted to God. O with what joy
must her husband meet her again in the kingdom of heaven ! and O happy day, in which she
was encouraged to seek after God. Last week,
another was buried in the like circumstances ;
and, blessed be God, in yonder burying-ground
are the remains of many precious souls, that in the
day of judgment will let the world know whether this Chapel was built for God or not.

O what an awful word is that in the
latter clause of the text, *he that believeth
not shall be damned.* Pause,—I will give you
time to think a little ; if you would have Christ
as good as his word of promise, remember he
will be as good as his word of threatning. You
hear the necessity of preaching the gospel, because upon believing or non-believing, our salvation or damnation will turn. What will you
laugh at the minister that cries out, Lord help
      , you

you to come; come, come, do you think that
we have nothing elfe to fay, and are at a lofs
for words, when we cry come, come, come,
to fill up our fermons? no, it is part of our
commiffion, it is one great part. And, my
fellow-finners, we are come to tell you, that
our Mafter has a two-edged fword as well as a
golden fcepter; and if you will not come under
the found of the word, and do not feel the converting power of it, you muft feel the confound-
ing weight of it. I repeat it again to you, *he that
believeth not fhall be damned*; the very word is
terrible, God grant you may never know how
terrible it is. You are condemned already;
he that believeth not is fo, *John* iii. 18. why?
*becaufe he hath not believed on the name of the
Son of God.* It is not his being a whore-mon-
ger or adulterer that will damn him, but his
unbelief is the damning fin; for this he will
be condemned; for ever banifhed from the prefence of the ever-bleffed God: and how will
you rave, how will you tear, and how will
you wring your hands, when you fee your
relations, your friends, thofe whom you defpifed, and were glad they were dead out of
your way, *fee them in Abraham's bofom, and
yourfelves lifting up your eyes in torment!* O

my

my dear hearers, do let me plead, let me intreat you; if that would do, I would down
on my knees; if that would do, I would come
down from the pulpit, I would hang on your
necks, I would not let you go, I would offer
myfelf to be trodden under your feet; I have
known what it is to be trodden under the foot
of men thirty years ago, and I am of the fame
temper ftill: ufe me as you will, I am a poor
finner; and if I was to be killed a thoufand
ways, I fuffer no more than my reward as an
unprofitable fervant of God: but don't tram-
ple the dear Jefus under foot; what has he
done to you? was it any harm to leave his father's bofom, come down and die, and plead
for finners? See him yonder hang on the tree!
behold him with his arm ftretched out! fee
him all of a bloody gore, and in his laft agony
preaching love! Would you give him a frefh
ftab? Are there any of you here that think the
fword did not pierce him enough; that they
did not knock the briers and thorns into his
head deep enough? and will you give him
the other flafh, the other thorns? and will
you pierce him afrefh, and go away without
believing he is love? I cannot help it; I am
free from the blood of you all. Oh that you
may

may not damn your own fouls! Don't be murderers; nor, like Efau, *fell your birth-right for a mefs of pottage.* God convince you; God convert you; God help thofe that never believed to believe; God help thofe that have believed to believe more; that they may experience more and more this falvation, till faith is turned into vifion, and hope into fruition; till we have all, with yonder faint, and all that have gone before us, experienced compleat falvation in the kingdom of heaven: even fo, Lord Jefus, Amen and Amen.

SERMON

✦✦✦✦✦✦✦✦✦✦✦✦✦✦✦✦✦✦✦✦✦✦✦✦

SERMON V.

Repentance and Converfion.

ACTS iii. ver. 19.

Repent ye therefore and be converted, that your fins may be blotted out, when the times of refrefhing fhall come from the prefence of the Lord.

WHAT a pity is it that modern preachers attend no more to the method thofe took who were firft infpired by the Holy Ghoft, in preaching Jefus Chrift! the fuccefs they were honoured with, gave a fanction to their manner of preaching, and the divine authority of their difcourfes, and energy of their elocution, one would think, fhould have more weight with thofe that are called to difpenfe the gofpel, than all modern fchemes whatever. If this was the cafe, minifters would then learn firft to fow, and then to reap; they would endeavour to plow up

the

the fallow ground, and thereby prepare the
people for God's raining down bleffings upon
them. Thus Peter preached when under a
divine influence, as I mentioned laft Wednefday night: he charged the audience home,
though many of them were learned and high
and great, with having been the murderers of
the Son of God. No doubt but the charge
entered deep into their confcience, and that
faithful monitor beginning to give them a proper fenfe of themfelves, the apoftle lets them
know that great as their fin was, it was not
unpardonable; that though they had been concerned in the horrid crime of murdering the
Lord of Life, notwithftanding they had thereby incurred the penalty of eternal death, yet
there was a mercy for them, the way to which
he points out in the text; *Repent ye therefore,*
fays he, *and be converted,* and adds, *that your
fins may be blotted out.* Though they are but
few words, they are weighty; a fhort fentence
this, but fweet: may God make it a bleffed
fweetnefs to every one of your hearts!

But muft we preach converfion to a profeffing people? Some of you, perhaps, are ready
to fay, go to America; go among the favages
and preach repentance and converfion there;

or,

or, if you muſt be a field-preacher, go to the
highways and hedges; go to the colliers; go
ramble up and down, as you uſed to do, preach
converſion to the drunkards: would to God
my commiſſion might be renewed, that I
might have ſtrength and ſpirit to take the
advice!

Poſſibly others will ſay, do not preach it to
us; pray who are you? I anſwer, one ſent to
call you to repentance; and although I might,
yet I will not come ſo cloſe to you at preſent,
as to inquire in my turn, who are you? yet
permit me to pray, that while I am preaching
God's Spirit may find you out; and not only
let you know who you are, but what you
are; and then you will not be eaſy with yourſelves, nor angry with a miniſter of Jeſus
Chriſt for preaching converſion to your ſouls.

Repentance and converſion are nearly the
ſame. The expreſſion in the text is complex,
and ſeems to include both what goes before
and follows *turning to God:* and if the Lord
is pleaſed to honour me ſo far to night to be
uſeful to ſinners, as well as ſaints, I will endeavour to ſhew you,

Firſt, what it is not to be converted: ſe-
condly, what it is to be truly converted: thirdly,

ly, offer fome motives why you fhould repent and be converted : and, fourthly, anfwer fome objections that have been made againft perfons repenting and being converted ; and may God fo blefs my preaching, and your hearing, that every one may go away and fay, Lord, con- vert me more and more.

First, I fhall endeavour to fhow you what it is not to be converted ; for I do verily be- lieve there are thoufands, and ten thoufands, that think themfelves converted, and yet at the fame time, if you come and examine them, they know not fo much as fpeculatively what real converfion is : the general notion many have of it is, a perfon's being a convert from the church of Rome to the church of Eng- land. There is a particular office in the large prayer book, to be ufed when any one publicly renounces popery in the great congregation. When this is done, that prayer read, and the perfon faid Amen to the collects upon the occafion, every body wifhes him joy, and thanks God he is converted ; whereas, if this is all, he is as much unconverted to God as ever ; he has in words renounced popery, but never took leave of the fins of his heart. Well, after this he looks into the church, and does

not like that white thing called a furplice ; he
looks, and thinks there are fome rags of the
whore of Babylon left ftill : now, fays he, I
will be converted ; how ? I will turn Diffenter : fo after he is converted from the church
of Rome to the church of England, he goes
to the diffenting church : may be, curiofity
may bring him to the Methodifts, thofe mon-
ftrous troublefome creatures, and, perhaps, he
may then be converted a third time, like their
preaching, like their finging ; O dear, I muft
have a Tabernacle-ticket, I muft have a Pfalm-
book, I will come as often as there is preaching, or at leaft as often as I can ; and there he
fits down, and becomes an outfide converted
Methodift, as demure as poffible. : this is
going a prodigious way, and yet all this is converfion from one party only to another. If
the minifter gives a rub or two he will take
miff perhaps, and be converted to fome other
perfuafion, and all the while Jefus Chrift is
left unthought of ; but this is converfion only
from party to party, not real, and that which
will bring a foul to heaven. Poffibly, a perfon may go further, and be converted from
one fet of principles to another ; he may, for
inftance, be born an Arminian, which all men
                                        naturally

naturally are; and one reason why I think Calvinism right is, because proud nature will not stoop to be saved by grace. You that are brought up in an orthodox belief, under an orthodox ministry, cannot easily make an allowance for thousands that have nothing ringing in their ears but Arminianism; you have suck'd in orthodoxy with your mother's milk; and that makes so many four and severe professors. I knew a rigid man that would beat Christianity into his wife; and so many beat people with their bibles, that they are likely, by their bitter proceeding, to hinder them from attending to the means God has designed for conversion. What is this but being converted from one set of principles to another? and I may be very zealous for them, without being transformed by them into the image of God. But some go further, they think they are converted because they are reformed: they say, *a reformed rake makes a good husband*, but I think a renewed rake will make a better. Reformation is not renovation: I may have the outside of the platter washed; I may be turned from prophaneness to a regard for morality; and because I do not swear, nor go to the play as I used to do; have left off cards;

Q   and

and perhaps put on a plain drefs; and fo believe, or rather fancy, that I am converted; yet the old man remains unmortified, and the heart is unrenewed ftill. Comparing myfelf with what I once was, and looking on my companions with difdain, I may there ftick fafter in felf, and get into a worfe and more dangerous ftate than I was before. If any of you think me too fevere, remember you are the perfon I mean; for you think me fo only becaufe I touch your cafe. The drunkards and fabbath-breakers, curfers and fwearers, fay to us, you can never preach but you preach againft us: as a good man once replied to a perfon, who complained againft us minifters for this preaching; I will put you in a way, faid he, that we fhall never preach againft you; how is that? why, leave off curfing and fwearing, &c. then your confciences will be clear, and the minifter will look over your heads: happy they that are convinced of it! You have not heard me, I hope, fpeak a word againft reformation; you have not heard me fpeak a word againft being converted from the church of Rome; againft being converted to the church of England; or, againft being good: no; all thefe are right in their place; but all

thefe

thefe converfions you may have, and yet never be truly converted at all. What is converfion then? I will not keep you longer in fufpenfe, my brethren: man muft be a new creature, and converted from his own righteoufnefs to the righteoufnefs of the Lord Jefus Chrift; conviction will always preceed fpiritual converfion; and therefore the Proteftant divines make this diftinction, you may be convinced and not converted, but you cannot be converted without being convinced; and if we are truly converted, we fhall not only be turned and converted from finful felf, but we fhall be converted from righteous felf; that is the devil of devils: for righteous felf can run and hide itfelf in its own doings, which is the reafon felf-righteous people are fo angry with gofpel preachers; there are no fuch enemies to the gofpel as thefe: *there were Jews who trufted in themfelves that they were righteous,* that fet all in an uproar, and raifed the mob on the apoftles. Our Lord denounced dreadful woes againft the felf-righteous Pharifees: fo minifters muft cut and hack them, and not fpare; but fay wo, wo, wo to all thofe that will not fubmit to the righteoufnefs of Jefus Chrift! I could almoft fay, this is the laft ftroke the

Q 2

Lord

Lord Jefus gave Paul, I mean in turning him to real Chriftianity; for having given him a blow as a perfecutor and injurious, he then brought him out of himfelf by revealing his perfon and office as a Saviour. *I am Jefus.*— Hence fays the apoftle, *I count all things but lofs—that I may win Chrift, and be found in him ; not having my own righteoufnefs, which is of the law, but that which is through the faith of Chrift ; the righteoufnefs which is of God by faith.* You hear him not only fpeak of himfelf as injurious, as a blafphemer, but alfo as a Pharifee ; and in vain we may talk of being converted till we are brought out of ourfelves; to come as poor loft, undone finners, to the Lord Jefus Chrift; to be wafhed in his blood; to be cloathed in his glorious imputed righteoufnefs: the confequence of this imputation, or application of a Mediator's righteoufnefs to the foul, will be a converfion from fin to holinefs. I am almoft tempted to fay, it is perverfenefs in people to preach againft the doctrine of imputed righteoufnefs, becaufe they love holinefs, and charge the Calvinifts with being enemies to it : how can they be charged with being enemies to Sanctification, who fo ftrenuoufly infift on its being the genuine

nuine fruit, and unqueſtionable proof of the imputation of the righteouſneſs of Chriſt, and application of it by the Spirit of grace? They that are truly converted to Jeſus, and are juſtified by faith in the Son of God, will take care to evidence their converſion, not only by the having grace implanted in their hearts, but by that grace diffuſing itſelf through every faculty of the ſoul, and making a univerſal change in the whole man. I am preaching from a bible that ſaith, *He that is in Chriſt is a new creature, old things,* not *will* be but, *are paſſed away, all things,* not only *will* but, *are become new.* As a child when born has all the ſeveral parts of a man, it will have no more limbs than it has now, if it lives to fourſcore years and ten; ſo when a perſon is converted to God, there are all the features of the new creature and growth, till he becomes a young man and a father in Chriſt; till he becomes ripe in grace, and God tranſlates him to glory. Any thing ſhort of this is but the ſhadow inſtead of the ſubſtance; and however perſons may charge us with being enthuſiaſts, yet we need not be moved either to anger or ſorrow, ſince St. Paul ſays, *I travel in birth till Chriſt be formed in your hearts.*

The

The author of this converſion is the Holy Ghoſt : it is not their own free will ; it is not moral ſwaſion ; nothing ſhort of the influence of the Spirit of the living God can effect this change in our hearts ; therefore we are ſaid to *be born again, born of God, of the Spirit, not of water only, but of the Holy Ghoſt ; that which is born of the fleſh is fleſh, but that which is born of the Spirit is ſpirit :* and tho' there is and will be a conteſt between theſe two oppoſites, fleſh and ſpirit, yet if we are truly converted, the ſpirit will get the aſcendency ; and though for a while nature and grace may ſtruggle in the womb of a converted ſoul, like Jacob and Eſau, yet the elder ſhall ſerve the younger, Jacob ſhall ſupplant and turn out Eſau, or at leaſt keep him under : God grant we may all thus prove that we are converted. This converſion, however it begins at home, will ſoon walk abroad ; as the Virgin Mary was ſoon found out to be with child, ſo it will be ſoon found out whether Chriſt is formed in the heart. There will be new principles, new ways, new company, new works ; there will be a thorough change in the heart and life ; this is converſion : at firſt it begins with terror and legal ſorrow, afterwards it leads to joyful-
neſs ;

nefs ; firſt we work for ſpiritual life, afterwards
from it : firſt we are in bondage, afterwards
we receive the Spirit of adoption to long and
thirſt for God, becauſe he has been pleaſed to
let us know that he will take us to heaven.
Converſion means a being turned from hell to
heaven, from the world to God. We have
not ſo much as aſked a perſon to ſell his all, to
leave his ſhop, to lay any thing at our feet:
when we talk of being converted from the
world, we mean being converted from the love
of it : the heart once touched with the magnet of divine love, ever after turns to the pole.
I think it is ſaid of a ſun-flower, though I queſtion whether it will always hold true, that it
turns to the ſun ; I am ſure it is true of the
Redeemer's flowers that grow in his garden,
they not only look to the ſun, but they find
freſh life, warmth, and transforming influence
from him who is their all in all. Here Chriſtianity appears in its glory ; here the work
done is worthy the Son of God. To be converted only to a party, is that worth Chriſt's
coming from heaven to earth for ; that we
might have a ſet of principles without having
them affect the heart ? for to be baptized when
young, or as ſome to come out of the water at

age,

age, and turn out as bad as ever, is a plain proof of the neceſſity of being baptized by the Holy Ghoſt.

What ſay you to this change, my dear ſouls? is it not god-like, is it not divine, is it not heaven brought down to the ſoul; have you felt it, have you experienced it? I begin to catechize you already, for I could ſpend a whole ſermon in ſpeaking of converſion; but I am afraid thoſe that ſit under the goſpel have more need of heat than light: would to God we had as much warmth in our hearts, as light in our underſtandings! But if there be any of you here that are not yet converted, upon what grounds do you hope for converſion? give me leave to ſay, that you ought to repent and be converted, for till then you never can, never will, never ſhall find true reſt for your ſouls. What wrong notions have people got of converſion! they think it is a wretched thing, and dread being converted; not knowing what it is, they think it is a frightful thing. I knew one ſometime ago that came to ſome Methodiſts; dear, ſays the perſon, you are chearful, I could be glad if I was a Methodiſt too, if there was a majority of them in the land: but God help us to go to heaven with the minority,

if

if the majority will not follow. But, my dear hearers, there is not a fingle foul of you all that are fatisfied in your ftations: is not the language of your hearts when apprentices, we think we fhall do very well when journeymen ; when journeymen, that we fhould do very well when mafters : when fingle, that we fhall do well when married ; and to be fure you think you fhall do well when you keep a carriage. I have heard of one who began low; he firft wanted a houfe, then, fays he, I want two, then four, then fix ; and when he had them, he faid, I think I want nothing elfe ; yes, fays his friend, you will foon want another thing, that is, a hearfe and fix to carry you to your grave ; and that made him tremble. O if you are Chriftians, if the Lord loves you, he will put a thorn in your flefh. I have often thought of what a good man fays in his Diary, the Lord put a thorn in my flefh. Among politicians, when they find a man ambitious, they fay, kick him up, that he may fall and break his neck : fo it is in every condition ; there is not one of you fifty years old, but have had many changes : have not you found thorns even on the rofe that fmelt fo fweet, and thorns perhaps that pricked you fo

R clofely,

closely, that you have forgot the scent of the rose by it? and what is all this for, but to teach you that happiness is only to be found in the Lord. If a soul is truly converted, there will be a battle, and an awful chasm that will never be filled up but with the love of God; and therefore when we say, Repent and be converted, it is no more than saying, repent and be happy. Indeed we shall never be compleatly happy till we get to heaven. O that every man could see the good of every thing of a sublunary nature drop off like leaves in autumn: God grant this may be known by every one of you.

If it is asked, why you should repent and be converted? I answer, because else you can never be happy hereafter. What do you think heaven is? why, says the covetous man, I think it is a place full of gold; so you think to steal some of the gold, do you? Others would like heaven very well if there was a good gaming-table in heaven; if there was card-playing in heaven. I have heard of a lady that was so fond of gaming, that though she had the pangs of death upon her, yet when in the midst of her fits, or just coming out of one, instead of asking after Jesus, where he

was

was to be found, ſhe aſked, what is trumps?
So the gameſter will aſk, where is the back-
gammon table? where is the box? he will
want to ſhake his ungodly hand in heaven; he
will ſay, let us have a gaming-table in heaven,
where, as he will find, he has loſt the game;
that God has damned him without an intereſt
in Chriſt. *Can two walk together unleſs they
are agreed?* If you die and do not love God
here, if you cannot love praying to God here,
and cannot watch one hour, ſuppoſe you was
to be ſtruck by death and be taken to heaven,
there is no ſuch language and amuſement
there, what would you do? Why, ſay you,
theſe Methodiſts are preſumptuous people, they
can tell us whether we are to go to heaven or
no. Good Mr. Rogers, a Welſh Boanerges,
preaching in the mountains, ſaid, Chriſt is heaven, if I worſhip God here, and do all to God,
and for God, without any hopes of reward
upon the earth. My dear brethren, the devils would never be troubled with ſuch a wretch
in hell, he would ſet all hell in an uproar; if
a true Methodiſt was to go to hell, the devil
would ſay, turn that Methodiſt out, he is come
to torment us: therefore, you muſt be converted if you will go to heaven. Dr. Scott

ſays,

says, if a natural man was to be put into heaven, it would be such a hell to him, that he would be glad to go to hell for shelter: angels they hate, God they hate; and as Adam was afraid to meet with God when he first fell from him, so his sons hate God and flee away.

I mention one thing more, which is, that you must be converted, or be damned, and that is plain English, but not plainer than my Master made use of, *He that believeth not shall be damned.* I did not speak that word strong enough that says, *He that believeth not shall be damned*; that is the language of our Lord; and it is said of one of the primitive preachers, that used to speak the word damned so that it struck all his auditory. We are afraid of speaking the word damned for fear of offending such and such a one; at the same time they despise the minister for not being honest to his master. Some have said, and stand to it, that hell is only a temporary punishment: Who told them so? A temporary punishment! nothing but a guilty conscience. O go to Bedlam! Do ask a child of God what he feels when his Lord is absent? Ask the spouse what she felt when she cries, *Saw ye him whom my soul loveth?* Ask a child of God when he is using this plaintive language,

language, *Why ftandeft thou afar off, O Lord?*
and he will tell you, it is hell to my foul to be
but one moment without the prefence of my
beloved. And if his abfence for a quarter of
an hour can fcarce be bore by a child of God,
what muft that foul undergo that is commanded to depart from him for ever? and yet
thefe very words were faid to thofe that thought
they bid fair for heaven; to thefe Jefus fays,
I know ye not. God grant you may never
know the meaning of thefe words by awful
experience! Now, what fay you? I could
make a hundred heads more, but I chufe to
make as few as poffible, that you may remember them. I fay, converfion makes you happy
hereafter, and without it you are damned for
ever.

Are thefe things fo? why then, my dear
hearers, do you think there can be any objection raifed againft converfion, do you think
there can be any argument raifed againft turning to God directly? is there any perfon here
that will give himfelf time to confider a moment that will not fay, though you fpeak in a
rough, incoherent manner, yet there is fome
truth in what you fay; I believe men ought
to be converted, but the common faying is, I
don't

don't care to be converted yet; we think it is
time enough to be converted. Is not this acting like the cardinal, when told he was elected
pope, and defired to come that night and have
the honour of pope conferred on him; becaufe
it was pretty late faid, it is not a work of darknefs, I will put it off till the morning; before
which they chofe another pope, and he loft
his triple crown. You may think to put it off
till the morning, though before the morning
you may be damned. Pray why will you not
be converted now? if you was in prifon, and
a perfon would take you out, you would chufe
to be let out to-night before morning, that you
might fleep the better; why will you not do
that for your foul you would for your body?
Well, I would be converted but I fhall be
laughed at: fuppofe you was to have it promifed, you fhould have a ten thoufand pound
lottery ticket, but you muft be laughed at all
your life-time; there is none but would fay,
give me the ten thoufand pounds, and call me
Methodift as long as I live: fo if you loved
God and your fouls, you would fay, give me
God and call me what you will. You are
afraid of being laughed at and nick-named,
and fkulk into this and that place, becaufe it

does

does not ſtink ſo much of Methodiſm as this.
Put your cockades in your hats, and let the
world ſee that you are not aſhamed of God's
badge: let the devil and his agents preach to
you ; they can proclaim their ſin like Sodom ;
they are not aſhamed of going to balls and
aſſemblies, to parties of pleaſure, and ſub-
ſcribing to horſe-races. Is the goſpel the glory of the land, and are you aſhamed of the
goſpel ? What think you, if you had given an
hundred pounds to learn ſuch a trade, would
you ſay, I ſhall never attain it ! no, you will
perſevere, and by giving diligence make an
excellent mechanic, an admirable tradeſman ;
and do you think to go to heaven without ſome
trouble ? do you think the leopard can change
his ſpots, the Ethiopian put his ſkin intirely
off? can we have any thing to nouriſh our bodies without the labour of particular perſons ?
and therefore we are commanded *to work out
our ſalvation with fear and trembling.* Remember our Redeemer *will not quench the
ſmoaking flax, nor break the bruiſed reed ; he
will gently lead thoſe that are with young.* We
are like poor ſwimmers; ſome people will put
one foot in and cry oh ! and then another,
but a good ſwimmer plunges in at once, and

comes

comes out braced up: would to God we could do fo, plunge into God at once, and God will bear up our fouls indeed.

But fay you, all in good time, I do not chufe to be converted yet; why, what age are you now? I will come down to a pretty moderate age; fuppofe you are fourteen: and do not you think it time to be converted? and yet there are a great many here, I dare fay, twenty years old, and not converted. Some are of opinion, that moft people that are converted, are fo before thirty. There was a young man buried laft night at Tottenham Court but feventeen, an early monument of free grace! Are you forty, or fifty, is not that time? Is it time for the poor prifoners to be converted that are to be hanged to-morrow morning? if it is time for them, it is time for you, for you may be dead before them. There was a poor woman, but two or three days ago, that was damning and curfing moft fhockingly, now fhe is a dead corpfe, was taken fuddenly, and died away. God grant, that may not be the cafe with any of you; the only way to prevent it is, to be enabled to think that *now is an accepted time, that now is the day of falvation.* Let me look round,

round, and what do you ſuppoſe I was thinking? why, that it is a mercy we have not
been in hell a thouſand times. How many
are there in hell that uſed to ſay, Lord convert me, but not now? One of the good old
Puritans ſays, Hell is paved with good inten-
tions. Now can you blame me, can you
blame the miniſters of Chriſt if this is the caſe,
can you blame us for calling after you, for
ſpending and being ſpent for your ſouls? it is
eaſy for you to come to hear the goſpel, but
you do not know what nights and days we
have; what pangs we have in our hearts, and
*how we travel in birth till Jeſus Chriſt be form-
ed in your ſouls.* Men, brethren, and fathers,
hearken, God help you, ſave, ſave, ſave *yourſelves from an untoward generation.* To-night
ſomebody ſits up with the priſoners; if they
find any of them aſleep, or no ſign of their
being awake, they knock and call, and the
keepers cry, awake! and I have heard that
the preſent ordinary ſits up with them all the
night before their execution: therefore, don't
be angry 'with me if I knock at your doors,
and cry, poor ſinners, awake! awake! and
God help thee to take care thou doſt not ſleep
in an unconverted ſtate to-night. The court

S   is

is juſt ſitting, the executioner ſtands ready,
and before to-morrow, long before to-morrow,
Jeſus may ſay of ſome of you, *Bind them hand
and foot.* The priſoners to-morrow will have
their hands tied behind them, their thumb-
ſtrings muſt be put on, and their fetters knocked off; they muſt be tied faſt to the cart, the
cap put over their faces, and the dreadful ſignal
given; if you were their relations would not
you weep? don't be angry then with a poor
miniſter for weeping over them that will not
weep for themſelves. If you laugh at me, I
know Jeſus ſmiles. I cannot force a cry when
I will; the Lord Jeſus Chriſt be praiſed, *I am
free from the blood of you all:* if you are
damned for want of converſion, remember
you are not damned for want of warning.
Thouſands that have no goſpel preached to
them, may ſay, Lord, we never heard what
converſion is; but you are goſpel-proof; and
if there is any deeper place in hell than other,
God will order a goſpel deſpiſing-Methodiſt to
be put in there. You will have dreadful torments; to whom ſo much is given, much
will be required. How dreadful to have miniſter after miniſter, preacher after preacher,
ſay, *Lord God, I preached but they would not
hear.* Think of this, profeſſors, and God make
you poſſeſſors!   You

You that do poſſeſs a little, and are really converted, God convert you and me every hour in the day; for there is not a believer in the world, but has got ſomething in him that he ſhould be converted from; the pulling down of the old houſe, and building up the new one, will be a work till death. Do not think I am ſpeaking to the unconverted only, but to you that are converted. God convert you from lying a-bed in the morning; God convert you from your conformity to the world; God convert you from lukewarmneſs; God convert us from ten thouſand things which our own hearts muſt ſay we want to be converted from; then you will have the Spirit of the living God. Do not get into a curſed Antinomian way of thinking, and ſay, I thank God, I have the root of the matter in me: I thank God, that I was converted twenty or thirty years ago; and once in Chriſt always in Chriſt; and though I can go to a public-houſe and play at cards, or the like, yet, I bleſs God, I am converted. Whether you was converted formerly or not, you are perverted now; and may God convert you all to cloſe Chriſtianity with God!

You

You that are old profeſſors, don't draw young ones back from God, by ſaying, ah! you will come down from the mount by and by; you will not always be ſo hot; and in-ſtead of encouraging poor ſouls, you will pull them down, becauſe you have left your firſt love: would you have Jeſus Chriſt catch you napping, with your lamps untrimmed?

O ye ſervants of the moſt high God, if any of you are here to-night, though I am the chief of ſinners, and the leaſt of all ſaints, ſuffer the word of exhortation. I am ſure I preach feelingly now; God knows I ſeldom ſleep after three in the morning; I pray every morning, Lord, convert me, and make me more a new creature to day. I know I want to be converted from a thouſand things, and from ten thouſand more: Lord God, confirm me; Lord God, revive his work.

You young people, I charge you to con-ſider; God help you to repent and be con-verted, who woo's and invites you. You middle-aged people, O that you would re-pent and be converted. You old grey-headed people, Lord make you repent and be con-verted, that you may thereby prove that your ſins are blotted out. O I could preach till I

preached

preached myſelf dead; I could be glad to preach myſelf dead, if God would convert you! O God bleſs his work on you, that you may bloſſom and bring forth fruits unto God. Amen and Amen.

SERMON VI.

Glorifying God in the Fire ; or, the right Improvement of Affliction.

IsAIAH xxiv. ver. 15.

Wherefore glorify ye the Lord in the fires.

YOU have oft, my dear hearers, let me tell you, met with affliction ; and I believe you may perfuade yourfelves affliction is at hand, which makes fuch deep impreffions, when fent and bleffed by heaven, as to thaw the very heart. Faith, like fome glaffes to view objects near us, fets them in fo ftrong a light, that we cannot help being affected with the weight of the impreffion ; hence the prophets, when under a divine impulfe, forefaw things at a diftance ; fpoke and wrote of them as though actually prefent. *They fung both of judgment and mercy*, in fuch ftrong and perfuafive ftrains, as to convince of the reality of their exiftence. Ifaiah, who had a

courtly

courtly education, being probably brother to a king, feems to excel in this kind of fpeaking; a perfon of good natural, as well as acquired abilities, which being tempered by the Holy Ghoft, made him a kind of an angel of an orator, of a writer, and a prophet. When he penned this chapter, he probably forefaw the dreadful calamities coming on the land; and fo ftrong was his perfuafion, that he writes as though he faw the things taking place. *Behold,* fays he, *the Lord maketh the earth empty, maketh it wafte, and turneth it upfide down, and fcattereth abroad the inhabitants thereof.* How much is expreffed in a few words! *As with the people fo with the priefts,* who perhaps, on account of their fituation in the church, might think they fhould be exempted; but if the priefts fin with the people, they fhall be punifhed with the people. *As with the fervant, fo with his mafter; as with the maid, fo with her miftrefs; as with the buyer, fo with the feller; as with the lender, fo with the borrower; as with the taker of ufury, fo with the giver of ufury to him.* So you fee that the vifitation would be univerfal; that it fhould fall on all forts of people. Ver. 3. *The land fhall be utterly emptied and utterly*
fpoiled;

spoiled; probably, by a foreign foe taking advantage of the domestic confusions, who shall destroy the fruits of the earth. Some may think, perhaps, that this will never come to pass; but, saith Isaiah, *the Lord hath spoken it.* It pleased God the nation should be devoted to a dreadful stroke: *The earth mourneth and fadeth away, the world languisheth and fadeth away, the haughty people of the earth do languish,* whose crimes, one would think, would never be brought to punishment, on account of the eminence of their stations; they thought themselves out of danger, but they shall feel the common scourge: *For the earth also,* as in the fifth verse, *is defiled under the inhabitants thereof; because they have transgressed the laws, changed the ordinances, broken the everlasting covenant.* God did not strike without a cause; for the earth groaned, as it were, under the sins of the inhabitants for their neglect of religion, for disowning God, for turning their back on the Most High. *Therefore hath the curse devoured the earth,* (ver. 6.) *and they that dwell therein are desolate.* He does not say it shall be, but it is done. *The inhabitants of the earth are burned,* with dreadful fire of consuming vengeance, *and few men left.*

All

All the merry hearted, that minded nothing but jollity and mirth, even *they do sigh. The joy of the harp ceaseth; they shall not drink wine with a song, strong drink shall be bitter to them that drink it.* The very great *city,* the metropolis, *is broken down; every house is shut up, because desolation is left in it.* The inhabitants forsake it, their houses are left, shut up, because they are afraid some foreign power should come to their destruction. *There is a crying for wine in the streets, all joy is darkened, the mirth of the land is gone:* no plays, no routs, no assemblies now; *the city is left desolate;* the court not excepted; desolation herself takes her seat and ravages there. *The earth shall reel to and fro like a drunkard, and shall be removed like a cottage; and the transgressions thereof shall be heavy upon it, and it shall fall, and not rise again.* What an amazing scene is this! enough to fill us with horror even at this distance of time and place! But is there no way for escape? is there no light breaking through this dark shade? blessed be God, there is; look at ver. 13, you will find in the midst of dangers, God shall lend his presence. *When thus it shall be,* pray mind that, *in the midst of the land among the people,*

T   what

what follows? *there shall be as the shaking of*
an olive tree, and as the gleaning grapes when
the vintage is done ; there shall be a few godly
people left, let the devil do what he will ; but
there will be but few. You know, after the
people have gathered the fruits from the tree,
they shake it to bring down the remainder ;
and after reaping of corn there are a few glean-
ings, so the Lord says, it shall deftroy moft
people, yet in fo difcriminating a way, that
God's people fhould be fafe.

I cannot well recollect how archbifhop
Ufher applies this ; but this I am fure he fays,
there will certainly come a time when the
world will undergo the greateft fcourge that
ever it felt, which fhall chiefly fall on the
outward-court worfhippers, upon thofe that
know not God ; God will take particular care
of fecuring his own ; and when the wicked
are all deftroyed, the Chriftians fhall go to a
little city, and there fhall dwell in Gofhen, till
God fhall call home his ancient people the
Jews. So God will take care of his people,
that they fhall be fafe : pray look to ver. 14,
they fhall lift up their voice ; what, to cry?
no, they have done with prayers, they have
done with fafting ; they have lifted up their
voice,

voice, and often exhorted their neighbours to *flee from the wrath to come*; but now they shall sing for the majesty of God; when all people are mourning, they shall rejoice. And at the great day, when Jesus Christ pronounces the wicked damned, *depart ye curfed*, God's people will then lift up their voices with majesty and triumph; which made a good man say to his son, just before he died, I am afraid I shall never see thee any more till I hear Jesus Christ say unto thee, *depart thou curfed!* Some years ago, being present at the trial of a very vile person at the Old-Bailey, and being in suspense whether he would be brought in guilty or no, when the word *guilty* came, and the people heard of it, they did in effect give an eclat to it; whether just or unjust, I thought it was an emblem of that awful day, when all the angels of God, and his saints, shall say Amen; when God consigns the wicked to hell: God grant this may not be any of your case. Says the prophet, *they shall cry aloud from the sea*; some of them may be on the other side of the water, gone abroad while others stay at home; but whether at home or abroad, though they have been banished by persecution, though they have been driven to

the

the other fide of the water, which has been the cafe of many perfons before now, *yet they fhall cry aloud*; they fhall find the fame God abroad as they did at home. A judge faid to a good old Chriftian that was perfecuted in Charles II.'s time, I will banifh you to America; fays fhe, Very well, you cannot fend me out of my Father's country. They fhall cry aloud from the fea, *wherefore glorify ye the Lord in the fires*; if this is the cafe, the prophet draws the inference; what muft they do under thefe circumftances; why, they muft ftudy how to glorify God in the fires, not how to efcape or run away from him, but how to glorify him; *wherefore*, faith he, *glorify me*, glorify me the Lord, *in the fires*; not the fire, in the fingular number, but in the plural number, fires. We are, my brethren, very much miftaken, if we think we have but one fire to go through.

The words imply, in order to bring them home to ourfelves, that all God's people muft be put into the fires. Fire fometimes denotes the love of God, fometimes the work of the Holy Ghoft, and very often it denotes affliction; therefore, the apoftle talks of a *fiery trial*; and let it be of whatever kind it will, let

let it be upon mind, body, or eftate; whether it comes from friend or foe, or whether it comes immediately from the hand of God himfelf upon the foul, it may well be compared to fire, for you all know that fire fcorches; God expects when he ftrikes, that we fhould feel. Of all things in the world to be avoided, a ftony heart, or a ftupidity under God's afflicting hand, is moft to be deprecated. I fuppofe you have heard of the Stoics *, with whom the apoftle Paul difputed in the place of public traffic in Athens. Paul did not take a walk to Change to talk on trade, he went to talk about Jefus Chrift, if he could meet with one to talk with: I wifh the clergy took no other walks but thefe. Every thing is to be tried by fire; we may talk what we pleafe, but we fhall never know what metal we are made of, till God puts us into the fire. It is very eafy talking what we can bear, and what we can do, but let God lay his hand on us, and we fhall fee what we are. We are apt to find fault, and be peevifh with our friends and relations under fuch circumftances; they are apt to fay,

you

---

* They taught that a wife man fhould be free from all affections and paffions whatfoever.

you fhould be patient, and patient, and patient; ah! put thefe reprovers into the fame
furnace, and fee how patient they will be:
they fay, there is no putting old mens heads
upon young mens fhoulders; and there is no
putting old heads upon fouls young in experience. The devil knew very well how it was
when he faid, *Haft thou not made an hedge
about Job, and about his houfe, and about all
that he hath on every fide; thou haft bleffed the
work of his hands, and his fubftance is increafed
in the land; but put forth thy hand now, and
touch all that he hath, and he will curfe thee
to thy face;* fo we fhould all do if God was
to leave us to ourfelves, and our faith is not
of the right fort.

How fhall we know if our faith is good?
we often pray, Lord, give us Abraham's faith,
but never pray, give us Abraham's trial at the
fame time. I was once in Scotland, at a great
man's houfe, where feveral rich people were
that knew Jefus Chrift; God having bleffed
my labours at a former vifit, I was defired by
the nobleman to pray; and I remember I prayed the Lord to give us great faith and patience;
—O faid Satan, as ftrong as if he had fpoke
to me, don't pray for that, for thou fhalt have

great

great trials. O, faid I, if that be the cafe, I will turn the devil's prayer againft himfelf; and I prayed, *O Lord, give us great grace, and never mind what trials.* Often when we are under temptations, God takes us at our words: O, fays one, what a prayer I had, I prayed for faith and patience; I was upon the mount, and never thought of coming down, and feeling a ftorm again.

Fire, my brethren, not only burns and purges, but you know it feparates one thing from another, and is made ufe of in chymiftry and mechanical bufineffes. What could we do without fire? it tries metal to purge it: God Almighty knows, we are often purged more in one hour by a good found trial, than by a thoufand manifeftations of his love. It is a fine thing to come purified, to come pardoned out of the furnace of affliction; it is intended to purge us, *to feparate the precious from the vile, the chaff from the wheat;* and God, in order to do this, is pleafed to put us into one fire after another, which makes me love to fee a good man under afflictions, becaufe it teaches fomething of the work of God in the heart. I remember fome years ago, when I firft preached in the north of England,

at

at Shields near Newcastle, I went into a glafs-
houfe, and ftanding very attentive, I faw feveral maffes of burning glafs of various forms:
the workman took one piece of glafs and put
it into one furnace, then he put it into a fecond, and then into a third: when I afked
him, why do you put this into fo many fires?
he anfwered, O, fir, the firft was not hot
enough, nor the fecond, and therefore we put
it into the third, and that will make it tranfparent. Taking leave of him in a proper
manner, it occurred to me, this would make
a good fermon: O, thought I, does this man
put this glafs into one furnace after another,
that we may fee through it; O may God put
me into one furnace after another, that my
foul may be tranfparent; that I may fee God
as he is. My brethren, we need to be purged;
how apt are we to want to go to heaven upon
a feather-bed; many go lying upon beds of
pain and languifhing, which is the King's
highway thither. You know there are fome
ways in London called the king's road, and
they are finely gravelled, but the King's road
to heaven is ftrowed with croffes and afflictions.
We are all apt to think well of being Chriftians; it is very pretty talking of being Chriftians,

tians, till we are put into one furnace after another; *think it not strange,* faith the apostle, *concerning the fiery trial which is to try you.* What must I do? why, since I must be in the fire, I must thank my corruptions for it; God will not put you or me into the fire if there was not something to be purged away; the grand thing is to learn to glorify God in the fire. *Wherefore glorify ye the Lord in the fires.*

When do we glorify him? when we endeavour to get such grace from the Lord, that we may not dishonour him when we are under the cross, and therefore we glorify God in the fire when we quietly endure it as a chastisement for our sins: if you keep watch now, and live near to God, you will never find that you are put into a fire, but you first brought yourselves into it; and I do verily believe from my heart, that our sin is always to be seen in our punishment. If any of you part from a child that he loves dearly, upon examination he will say, I find now the creature's gone, that the ivy twined too much about the oak; and then he turns off; ah! says he, God has met with me now. And you will find in all the Old and New Testament, that the afflictions of God's people were suitable to their faults: Ja-

U   cob

cob was over-perfuaded by his mother to get
the bleffing by a lie; but he was a fimple-
hearted poor creature. Some perfons think
nothing of a lie; if they can but get by it,
they do not mind it; but an honeft man will
fhun it. Jacob argues with his mother againft
it; O, fays fhe, *the curfe be on me, my fon!*
O dreadful! for a good woman to fay fo.
Doubtlefs, fhe was perfuaded God would give
Jacob the bleffing, but fhe took a wrong way
to obtain it; fhe might have waited for the
bleffing to come with a bleffing. How did
God punifh Jacob? why, in a night afterwards poor Jacob was impofed upon by a
wrong wife, he got a Leah inftead of a Ra-
chel; the poor creature was impofed upon
there, and fo all along almoft to the end of his
life; he had a furnace of afflicton. Happy
they who pray in the furnace, Lord, let me
know why thou doft contend with me. Therefore God fends this meffage to Ely by Samuel,
the thing that thou knoweft, feems to me to
refer to his too great lenity to his fons; *the
thing that thou knoweft;* thou doft not act like
a magiftrate. Thefe fons were the means of
bringing a judgment on his houfe, and breaking their father's neck: God Almighty keep
us from bringing a rod upon ourfelves.

We

We glorify God in the fire when we bear it patiently. It is a dreadful thing when we are saying with Cain, *My punishment is greater than I can bear*; but the language of a soul that glorifies God in the fire is this, shall I, Lord, shall I a sinful man, complain for the punishment of my sins? It is a glorious thing when we can say with a good man, one of whose particular friends told me more than once, that when he was racked with pain, and groaning all night with trouble, he would often say, Lord, I groan; Lord, I groan; Lord, I groan; but, Lord Jesus, I appeal to thee, thou knowest I do not grumble. Then we glorify God in the fire, when, though we feel pain and anguish, we at the same time say, Lord, we deserve this and ten thousand times more.

We glorify God in the fire also, when we are really and fully persuaded, God will not put us in the fire but for our good, and his own glory. I am afraid some people think God does as some cheating apothecaries, that bring five things when they need not bring but one, especially when they have some silly patients that love to be taking physic; they send one after another, when, perhaps, the best

thing

thing would be to throw them all away; fo
we think of God, but it is a miſtake; he never ſends one but what is neceſſary, and ſomething to be purged away.

We glorify God in the fire when we ſay,
Lord, don't let the fire go out till it has
purged away all my drofs.   Then we glorify
God when we wiſh for the good of the fire,
and not to have it extinguiſhed; when the
ſoul can ſay, *Here I am, my God, do with me
as ſeemeth good in thy ſight*; I know I ſhall
not have one ſtroke but thou will give me a
plaiſter, and let me know wherefore thou
contendeſt with me.

We glorify God in the fire when we are
content to ſay, *I know not what God does with
me now, but I ſhall know hereafter.*   Do you
tell your children that are five years old the
reaſon of things, no; and do you think God
will tell us? *What ſhall this man do?* ſaith
the difciples; *what is that to thee?* ſaith
Chriſt, *follow thou me.*   You glorify God in
the fire, when you are content to walk by
faith and not by ſight,

You glorify God in the fire when you are
not grumbling, but humbly ſubmitting to his
will; a humble ſpirit walks not in ſulkineſs
                                                          and

and ftubbornnefs: there are fome fpirits too ftout, they will not fpeak. When that awful meffage was brought to Ely, what does he fay? *It is the Lord, let him do what feemeth him good;* let my children be killed, whatever be done it is the Lord's doing; only, Lord, fave my foul at laft.

We glorify God in the fire, when in the midft of the fire we can fing God's high praifes. Thus the children of Ifrael glorified the Lord; the fong of the three children in the fiery furnace is a fweet fong; as are all that are made in the fire. *O all the works of the Lord, praife and magnify him for ever!* Then we glorify God in the fire when we rejoice in him, when we not only think, but know it beft, and can thank God for ftriking us; can thank God for whipping us; can blefs God for not letting us alone; thank God for not faying, *let him alone:* this is to glorify God in the fire. *Not only fo,* faith the apoftle, *but we glory in tribulation, knowing that tribulation worketh patience.*

In a word, we glorify the Lord in the fire when we have in exercife, patience, meeknefs, humility; learning more to diftruft ourfelves, having a deeper knowledge of our own weak-

weakneſs, and of God's omnipotence and grace. Happy when we can look back and ſay, thus have I been enabled to glorify God in the fire. Who can put his hand to his heart and ſay, I have glorified God in the fire as I ought? inſtead of that I am afraid the ſoul muſt ſay, that inſtead of being thankful and reſigned, I have been fretful; and becauſe I will not find fault with myſelf, nor let the world know I find fault with God, I find fault with all about me. Did you never find yourſelf in ſuch a humour when your ſpirits were low? I heard a good man once ſpeak on thoſe words, *they ſhall bring forth fruit in old age:* O the fruit, ſaid he, is peviſhneſs; I thought it was the infirmity of old age, the fruit of which ought to be heavenly-mindedneſs, deadneſs to the world, and a livelineſs to God.

My brethren, let us humble ourſelves to-night, and let us be aſhamed and abaſhed before God, and wonder he hath not ſtruck us into hell when we have been complaining the fire was too hot, that God ſent us not to the devil. Let us weep, let us weep, let us weep for our ſtubbornneſs. Happy they who are uſed to be put into the fire betimes! *It is good for a man to bear the yoke in his youth.* Some
years

years ago, when I was at the Orphan-houfe, they told me they were going to yoke two fteers together, one fturdy and old, the other a little one, on which they no fooner put the yoke, but he kicked once or twice, and then bore it very well : O, thought I, it is a good thing to have the yoke betimes.

Are any of you now in the furnace, are any of you troubled, or can any of you fay, I have no trouble; a calm is fometimes the fore-runner of a ftorm; thank God, you are not in the fire; furely you have been in the fire. There is the devil's fire; the fires of *the luft of the flefh, the luft of the eye, and the pride of life :* God help you to come out of thefe fires, left they damn your fouls for ever. You muft be put either in the devil's fire or God's fire, and the devil's fires are hotteft, becaufe there is no God to fupport under the trouble they bring upon the foul. O what a dreadful thing it is to be in the devil's fire continually, and to go out of the fire of the devil here to burn with the devil in hell hereafter ! If there are any of you in this cafe, Lord Jefus Chrift fhorten them, Lord Jefus Chrift fanctify his afflictions to his people, as he did to one of the prifoners laft Wednefday : how fweetly he behaved !

while

while the others were curfing and fwearing,
toffing up who fhould fit on the right hand in
the cart, he was glorifying God, thanking
God he was fent there, and going to be executed : God, faith he, hath ftopt me, I might
have gone on in fin to ruin. O fend to my
father, go to him, warn him to *flee from the
wrath to come :* fomebody went to his parent,
and the father fent back this *loving* meffage ;
tell him to mind his own foul, and be damn'd !
O, dear Lord, what lengths has man gone !
never was fuch a meffage fent to a fon before ;
he bid him mind his own foul and be damn'd !
God grant none of you may ever have fuch a
frame of mind as that ! O remember fire har-
dens as well as foftens; and if you are not
better by afflictions you will be worfe: and
indeed you will know you cannot come out of
the furnace as you went in, you will either be
hardened or elfe be purified ; and if this be
the cafe, the Lord Jefus Chrift help you to
bear the fire now, that you may never be caft
into the fire of hell. God hafte you, haften
you that are out of the devil's fire to flee, flee,
ye weary fouls, to Jefus Chrift ; fly to the
Lamb of God, from hell to heaven, as far as
you can from thefe hellifh fires, to the fire of
his bleffed merit and love.

Happy

Happy you that have got into Chrift's fire! happy you that have found his fires in your fouls! I believe many fouls have: O Lord Jefus Chrift help you to glorify him in whatever fires he fhall be pleafed to fend you, and into whatever furnaces he fhall be pleafed to put you: we fhall then fing " *the church triumphant,*" much better than we fing to-night; we fhall fee Jefus Chrift ready to help us when we are in the furnace: O that this thought may make every poor finner fay, by the help of God I will be a Chriftian; by the help of God, if I muft burn, it fhall be burning with the love of Chrift. I will fay then, O Lord, glorify thyfelf by fnatching me as a brand from the devil's fire. O that this might be the cry of every heart!

I am going to afk a favour of you to-night which I never did before, and, perhaps, may not again for fome time: I have had complaints made to me by the perfons that take care of the poor, that the poor's ftock is very low; though I cannot fpeak on Sunday night, yet I will fpeak a word to the poor on Wednefday evening. There are numbers of poor that are ready to perifh, and if you drop fomething to them in love, God will take

X care

care to repay you when you come to judgment. We fhall not only glorify God by a
fubmiffion to his will, when he is putting us
in the fire, but in doing any good, when we
lay all the glory at the foot of Jefus ; which
God grant for Chrift's fake. Amen.

SERMON

✤✤✤✤✤✤✤✤✤✤✤✤✤✤✤✤✤✤✤✤✤✤✤✤✤✤✤

SERMON VII.

The Beloved of God.

DEUT. xxxiii. ver. 12.

And of Benjamin, he faid, The beloved of the Lord fhall dwell in fafety, by him ; and the Lord fhall cover him all the day long, and he fhall dwell between his fhoulders.

OH! what a difmal fight is it, to fee an old man with his hoary head grown grey in fin, and hardened in iniquity.

On the other hand, I believe to all that confider rightly, there is no grander fight almoft under the fun, than to fee an old grey-headed man keeping up a confiftent character; and proving, by his conduct, that *his path,* like that of the juft, *is as the fhining light, that fhineth more and more to the perfect day* ; efpecially when perfons have been called to act in a public character; when they have been eminent either for the highnefs of their ftation,

or

or for the largenefs of their income. It is on this account that I admire old Jacob; how grand he looked when leaning on his ftaff, with all the compofure in the world, under a divine influence, blefling his children ftanding round him. But, methinks, there is one who was called to act a more public part, namely, Mofes, who was honoured of God to be a great legiflator, king in Jefhurun, a lawgiver be-tween Judah's feet, as pupils ufed to be at the feet of their teachers, to receive their inftruc-tion; if you have a mind to fee how bright he fhines, you muft read Deut. xxxii. indeed you muft read all Deuteronomy, which is nothing but a fermon that Mofes, at various times, preached to the children of Ifrael; and having done preaching, he fang a hymn of his own compofing, and that too at a time when he knew, at the very finifhing the fong, he fhould immediately have his foul kiffed away, and be called to fing a better fong in the kingdom of heaven. A perfon would need a good deal of compofure, a good deal of the Spirit's in-fluences, a large meafure of it, chearfully thus to ftand in view of death, juft on the very bor-ders of the grave; you fee this in chap. xxxii. and here in chap. xxxiii. One would have

thought

thought he had faid enough, yet he feems as it were not to know how to leave off; he parted from the people blefling them; they had ufed him ill, they provoked him in the wildernefs; he had bore with them many, many long years; fure you would have thought he would have went away in a huff; no, that eminent fun by no means goes down in wrath; his eyes did not fo much as wax dim, nor his intellectual powers impair in all that time: he fweetly gives them all a blefling before he goes. If you read this chap. xxxiii. you will find how various, yet fpecial, are the bleffings which, in a prophetic ftrain, he foretels fhould attend particular perfons, or tribes. I have been reading them over, and though I admire them all, I was at a lofs which to fpeak from, till the blefling of Benjamin fixed my attention, not only as fweet, but inftructing. *The be-loved of the Lord fhall dwell in fafety, by him; and the Lord fhall cover him all the day long, he fhall dwell between his fhoulders.* This is a blefling indeed, if we look only to the literal interpretation of the words, and a literal com-mentator can go no further; he muft confine them to Benjamin; and will tell us, that this fcripture was fulfilled at the building of the

Temple,

Temple. The Temple was built upon two hills, one in the tribe of Benjamin, the other in the tribe of Judah; the Temple being built there, and Benjamin being placed near it, then Benjamin dwells in safety by the Lord, by having his lot cast near the Temple. How often, alas! is it the case, I am sure it is very often the case in London, the nearer the church the further from God; but some make good use of it, and are glad to get near the church that they may be nearer God. The Temple being placed between two hills, so Benjamin as it were dwells between God's shoulders; so far a literal commentator can go, here he stops; a spiritual commentator, and a spiritual reader, go further; O, says he, this is true, but at the same time this is not the whole truth; and I am persuaded, when a person is helped by the Spirit to read the scriptures, the declarations that are made, and those particular promises, the true believer applies with great propriety to himself; and therefore I think I may venture to aver, that the blessing which Moses here pronounces upon him in the name of the Lord, belongs to God's people in all ages whatever; God, in his infinite mercy, grant that this blessing may descend upon us and

ours,

ours, that it may defcend to your lateft pofterity.

Obferve how wonderfully the perfons, to
whom the blefling is given, are characterized :
of Benjamin it is faid, *the beloved of the Lord* ;
the beloved of the Lord, pray who are they ?
why, the men that the fcriptures always fpeak
of, whofe conftant uniform character is, they
love God in all ages. It is not faid, the Prefbyterians fhall dwell in fafety ; Mofes never
heard of a Prefbyterian in his life ; he never
heard of the name ; nor it is faid the Independents fhall dwell in fafety ; he never heard
of that word ; nor is it faid the Papifts fhall
dwell in fafety ; he never heard of Papifts,
nor of the pope ; nor is it faid that the Church
of England fhall dwell in fafety, no ; neither
is it faid that the Methodifts fhall dwell in fafety, though I truft there are a great many good
people among thefe mongrels of the church ;
but it is fpoken of all the people of God ;
God help us all to apply it to ourfelves.

Here is a difpute between the Arminians
and the Calvinifts : afk an Arminian what is
meant by *the beloved of the Lord* ; O, fay they
that are for general redemption, the beloved of
the Lord fignifies, all the men that were ever
born

born into the world ; that is a good broad bridge
to take them in ; but broad bridges are not
always the ſtrongeſt bridges in the world.
The Arminians will aſſert it, that Judas was
as much beloved of God as Peter, or any other
of the apoſtles ; and thoſe that are not Arminians, but are what you call Quakers, and
there are a good many, I believe, among them,
that have better hearts than heads, they ſay,
that we are all alike, that we all come into the
world with a ſeed of grace, and ſhall be happy according to the improvement of that grace ;
hence they talk nothing of a Chriſt *without*
but *within*; happy they that experience a
Chriſt within ! God's mercy is ſure, and over
all his works ; and in one ſenſe, our Lord Jeſus
Chriſt is the Saviour of all men, that is, of all
ſorts of men ; even the wicked are beholden
to Jeſus Chriſt, whom they deſpiſe, for every
worldly comfort they enjoy ; in this ſenſe we
ſhould learn to love as our Lord, we are told,
loved the young man when he ſaw he had
been a harmleſs and good liver : but we muſt
go more to what we call Calviniſm, what I
call ſcriptural truth. The love which Jeſus
Chriſt bore for the young man, quite differed
from that love with which he loved Martha,

Mary,

Mary, and their brother; there was a cargo for you! three in one family; God grant it may be your happy lot and mine! two fifters and one brother, three to entertain Jefus Chrift, all in a peculiar manner beloved of the Lord. It is not faid of Benjamin, they fhall, that is, they that love the Lord, they fhall dwell in fafety; no; it would not be fo ftrong to them, as to fay *the beloved of the Lord*; for God knows our love is not worth a fhilling; all the faith of God's people, fays bifhop Hall, is but meer infidelity; and all the love of the people of God is but meer hatred, compared with God's love, or that which his law juftly requires; therefore it is faid, *beloved of the Lord*, and that becaufe if ever we love God, he firft loved us, which is what Mofes's very expreffion means; as ftreams flow from the fountain, fo they fhall return to it. Hence the apoftle fays, *Knowing your election, brethren, beloved of God.* I know very well the Myfticks talk of loving God with a love for himfelf only, without any refpect to the creature at all; that is, we muft love God without any regard at all for what God has done for us; nay, fome go fo far as to fay, that if we do not fo love God, we are not converted,

Y   though

though we have as much grace as we can have; that we do not love God properly till we love him for what he is, not what he has done for us: I verily believe, the angels do not love God in that manner; and we cannot love God till we are made partakers of a divine nature, and have eyes given us to fee his glory.

The grand enquiry is then, how fhall I know that I am one of the beloved of the Lord? The natural man never minds the love of God; he flatters himfelf he loves God naturally, that the love of God is a plant that grows in nature's garden; but a fpiritual perfon does not fo. What does the king take notice of me? does the king look pleafant upon me in a drawing-room? am I called to wait upon him? am I beloved of this, and that, and the other perfon? if I am, let God go, I care not; if I have but the love of this and that courtier, I care not whether God loves me or no; this will not do for an awakened foul; and therefore the grand enquiry, and one proof of a perfon's being awakened is, how fhall I know whether God loves me or not? why try; I am perfuaded of it, that we may as well know that God loves us, and we love God, as we may know that the fun fhines at noon

noon-day; how fhall I know it but by the effects of this love, by the fruits of it? That great man, Dr. Watts, who was called the fweet finger of Ifrael, fays, " we fhould go firft to the grammar-fchool of faith and repentance, before we go to the univerfity of predeftination :" whereas, the devil would have them go firft to the univerfity, to examine whether they were elected or rejected, or no: they fhould do as a good woman once did, when fatan tempted her, and wanted to diftrefs her, that there were but few to be faved; fhe faid, if there were but two to be faved, fhe would ftrive to be one of them. Surely I am beloved of the Lord, if my natural enmity againft the Lord is flain. How do I know I love a perfon? how can you prove that you love me? why, fay you, I hated you the other day: how many people met I with the other day, that could a few weeks ago have pulled me out of Tottenham-court, but God has overcome their hearts. The perfon now confeffes his former enmity, and when that enmity is removed, and you are reconciled to them, cannot you know that you love them? and if God has removed that enmity to Chrift out of your hearts, furely you are one of the beloved of the Lord.

We

We are the beloved of the Lord, if we are brought to abhor and renounce that which ftands between us and the Lord; I mean, our curfed felf-righteoufnefs. Can I prove that I have renounced my own duties, that I am fick of my duties as well as my fins; none but the beloved of the Lord fee this: an enemy to the Lord may have this in his head, but it is only a friend of the Lord that has this in his heart: a talkative profeffor can fpeak of it; you may teach, perhaps, a parrot to pray, but it is odds to talk like a parrot, and experience like a Chriftian. Now if I have renounced my own righteoufnefs, and been helped to truft to Chrift's, to believe on the Son of God, let fatan fay what he will, I am fure I am the beloved of the Lord, for none but thofe that are beloved by him with an everlafting love, are brought to believe on him.

I may know I am beloved of the Lord, from what? why, experiencing *his love fhed abroad in my heart by the Holy Ghoft.* Jonathan loved David as his own foul. Moft of you know what love is in a carnal fenfe; and if there be a union of fouls between creature and creature, furely there muft be a union of fouls between the Creator and the creature

beloved

beloved of God; it cannot be otherwise; this love will have its effects.

If I am beloved of the Lord, if having his love in my heart, I show it by loving those he has loved, Some people may say, I love you, but I do not love those about you, your friends ; why you are not bound to love all alike, but it may teach you to be civil to that person's beloved. As soon as ever we hear of a Christian, as soon as ever we hear of a believer, as soon as ever we hear of a sinner turning to God, O it will rejoice us; and we shall be like the angels in heaven, who *rejoice over one sinner's repentance, more than over ninety-nine just persons that need no repentance.* Some people may say, I love dearly to hear of a person's being converted by such a minister; I love dearly to hear of persons converted by a dissenter; I love dearly to hear of persons converted by a churchman, but I do not like people should be converted by this and that person ; why I believe there are a great many people whose hearts are thus narrow, but this mixture is not of God ; and I pray God they may know it by experience; that they may know they are beloved of God, then they will rejoice when other people are brought to believe on

him,

him, whoever is made the inftrument. *Grace and mercy be with all them that love the Lord Jefus Chrift in fincerity.* What would have become of poor Paul if he had only loved his own followers: the Romans he never faw till he was taken there a prifoner, but he loved all the reft of the apoftles, writ letters to all forts, not to their particular parties or churches, but to all thofe *that loved the Lord Jefus in fincerity*; and if we do love in this manner, we may be affured we are beloved of the Lord, for none but the Lord could beget fuch love in us.

If we are beloved of the Lord, we fhall be hated by the world. *If you were of the world, the world would love you, but becaufe you are not of the world, but I have chofen you out of the world, therefore the world hateth you.* Will you make me believe that any of you are beloved of the Lord, that never loft your good character by it; why you may as well make me believe that you are emperors of the world: where is the bleffing the fermon on the mount fpeaks of; where is the bleffing of perfecution; where is the bleffing of being hated of all men; where is the bleffing of being hated for the crofs? you love the Lord,
and

and not carry the crofs after you ; you love the Lord, and not be hated as your Lord was ? I don't fay all are hated alike; poor minifters are fet in the front of the battle ; in proportion to our fucceffes we fhall be hated. There are numbers of minifters now fleep in whole fkins, that were formerly in a worfe plight; the devil difturbs them not becaufe they are quite civil, and do not trouble and contradict him ; but if you oppofe the world and the devil, the world will hate you ; and no greater proof of being beloved of the Lord, than the world hating you, but it muft be for Chrift's fake. So Ahab faid of the prophet, *all his prophefying is againft me* ; I hate him ; the world hated him ; *the world hated me,* fays our Lord, *before it hated you* ; and the apoftles, when they began to fpeak for God too, they were hated like their Lord; and glory to God for it, for it is a bleffed mark of their belonging to God, when they are honoured to fuffer for him, and we are never right till we are bearing the crofs : to fee men or women fleeping under the crofs, fculking and hiding from it, is this love ? give me a profeffor that will wear a cockade in his hat, and is never eafier than when he is combating the enemies of his King.

If

If I am the beloved of the Lord, I really
shall live above the world. You may say what
you will, and you may bring the scriptures as
low as you think proper; *but the friendship of
the world is hatred to God ; and if any man love
the world, the love of the Father is not in him.*
Now by not loving the world, I don't mean
that you should shut up your shops, and run
into a convent: how idle for persons to say
they love God, and hide themselves from the
world; that is no religion at all. But the
greatest proof of a Christian's loving God is,
I am in the world, but not of it; I work
with my hands all the day, but my heart is
from it. I remember a dear friend once sent
me word, many years ago, how busy he was
morning and night, up early and late; perhaps, says he, you will think by this account,
I am worldly; he said, no, sir, I thank God
that my heart is above the world : God grant
we may thus prove we love God ! I don't say,
but many that love the Lord may be in another
situation ; but when persons are enabled to
leave all for Christ, it is a great mercy: God
be praised, we have some such ; God add to
their happiness.

They

They that love the Lord, will ſtudy to keep from offending God, not for fear of being damned, but becauſe ſin murdered his dear Son; there are a great many people abſtain from ſin for fear of puniſhment; but hear what Joſeph ſaid, *My maſter has done thus and thus by me, how can I therefore do this great wick-edneſs and ſin againſt God?* my God that loves me; ſo they would not ſtab him, becauſe he has been wounded enough already.

If we are the beloved of the Lord, we ſhall be willing to work for the Lord; faith with-out works is the religion of every carnal man; make an end of one good work and then be-gin another, and lay it down and wonder that Jeſus Chriſt ſhould accept any thing at your hands. I knew a lady ſometime ago, that wanted ſtill more to be employed for God; ſays ſhe, if Jeſus Chriſt would but help me to do ſuch and ſuch a thing I have in view, O I would kiſs his feet, and dedicate myſelf more and more to his honour: a true Chriſtian loves to be thus employed, but above all he is glad he has the blood of Chriſt to waſh his duties in.

I ſhall mention but one thing more, though I might mention twenty; if we have the love of God in our hearts, though we cannot get

Z   over

over the fears of death at all times, yet I think
the bent of the mind of such a person will be,
when shall I see the object of my love, *him
whom my soul loves?* they sit at ordinances,
and long to be led to the fountain head. *I am
in a strait between two,* says Paul ; the word
signifies a strong, an intense desire to be with
Christ: he does not say to be in heaven, but
to be with Christ, which is far better ; but to
stay here is better for you, therefore you should
be content to stay, not because you love the
world, but as willing to wait your Master's
call. I could not help admiring while I was
reading it, that when Christ ascended to heaven, one angel, one particular angel, it must
have been a blessed one, left those that were
attending Christ into glory, stopped in the
way, for what ? why, to preach to the apostles: *Why stand ye thus gazing into heaven?*
I am ashamed of you, says he; here is an angel, one of the convoy, waiting upon them:
he does not say, let me go to heaven with thee,
and let me come down again and preach, no;
he stays down thus to preach to a few poor
fishermen. Lord search us, Lord try us, Lord
God Almighty help us to examine ourselves,
that we may know whether we are beloved of
the Lord or not. So

So that fome may fay, I think I can apply all the marks, though I don't depend upon marks. I have a number of bills here to-night; one fays, if I am beloved of the Lord, why am I fo poor? another fays, if I am beloved of the Lord, why am I fo afflicted? fays another, if I am beloved of the Lord, why am I left to ftarve; can I think God loves me, when I fee thoufands and thoufands fquandered away every day, and yet my poor babes groaning, my poor children quite emaciated, for want only of a little bread that I fee in the baker's fhop as I go along; if I am beloved of the Lord, how is it that my poor children are ready to cry for bread, and I have none to give them; that others are adorned with diamonds, but I have not fo much as a rag to put on my little one's back. If I am beloved of the Lord, how is it that my friends are againft me; my children, inftead of being a bleffing, are a curfe, and break my heart. If I am beloved of the Lord, how is it that I have fo many domeftic trials that caufe me to cry out, *Wo is me that I fo-journ in Mefheck, and dwell in the tents of Kedar.* If I am beloved of the Lord, how is it that I am harraffed with blafphemous thoughts thus; the trials I meet with in bringing down

the

the outward man. If I am beloved of the Lord, how is it that inftead of living in plenty, I now want bread to eat, and fhould be glad to have it from thofe *I once fcorned to fet with the dogs of my flock? Whom the Lord loveth he chafteneth, and fcourgeth every fon whom he receiveth.* Our dear Jefus was never more be-loved of his father than when he cried out, *My God! my God! why haft thou forfaken me?* never more beloved of his father than when he was fweating great drops of blood, when he cried, *Father, if it be poffible let this cup pafs from me.* I remember a dear mini-fter of Chrift, now in Suffolk, told me, when he was in Scotland, going to receive the facra-ment, he was fo dry and dark, and benumbed and tempted, that he thought he would go away; as he was going this word came to his mind, when was Jefus Chrift moft acceptable to his Father? when did he give the greateft trial of his love? when he cried out, *My God! my God! why haft thou forfaken me?* Why then, fays he, upon this I will venture; if I perifh, I perifh at Chrift's feet; and he came away filled with comfort from his bleffed God and Father in Chrift.

Well

Well then, what is to be done to thofe that are beloved of the Lord? here's for you, *they fhall dwell in fafety*; why? *they fhall dwell between his fhoulders*; obferve the expreffion, the prophet fays *they fhall dwell in love.* *Will God indeed dwell on earth?* fays Solomon; yes, God, fays he, dwells in my earthly heart, made heavenly by the grace of God. Did ever any hear fuch an expreffion from the mouth of God, *I will be thy God*; *I am thy fhield, and thy exceeding great reward?* He does not fay an angel fhall go; if God had only faid in his word, that I was to be kept by angels, I am fure my wicked heart would defpair, becaufe it would deceive all the angels in heaven: but God faith, *I will be thy keeper*; fo they that would hurt his people, muft go through God himfelf. *They fhall dwell on high*; *bread fhall be given to them, and their waters fhall be fure.* *They are kept by the mighty power of God through faith, to everlafting falvation.* It is faid, *they fhall dwell between his fhoulders:* the government of the church, and the world, and all, are upon the Redeemer's fhoulders, and the Lord's everlafting arms are under his people. Obferve it is faid, *they dwell in fafety*; and very often we are fafeft when we think we are moft in danger.

They

They shall dwell in safety; those that are lovers of the Lord Jesus shall dwell safely with God on earth, and eternally with him in heaven. O may God bless this foolishness of preaching to some of God's poor, and, perhaps, doubting beloved ones. Come you poor souls, I often think that this *field* preaching is particularly comfortable to the poor; whenever *field* preaching is stopped, farewel to the power of religion. When poor people have been working hard all day, how sweet must it be for them to come to a place of worship, and get a lift for to-morrow: may the Lord God bless this barley-bread! If you can wrap yourselves in God, let the world hate you; God's children are the greatest plagues and trials one to another, but God loves them, God smiles upon them, and therefore they shall dwell in safety. The devil told me I should not dwell in safety, but I bid him defiance, and turned him to Deut. xxxiii. and told him Benjamin's lot was mine; *the beloved of the Lord shall dwell in safety by him.*

Wo, wo, wo be to you that have no marks of being beloved of the Lord. Have we any prophane Esaus here to-night, that are saying, do not tell me of your being beloved of the

Lord;

Lord; if I can have the love of fuch a perfon, I don't care whether God loves me or not; you may tell me God loves people when they are afflicted, I want none of thefe marks, I think God loves me becaufe I am in a good frame; I think God loves me becaufe I profper; I think God loves me becaufe I am very healthy and ftrong; I do not care whether I wait upon God or not, or give to the poor or not. I will not foften the matter, there is no going to heaven without wearing a fool's coat. O, you may fay, that is owing to your imprudence; you make people uneafy, and fet them upon a falfe fcent, and make them their own perfecutors; thank God, I can go into a hundred companies, and not give them reafon to fay I am a Methodift: I can go into company and fing an innocent fong, I don't tell them I have a Tabernacle hymn-book in my pocket. There are few have the courage that the gentleman had who loved God, and went to fee fome carnal relations after he became a fool for Chrift's fake: fays one of the relations, it is always our cuftom after dinner to fing a fong, and afked him to fing; he faid, he would in his turn; two of them fung; his relation faid to him, come, coufin, fing; fays he, I have

not

not fung a fong a good while, but, if you
pleafe, I will fing a hymn: he fung it out,
but they never afked him to fing again, nor
did they fing afterwards.   How fweet it is to
go through boldly with a thing for Chrift! Do
not you think you are a coward? are you not
afhamed? are any of you fuch cowards as to
plead your prudence: God help you to be
unmafked to-night.   I do not know whether
you go to a mafquerade, but you have a dreadful mafque upon your fouls, a dreadful religious vifage.   I heard fomebody appeared the
other night, in order to bring contempt upon
us, in a Methodift drefs, that was one of the
dreffes.   O how can they do fo? fay you;
how canft thou do fo? pretend to be a Methodift among God's people, and behave light
and foolifh among the children of the devil;
for fhame unmafk yourfelves, for God will,
by death, unmafk your foul, and fhow your
hypocrify.   The word hypocrite is taken from
a ftage-player, who acts that part he is not:
God, of his infinite mercy, keep all here from
ftopping fhort.   (

If any of you are awakened and convinced,
the Lord grant you may never reft till you
know you are the beloved of the Lord.   Ah!
                                                    fays

fay you, I fhall never know that, that I am
the beloved of the Lord: I am that old grey-
headed wretch you mentioned at the beginning
of your fermon; can God love me a drunkard,
fabbath-breaker, a whoremonger, an adulterer,
an unclean wretch as ever trod on the ground!
Pray what was Paul? what was the jailor?
what were all the three thoufand that were
converted at once; what was their cafe? nay,
what was Adam the firft finner? and yet Adam
and Eve both, I believe, received mercy of
God; fhe is therefore called *the mother of all
living*, becaufe fhe is the mother of all believers.   Come then at a venture, come then,
throw thyfelf upon Chrift; do not fay, Pardon my iniquities becaufe they are fmall, but
fay, *Lord, pardon my iniquities for they are
great*.   One that was executed to-day for forg-
ing fomething to rob his father; what a father
deal thus with his fon? well, faid I, it is fo
with a man, but our heavenly father will pardon; and though the law is called a fiery law,
yet there is, bleffed be God, a new and living
way.   Oh finners! oh finners! God help you
to come and venture, and ftrive, though you
have none of the marks that have been mentioned, yet fay, God can put thefe marks

A a   upon

upon me. I have been courting this and that perſon's love; nay, I made no other uſe of coming to worſhip, but to look out for ſomething to advance myſelf. I have been looking out for nothing but beauty; I have been looking out for nothing but money, or ſomething or other to make my fortune; but now begone, vain world; now, Lord, I would look after thee. That you may know you are the beloved of the Lord, dwell in ſafety on earth, and after death be conveyed to dwell with, and love him to all eternity, God grant for Chriſt's ſake. Amen.

SERMON

SERMON VIII.

The Furnace of Affliction.

IsAIAH xlviii. ver. 10.

I have chosen thee in the furnace of affliction.

GRACIOUS words indeed ! words
worthy of a God ! who has promised
that *he will not always chastise, that
he will not keep his anger for ever*; but, on
the contrary, will take care in the midst of
judgment to remember mercy ; and if he strikes
with one hand, will uphold with the other.

I hope I need not tell you, my dear hearers, that these words were spoken to comfort
the captives in Babylon, who, for their various
sins and great backslidings, constrained the God
of love, the God of mercy, their covenant
God, to send them captives into a foreign soil;
upon this their enemies take occasion to insult
them, *where are now your songs ?* say they ;
give us one of your Temple songs, with which

A a 2   you

you ufed to pour out your allelujahs; let us fee now whether you can praife him in a ftrange land. The enemy of fouls joining inwardly with them without, makes fome that can fing, even afraid *that God hath forgotten to be gracious, that he hath fhut up his loving kindnefs in difpleafure,* that the darknefs in which they were now involved would not be a temporary, but a perpetual one; and notwithftanding the prophets were fent in mercy of God to comfort them in their trouble, yet many of them were tempted to fay, *all men,* yea the prophets, *were liars;* it is very well if they ftopped there, and did not fay, God is a liar too. The enemy being thus fuffered to break in upon them like a flood, it was high time for the bleffed God to lift up a ftandard againft him; and therefore the great Redeemer, the angel of the everlafting covenant, lets them know that he would fome time or other, nay, very fpeedily, appear to relieve his afflicted people: he affures them, that however for a while he might fuffer them to be tried, he would caufe a fpeedy deliverance, that fhould make them look upon him as their God; and this not for any merit found in this people, not for any good forefeen, but he fays,

for

for my own name's fake; that the heathen might not fay God had utterly forfaken them, he will appear for their relief, and *make them more than conquerors through him that loved them*; that however dark the feafon of afflic-tion might be, yet he would let his own peo-ple know that all that happened, happened out of love; that it was fo far from being true, that they were really caft off from God, that, on the contrary, he intended to over-rule thefe troubles, both foreign and domeftic, to bring them nearer to, and at laft to lodge them fafe in the world above: well therefore for their comfort might it be ufhered in thus, *for my name's fake will I defer my anger, and for my praife will I refrain for thee, that I cut thee not off.* And to fix their attention and gratitude, 'tis added, *behold I have refined thee, but not with filver*; for this is fo far from being contrary to the everlafting decree, or pur-pofe, hid in my bofom, that, on the contrary, it is the fulfilling it; for, faith God in the words of our text, *I have chofen thee in the furnace of affliction.*

Though the words are fpoken in the fingu-lar number, yet they are of a complex and large import; the great God not only fpeaks

to

to them as a people collectively confidered, but particularizes them in this manner; not *I have chofen you, but I have chofen thee*; for the word of God itfelf will never, never, never do us good, if it is not applied by the bleffed Spirit of God to you and I. The wifdom and kindnefs of the Holy Ghoft deferves our notice; had the prophet gone on and faid, *I have chofen you*, unbelief might have faid, ah, this prophefy belongs only to the people of Ifrael, the words were addreffed to thofe who were under the Jewifh difpenfation, what have I to do with them? or unbelief would perfuade us to fay fo of fuch a general promife as this; but when it is faid I have chofen *thee*, and we know that no fcripture is of private interpretation, but, like its bleffed author, is *the fame yefterday, to-day, and for ever*, there is no loop-hole, as it were, for unbelief to creep out at; but every believer may, in all ages, in the words of the text, fay to himfelf, *God has chofen me in the furnace of affliction.* Perhaps, there is not a more comfortable paffage in the whole book of God; I do not know of one that has a greater tendency to filence a complaining child of God, or to make a poor fuffering believer happy, and to reft under

the

the promiſe, to kiſs the rod of God that ſtrikes the blow.

Where ſhall I begin, where ſhall I end? the very firſt words open ſuch a field, that eternity itſelf will be but juſt long enough for us to take a view of it; the time is come that even ſome good people that have the grace of God in their hearts, have ſuch muddy heads as to kick at the doctrine of election, and look upon it as having a tendency to make us bad in our heads, or Antinomians in our hearts; but if we have eyes to ſee, and ears to hear, and if our hearts are really informed by the Spirit; if we have been anointed with his eye-ſalve, O then electing, ſovereign, diſtinguiſhing love flows in ſuch a ſcene, ſuch a tranſporting ſcene, as will make a believer's heart leap for joy. For my own part, I know no other doctrine that can truly humble the man; for either God muſt chuſe us, or we muſt chuſe God; either God muſt be the firſt mover, or man muſt be the firſt mover; either God muſt chuſe them on account of ſome goodneſs, on account of ſome purity, or acts of piety, or God muſt chuſe them merely of his grace, for his own name's ſake, and to let us know that we have not choſen him, but he has choſen us. I verily
believe,

believe, that the grand reason why such doctrine is so spurned at, and hated by carnal people, is, that it strikes at the very root of human pride, cuts the sinews of free-will all to
pieces, and brings the poor sinner to lie down
at the foot of sovereign grace; and, let his at-
tainments in the school of Christ be ever so
great, it constrains him to cry out, Lord, why
me! why me! Our Master, and I think we
should not attempt to be wiser than our Master
was, speaks particularly of and to his own
school, his little college of apostles: *Thine
they were, and thou gavest them me; I have
chosen you, but ye have not chosen me.—Because I
have chosen you out of the world, therefore the
world hateth you.* Before they were fully
enlightened, though they were afterwards
brought more to the light, two of them at first
said, *we have found the Messiah;* yet when
they were sunk deeper in the knowledge of
themselves, they changed their note, and said,
the Messiah has found us. Observe the manner of the Redeemer's addressing our first parent, when their guilt had caused them to hide
themselves, *Adam, where art thou?* Pray who
called first, did Adam call after Christ, or did
Christ call after him; or do you think there is
any

any difference between us and Adam, or that we have got better hearts than Adam had; do you think we are wifer and better now? Adam run away from God, and fo fhould we to this very day, unlefs Jefus Chrift had called us to himfelf.

Some perfons, perhaps, may fay, Well, I like your doctrine very well; God chufes us, you fay, when we have no regard to any good works at all, therefore I will go on finning, becaufe the fitter I fhall be for God's grace; and the fitter thou mayft be for hell.—Grace does not deftroy the ufe of the law; an honeft heart will draw that inference from it, as a good woman once did when the devil told her, that either God had chofen her and fhe fhould be faved, or if fhe was rejected fhe fhould be damned, fo, faid he, you need not ftrive; fhe anfwered, if there were but two to be faved, I would ftrive to be one of them: God help us to draw that inference.

Now this word *chofen*, refers us to God's eternal election; it comprehends, and is the fource of all that God has done for believers, for every individual believer in particular when Jefus bowed his head and gave up the ghoft. Hence the apoftle, in the eighth of the Ro-

B b   mans,

mans, mentioning this doctrine in the cleareſt manner, triumphs over the accuſer by aſking, *Who ſhall lay any thing to the charge of God's elect?* and in the ſame chapter declares, *that it is God that glorifies:* for though glorification is the laſt thing done to us, yet it is the firſt thing God deſigns for us. What is the great thing for a natural man to hear? what is it? why, not only that God has choſen us, but *choſen us in the furnace of affliction:* O that the Spirit of God may vouchſafe to tranſcribe theſe words into our hearts! God help thee to take it to thyſelf, O man; to take it to thyſelf, O woman; to take it to thyſelf whoever thou art that art either a Chriſtian now, or deſires or hopes to be a Chriſtian before thou dieſt, *I have choſen thee in the furnace of affliction.*

What can be the meaning of the words? why, 'tis very plain that the import of them muſt be this; I have choſen thee, and it is my determination from everlaſting to the end of time, and for ever. I have choſen thee with this determination, that the way to heaven ſhould be through the road of affliction: this is the believer's way, eſpecially the miniſters of Chriſt. When Paul was converted, pray what preferment did God promife him? was it to be a great dignitary in the church? no, nothing about the church? was it any more eafe, was it to wear a triple crown, were perfons to come and kifs his toe, what preferment did God chufe him to? what? fays God, *I will fhow him what great things he muft fuffer for my name's fake.* I verily believe, that if we were to have no other preferment than this of Paul, there is not one in a thoufand of the minifters that would afk for a living, if they knew they were to have fuch poor wages as Paul had. Minifters that hold the ftandard up, muft expect the enemy will fire on them from every quarter; and if they happen to be inftrumental in comforting others, *with the fame comforts wherewith they themfelves are comforted of God,* they muft expect to bear their part, not only for their own purification, but for the benefit of thofe to whom they minifter; and I believe audiences find that minifters minifter beft, and the bread comes beft, when it comes out of the furnace of a minifter's affliction.

The word affliction is of a very complex kind; it is like the word tribulation, which comes from the latin *tribulus*, fignifying a

pricking

pricking thorn, a fcratching briar, or wound-
ing fpikes concealed in the way ; and the word
affliction arifes from a word that fignifies fomething that beats down, preffes fore, and is
very grievous and tormenting ; it is a word of
fo general import, that it takes in all the trouble we meet with from men, all the wounds
we receive from enemies, as well as in the
houfe of our friends ; it takes in all our domeftic trials, all our inward ftruggles and dreadful
temptations occafioned by the fiery darts of a
watchful devil ; and if I am not miftaken,
when the great God faid, *I have chofen thee
in the furnace of affliction*, it implys, that this
is really to continue with us even to the very
end of our days : this is what young converts,
in the time of their firft love, do not fee ; that
is, do not wholly fee it ; for if young Chriftians were to know all they have to fuffer, it
would dreadfully difcourage them.   God fays,
his people fhall not do fo and fo, becaufe at
their firft fetting out they would be difheart-
ned, and think of going back.   It is our happinefs God lets us know our trials but very
little before-hand, very little notice of them
have we before the time, and then, perhaps,
gives us but little refpite ; but O when one
                                    trial

trial is gone, God does with us as mafters do
with their fcholars, turns over a new leaf with
us; and when one trial is over, teaches us another; hence our trials are not only new, but
conftant; hence many a believer is apt to fay,
My trials rife out of the ground; and many
believers are faying, who would have thought
fuch a trial would have befallen me at fuch a
time, from fuch a hand? this may, perhaps,
open to us a gloomy fcene; it would be
gloomy indeed, if we were not living in a ftate
of preparation; it would be gloomy indeed, if
God was to afflict without a caufe; but there
is fo much corruption, fuch remainders of indwelling fin, even in God's own children that
are to ftand neareft to him in glory, that are
the deareft to him, and who are to be bleffed
with being in his bofom, that if God was not
to fend them afflictions, there is not a child of
God but would overfet even with the comforts
God vouchfafes to them. We find it fo with
our bodies, that if we live without exercife
we are liable to have a variety of difeafes, we
therefore fubmit to various ways and means
that a phyfician can prefcribe; and if the diforders to which we are expofed in our bodies,
make us willing to fubmit to a regimen pre-
fcribed

scribed by a skilful physician, does it not follow by a parity of reasoning, that we for our souls want sometimes lenitives, and corrosives, and something like a caustic to eat off the proud flesh that cleaves to us? and it vindicates God's ways to man, that there is an hereafter appointed for us, that there is another world, to which, perhaps, we shall be called to go before the morning, *where the inhabitants shall no more say, I am sick.* Believers know this, and if they cannot keep a ledger book, if they cannot post a merchant's book, they may learn so much of divine arithmetic, as to know that *the light afflictions which are but for a moment, work for us a far more exceeding and eternal weight of glory.* The way to heaven, good bishop Beveridge says, is narrow, but it is not long; the gates are strait, but open to everlasting life; and therefore *God has chosen us in the furnace of affliction,* because if we were not afflicted, we should never know what we were made of. Mr. Bohem, who was chaplain to the prince of Denmark, that was married to queen Anne, in one of his excellent sermons upon affliction, has this observation, " Afflictions and temptations are like sunbeams falling upon a dunghill; they do not bring

bring vapours into the dunghill, but they exhale the vapours." So afflictions do not bring the corruptions into us; we blame such and such a one for stirring up such and such corruptions in us, but these tend to draw out the vapours, and prepare us for the more lasting sunshine of a smiling God. God does not intend to destroy thee, but to refine thee, and to humble thee by it. The devil wants to sift thee as wheat; he thinks to let the grain go through the sieve, but Christ will only let the chaff fall through, and the sooner that is gone the better: so it is no ways derogatory to the honour of Christ, but agreeable to the state in which we are, agreeable to the state and the preparations to be made for eternity, agreeable to the militant disposition that our graces must retain. Hence our Lord was content to be called God's servant, *Behold my servant whom I have chosen, mine elect in whom my soul delighteth.*—*Though he was a son, he learned obedience by the things that he suffered;* he was made perfect by his sufferings. We cannot avoid trouble as men, as Christians we should not attempt it: *man is born to trouble as the sparks fly upwards;* and Christians, especially the man new-born. *If these things were done*

to

to the green tree, what shall be done to the dry?
The crofs is the high-road to heaven, and fo
the king's highway : you know there is always
a bar upon the king's road, the king has a
particular road for himfelf; but the King of
kings will make all bars to be removed, and
then his people go the fame road he himfelf
went: this was the road of all the children of
God; there is not an heir of God in heaven,
but is now thanking God for his fufferings here
below; there is not a child of God ever received into glory, but, I believe, as foon as
he comes there, is made to know why he met
with fuch a trial, and from fuch a quarter;
why he was under fuch a rod, why under it
fo long; why it was fhifted, why it was changed, why the whip fometimes was turned to a
fcorpion, and the furnace heated feven times
hotter; then the believer fees the need of it:
in heaven, it makes him wonder he was not
afflicted feven times more on earth. I remember Virgil makes his hero in the Æneid to
fay, *'twould all end well**. He comforts himfelf with this confideration under his trouble,
that the difcharge from it would be the better;

and

---

* Dabit Deus his quoque finem,
  Forfan et hæc olim meminiffe juvabit,
  Per varios cafus, per tot difcrimina rerum,
  Tendimus in Latium.

and if a child of God would think of that, hereafter he will look with pleafure on what he fuffered here; much more a Chriftian enriched with the grace of God, will be willing to die when he confiders he is hereafter to fit in Abraham's bofom, and God fays to him, *Remember thou in thy life-time received thy evil things.* O my brethren, a fine fchool is the fchool of Chrift! I never knew any one of my acquaintance that were believers, and I have been acquainted with fome thefe twenty-eight years laft paft, but what flourifhed moft under the afflicting hand of God. I believe if the devil had his will, he would bid too high for every believer; he does not love money; a covetous man is worfe than the devil, he loves that which the devil fquanders away; but fay they, we think we fhould be very good if we had a coach and fix; fo when they have it, they think they are too good to go to that chapel or foundery; it was a good place when we walked a-foot, but now we have a coach we will drive by. Happy is it for us that we are chofen in the furnace of affliction; that is a glorious petition in our litany, *That in all time of our tribulation, good Lord deliver us!* You may very well excufe me for preaching

C c

from

from fuch a text as this, becaufe I have been
in the furnace, and I find it is very fweet; it
is very fweet walking in a burning fiery furnace when the Son of God leads by the arm.
In the account we have of the three children
being in the fiery furnace, the king could fay,
I fee one walking with them : what an emblem
of the children of God! O, fay you, does the
Son of God walk with you in the furnace? I
anfwer, yes; make the worft of it, tell them
the enthufiaft, the babler fays, God walks
with his people in the furnace; he walks with
all that walk with him, and never walks clofer
with them than when they are in the furnace.
Daniel is generally painted young, but he was
four-fcore years old when he was thrown in
among the lions, there he fits as fweet and
eafy, and no lion dare to touch one of his
grey hairs. Nothing proves the truth of grace,
and fhows the love of God more, and you
may be affured of it as you are of being in
this place alive, that fanctified afflictions are
the greateft evidence God can give you of his
love; fo that if we are chofen in the furnace
of affliction, we are to expect it; and is it not
a great fhame for us, that the heathens out-
do us? when one came and told one of the
                                        .heathens

heathens that his fon, a darling fon, was dead, he faid, " I know that I begot him mortal." So Job faid, *The Lord hath given, and the Lord hath taken away.* O that God may blefs this poor preaching to the raifing up fome drooping foul. Underneath thee, O believer, O fufferer, are God's everlafting arms; there- fore *the beloved of the Lord fhall dwell in fafety,* becaufe they dwell near him, and *he that toucheth them, toucheth the apple of God's eye.*

This may teach us, when one trouble is over to expect another; none of your re- quiems here. Abraham, I believe, thought when he had got his Ifaac, he was to be tried no more; but *after thefe things God did tempt Abraham.* We know not what trials we are to have, but remember they are marks of our adoption: not that all afflictions do prove us children of God, becaufe there are fome afflic- tions that are not fanctified: God give us all to have fanctified afflictions!

If this is the cafe, let young believers know what they are to meet with; God forgive thofe, and vifible churches are too much pef- tered with them, that daub with untempered mortar: formerly, when the church was un- der perfecution, they would forfake father,

mother,

mother, and all ; but *now, bleſſed be God, we are for becoming Chriſtians* ; *we live in London, we live where the church is ſmiled upon, we may live where we are at eaſe.*—My dear hearers, do you think that all the Londoners are converted ? do you think they all bring forth the fruits of the Spirit ; or have you heard that the devil is converted ? can any body prove to me that the devil is not the ſame ; can you prove that God is not the ſame ; can you prove that the world is not the ſame, that the human heart is not the ſame ? if you can prove that neither of theſe are what they were when Chriſt came into the world, I will give up the point ; but if they are the ſame, we muſt expect the ſame trials our forefathers met with, if ever we hope to meet with them in glory ; *God forbid I ſhould glory, ſave in the croſs of Jeſus Chriſt.* Therefore, if any of us have a mind to ſet out for heaven, expect trouble. Indeed, if we have enliſted under the devil's banner, he ſhows you the kingdoms of the world, and the glory of them. When Peter ſaid to our Lord, concerning his ſufferings, *far be that from thee* ; after having ſhown his diſpleaſure at it, as a ſuggeſtion of ſatan's, he ſays to all his diſciples, *If any man will*

come

come after me, let him take up his crofs and follow me. And I remember Mr. Law, who was a great man, notwithftanding fome great blunders and miftakes, told me thirty-two years ago, all principles, all doctrines, are comprehended in thefe few words, *If any man will come after me, let him deny himfelf and take up his crofs and follow me.* And if you do not chufe the furnace of affliction, if you are too nice to enter in, you forfake the Lord, and are only preparing to be company for the damned in hell. This was the cafe with Dives; *Son, thou in thy life-time received thy good things:* and for a man that fares fumptuous every day; for a man that is cloathed in fine linen, to be tormented by the devil; to fee God, Chrift, heaven, with all he had, loft; and the torments muft never ceafe. One moments thought of this is very awful! God grant this may not be the lot of any of us! Come, my dear hearers, may God of his infinite mercy grant this night, that fome poor foul may be refcued from the devil, and enlift under Chrift's banner! I have bore the crofs thirty-four years; I never wore it long, but I found to my great comfort it was lined with the love of God. *My yoke is eafy, my*

burden

burden is light, faith our bleffed Lord. Suffering grace is given for fuffering times; the
reafon we have not more comfort is, becaufe
we have not more croffes: happy they that
fay in this vifitation, my Jefus, my Lord, I
give up all for thee ; my life, and all things,
I caft behind.

> *A heart that no defire will move,*
> *But ftill to adore, obey, and love,*
> *Give me, my Lord, my life, my all.*

I wifh you joy that run this courfe; don't
be weary of it, don't think hard of God, don't
fay, never was any body tried as I am, never
was any body tempted as I am, for if you was
to go and tell your crofs, there are a thoufand
in the congregation would, perhaps, fay, dear
I have had that and ten times worfe. One
Mr. Buchanan, a Scotchman, who died the
other day, having loft his laft child, faid, " I
am now childlefs, but, bleffed be God, I am
not Chriftlefs." A noble lady told me herfelf,
that when fhe was crying on account of one of
her children's death, her little daughter came
innocently to her one day and faid, " Mamma,
is God Almighty dead, you cry fo? the lady
blufhing, faid, no; fhe replied, Madam, will
you lend me your glove? fhe let her take it,
and

and after that afked for it again; upon which the child faid, Now you have taken the glove from me, fhall I cry becaufe you have taken away your own glove? and fhall you cry becaufe God has taken away my fifter." *Out of the mouths of babes has God perfected praife,* and will for ever. O glorify God in the furnace!

If any of you are faying, don't tell me of your afflictions, I will live, I will drink, *to-morrow fhall be as to-day, and fo much the more.* If there be any of you that fay fo, take care, take care, God himfelf can't iffue out a worfe fentence againft you than this, *Let him alone, let him alone;* whom the Lord loves he chaftens. What a pretty creature would you make in heaven, if you was to go there, without one of Chrift's croffes on your back, you would be turned out; no, there are none fuch there.

Chriftians endure the crofs; happy ye that are tried, and happy they that are gone to glory. Where is Mr. Middleton now? where is my dear fellow-labourer, that honeft, that fteady man of God? Oh! he was thanking God for the gout in his head, in his feet, in his ftomach, all decays; thanking God for

that

that laft trouble that cut the thread of life, and
gave the foul a paffage for heaven; if, in the
midft of that torture, he could anfwer his
daughter and fay, *heaven upon earth, heaven
upon earth,* and went to heaven but a little
after; now furely he muft fay, *heaven in heaven*; muft he not now he fees God, and fees
Chrift? and by his comfort, though in fuch
great pain, it fhows that God was kiffing away
his foul, he died at the very mouth of God.
O may the bleffed God blefs his parents and
children that are here to-night; I believe you
may be glad that God has chofen him in the
furnace of affliction. I am glad to hear that
fo many are defirous that fomething may be
done for his family, and Mr. ——, and Mr.
——, and Mr. ——, are willing to take in the
fubfcriptions that any may be inclined to fend
them. May God blefs the family, and grant
that his children may not difgrace the memory
of their father; that they may live as followers
of his faith, who is now gone to inherit the
promifes of God. You know not how your
children may be left by you, though there is
not one of you here but may be called that
have children, to fay, by and by my children
muft be left to the goodnefs of God; and it is
a great

a great happinefs to fee fo many fatherlefs
children provided for of late: there was never
a time when perfons were more beneficent to
the diftreffed; let it not be faid that believers
in London live on bread alone, but may they
be continuing to lay up treafure in heaven!
when we plead, not by way of merit, remember me, O Lord, I did fo and fo when others
were in trouble. Lord Jefus, I plead thy
promifes, if thou haft chofen me in the furnace of affliction; O Lord, help me to lay
hold on thee: O that this may be your and
my lot. I am haftning to the grave; I am
aftonifhed that I have again an opportunity to
preach the word of God. May God prepare
us to follow thofe that have gone before
us, *where the wicked ceafe from troubling,*
and the weary foul enjoys everlafting reft with
thee, O Father, with thee, O Son, and with
the Holy Ghoft; to whom, three perfons but
one God, be all honour and glory, now and
for evermore. Amen.

D d   SERMON

SERMON IX.

The Lord our Light.

ISAIAH lx. ver. 19, 20.

The sun shall be no more thy light by day, nei-
ther for brightness shall the moon give light
unto thee, but the Lord shall be unto thee an
everlasting light, and thy God thy glory.
Thy sun shall no more go down, neither shall
thy moon withdraw itself, for the Lord shall
be thine everlasting light, and the days of
thy mourning shall be ended.

UPON reading these words, I cannot
help thinking of what the royal
Psalmist said, *Glorious things are spo-*
ken of thee, O city of God. Selah. I am afraid,
my dear hearers, that even believers themselves, who have tasted of the grace of God,
reflect not and meditate as they ought, on
the glorious and amazing felicity they are
called

called by the Spirit of God to experience in this life. We content ourselves too much with our hopes, and if we attain to *a good hope through grace*, we are ready to think we have got up to the last step of the gospel ladder, and have nothing more to do but to rest in that hope, without ever attaining to an abiding, full assurance of faith. If we would examine the scriptures, and not chuse to bring them down to us, but beg of God to raise our hearts up to them, we shall find the believer is made partaker of the grace of life, as well as an heir of it; the one is on earth, the other in heaven, and one is only a prelibation of the other. This blessed prophet Isaiah, speaking of the privileges of the children of God, saith, *Eye hath not seen, nor ear heard, neither hath it entered into the heart of man to conceive the things that God hath prepared* (and that even here below) *for those that love him:* God grant that we may be of that happy number! Hence, like an evangelist, the prophet draws aside the veil, and as one inspired by the Spirit of God, and filled with the rays of divine light, gives us a transporting view of the gospel state, and the glory which the church militant enjoys below, before its triumphant state above.

The

The text, probably, refers to the great change that fhould be made in the affairs of the Jews after their captivity, how wonderfully God would appear for them, after their harps had been long hanging on the willows, and they could make no other anfwer to their infulting foes than this mournful one, *How can we fing the Lord's fong in a ftrange land?* The gofpel is, doubtlefs, glad tidings of great joy; and however the people of God might be encouraged to hope that the time would come, when they fhould tread on the necks of their enemies, the prophet teaches them to look further, and lets them know that their happinefs was not to confift in any external created good, but in a larger poffeffion of the graces and comforts of the Holy Ghoft. So that this chapter fpeaks not only of a temporal deliverance and reft, which they fhould enjoy after their trouble, but a fpiritual reft, which, by faith, they fhould enter into here, as the earneft and pledge of the reft and enjoyment of the better world hereafter. As we know no more of heaven than is difcovered by the eye of faith, for even St. Paul acknowledges, that the things he faw were unutterable, 'tis obfervable that heaven in fcripture is defcribed

to

to us more by what it is not, than by what it is. So in the words of the text, *Thy sun shall no more go down, neither shall thy moon withdraw itself, for the Lord shall be thine everlasting light, and the days of thy mourning shall be ended.* Here are three negatives, and but one positive, namely, *the Lord shall be thy everlasting light*, which is a beautiful allusion to the sun, that should teach us to spiritualize natural things; and if we feared God, and lived near to him as we ought, there is no object of our bodily eyes but might improve our spiritual sight. You cannot suppose the prophet meant a time should come, when the sun should not literally go down, that there should not be night and day as now; God indeed permitted a man once to say, *sun, stand thou still,* and it was done; but, perhaps, there never will be any such thing again till the sun is removed from its station, and the moon forsake her orbit, and be turned into blood. The word must therefore be understood in a figurative sense; and then comparing spiritual things with spiritual, it must certainly import, that Jesus Christ, the Sun of Righteousness, shall be what the sun is to the visible world, that is, the light and life of all his

people;

people; I fay, all the people of God. You fee now, the fun fhines on us all: I never heard that the fun faid, Lord, I will not fhine on the Prefbyterians, I will not fhine on the Independants, I will not fhine on the people called Methodifts, thofe great enthufiafts; the fun never faid yet, I will not fhine on the Papifts; the fun fhines on all, which fhows that Jefus Chrift's love is open to all that are made willing by the Holy Ghoft to accept of him; and therefore it is faid, *the fun of righteoufnefs fhall arife with healing under his wings.* If you were all up this morning before the fun arofe at five o'clock, how beautiful was his firft appearance! how pleafant to behold the flowers opening to the rifing fun! I appeal to you yourfelves, when you were looking out at window, or walking about, or opening your fhop, if in a fpiritual frame, whether you did not fay, Arife thou fun of righteoufnefs with healing under thy wings, on me. All that the natural fun is to the world, Jefus Chrift is, and more, to his people; without the fun we fhould have no corn, or fruit of any kind: what a dark place would the world be without the fun, and how dark would the world be without Jefus Chrift; and as the fun does

really

really communicate its rays to the earth, the plants, and to all this lower creation, fo the Son of God does really communicate his life and power to every new created foul, otherwife Chrift is but a painted fun; and is Chrift nothing but a painted Chrift to us, while we receive heat and benefit by the Holy Ghoft, on account of the virtue of his blood? Sometimes the fun fhines brighter than at other times, and does not always appear alike; clouds intervene and interrupt its rays; fo it is between a renewed foul and the Lord Jefus, the fun of righteouf-nefs; O my brethren, I believe you know it by fatal experience: hold but your hand now, when the fun fhines in its meridian, between it and you, and if by the breadth of that you can keep the fun from you, ah! how very little earth will keep off thy heart from Jefus Chrift! It was a very excellent faying of one of the antients, that God never leaves a perfon till he firft leaves him. Some people think God does fo of his fovereignty, but I am apt to think when the fun fhines, we fhall find fome people have taken up with fomething fhort of the fun of righteoufnefs; and I believe there are times, when the poor believer thinks his fun will quite go down, and rife no more:

he

he lofes his relifh, his tafte and evidence of divine things; not only are the rays intercepted for a while, but doubts and fears, a dreadful cloud of them, come on. Though I hold with a full affurance of faith, yet I am of opinion that 'tis not always in a like exercife; and therefore pray that doubting people will not take hold of that, and fay, Bleffed be God, I am in a doubting ftate, and I am content. The Lord deliver you from a mind to ftay in prifon, and prevent the devil from locking the door upon you, and keeping you there as long as he can. The Lord help you to come; come, come, and break out of prifon, that you may know how pleafant it is to behold the Sun, and praife his name.

Sometimes, inftead of the fun there is only moon-light, which fhews the difference a believer feels in his foul, both in relation to grace and comfort. Both fun and moon give light, but O how far fuperior is the one to the other: the moon gives a very faint, uncertain light, waxes and wanes, and at beft is almoft nothing when compared with the light, and the bleffed reviving heat of the fun. Hence, my brethren, this world fometimes is a world of mourners: it is faid, *that the days of our mourn-*

mourning shall be ended; for if the text refers to the future state, as no doubt it does, it means that the days of believers here below are very often mournful, trying, and afflicting, though they end in joy, as our Lord intimates in his opening his gospel-sermon almost with these very words, *Blessed are they that mourn, for they shall be comforted.* Some, perhaps, may think it is an odd kind of blessing; and though worldly people are fond of the fifth of Matthew, and wonder that Methodists and gospel-ministers do not preach oftner on that chapter, I am apt to believe, when you come to preach and open that word, they will not like that chapter any more than any other, because they are for a joyful Christ, and not for any mourning at all. Do you know God in Christ? let me tell you, the more you are acquainted with him, the more your souls will be kept in a mourning state. A mournful state!—O, say you, people will mourn before they are converted.—Ah, that they will.—I don't love to hear of conversions without any secret mourning; I seldom see such souls established. I have heard of a person who was in company once with fourteen ministers of the gospel, some of whom were eminent servants

of

of Chrift, and yet not one of them could tell
the time God firft manifefted himfelf to their
foul. Zaccheus's was a very quick converfion, perhaps not a quarter of an hour's conviction : this I mention, that we may not condemn one another.   We do not love the pope,
becaufe we love to be popes ourfelves, and fet
up our own experience as a ftandard to others.
Thofe that had fuch a converfion as the jay-
lor, or the Jews: O, fay you, we do not like
to hear you talk of fhaking over hell, we love
to hear of converfion by the love of God;
while others that were fo fhaken, as Mr. Bol-
ton and other eminent men were, may fay,
you are not Chriftians becaufe you had not the
like terrible experience.   You may as well
fay to your neighbour, you have not had a child,
for you were not in labour all night.   The
queftion is, whether a real child is born, not
how long was the preceding pain, but whether
it was productive of a new birth, and whether
Chrift has been formed in your hearts; it is
the birth proves the reality of the thing.

Some allow that there is mourning before,
but no mourning after converfion; pray who
fays fo? none but an Antinomian, a rank Antinomian; and when you hear a perfon fay,

that

that after converfion you will have no mourning, you may be affured that perfon is at beft
walking by moon-light; he does not walk by
the fun, he has got fome doctrine in his head,
but very little grace, I am afraid, in his heart.
How! how! my brethren, not mourn after
we are converted; why, till then there is no
true mourning at all. The damned in hell are
mourning now, they put on their mourning
as foon as they get there. How am I tormented in this flame, fays Dives; and Cain, my
punifhment is greater than I can bear. How
many worldly people break their hearts for
the lofs of the world: they cannot keep their
ufual equipage, nor do as they would; and
come not to worfhip on Sunday, becaufe they
cannot appear fo fine as formerly they did:
this is a forrow of the world that worketh
death; but there is a bleffed, a more evangelical mourning, which is the habitual, bleffed
ftate and frame of a converted foul. How
ftrong the expreffion, *They fhall look on him
whom they have pierced, and fhall mourn:* how
fhall they mourn? *as one mourneth for a firft-
born, an only child.* Have you ever been
called to bury a child? is there any tender
mother here? were you merry directly after

the child was dead? no, perhaps till this very day, you continually call to remembrance your little one and fhed a tear; every thing relating to it, caufes the repetition of your forrow. When a poor believer is acquainted with Jefus Chrift, he mourns for having crucified the Son of God, and you will mourn for the fame fin after converfion as before. Surely, fays fome, I mourn for my fins I committed before my converfion. I do not know whether you do or no, but I know you fhould. O, fays David, *Remember not againft me the fins of my youth,* in a Pfalm which was wrote when he was an old man; and Paul fays, *I was a blaf- phemer and injurious, and therefore not worthy to be called an apoftle, becaufe I perfecuted the church of God;* and this after he had been wrapped up to the third heaven. See Mary rufhing into the houfe, wafhing her Lord's feet with her tears, and wiping them with her hair: I don't fuppofe fhe was dreffed as our ladies are now; they did not make fuch apes of themfelves; but her hair was very fine in an honeft way: though fhe breaks the allibafter box of ointment given her, perhaps by fome poor filly creature that would die by her frowns, and live upon her fmiles, fee her at the feet of

her

her Saviour; and Jesus Christ answers for her, some having thought she was profuse, that having had much forgiven, she loved much. The more the love of God is manifested, the more it will melt the soul down: I appeal to you Christians, whether the sweetest times you ever enjoyed, were not those when you were much melted at the sight of a crucified Saviour; when you could say, Lord, thou forgavest me, I feel it, I know it, but I cannot forgive myself; this will always be the effect of an ingenuous mind; and a person that is really converted will thus mourn, and if you do not know this, you may be assured you know nothing savingly of Jesus Christ. You may go and hear this and that warning, and you are right to gather honey from every flower, but you have not got within the inner court, but are yet without. God give you to see your folly herein.

A true believer will mourn over his corruptions: I wonder what they can think, who suppose they have no corruptions. I remember a poor creature of Rhode-Island, who looked the most like the old Puritans I ever saw, when I was talking with him, and said, some people say there are some men that have

no

no fin; he faid, if you fend fuch a man to me, I will pay his charges even from England and back again. I have often learned fome-thing from the difference of glaffes: you look into the common glaffes, and fee yourfelves there fo fine, and admire your perfon, drefs, &c. but when you view yourfelves through a microfcope, how many worms are difcovered in that fine fkin of yours, enough to make you afhamed of the vermin and filth that is feated there: fo it is in faith, that glafs would fhow you fo much corruption cleaving to every ac-tion of your lives, that would make you fin-fick, and mourn that you have known God fo long, and are like him fo little. What fays Paul? *Who fhall deliver me from the body of this death?* Notwithftanding he knew that *there is no condemnation to them that are in Chrift Jefus,* yet cries out, *O wretched man that I am!* I fhould have thought, O happy man that thou art! formerly a perfecutor, and now a preacher; a man that has been honoured fo much above every man in planting churches, which is the higheft honour a man can have under heaven; here is a man that hath been wrapt up to the third heaven,—what of him? *O wretched man that I am, who fhall deliver*

me

me from this body of sin and death? Do you think that it was only a little qualm of conscience? no, it was the habitual temper of his heart. Some people are much humbled by fits and starts, but Paul felt this daily: many things that we are not concerned about, Paul looked upon them as such that made his heart ach, because he thought he could not live near enough to God. He not only watched to do good, but he watched how he did that good; and nature was so mixed with it, that he said, I cannot do as I would do, I would have served God like an angel, but I find myself to be a poor sinner after all; and if we are like-minded with Paul, we shall mourn over our corruptions, we shall mourn over our hidden sins that none know but God and ourselves. It is a very dangerous thing to trust gospel-gossips, who being strangers to themselves, hear with wonder and contempt, and often betray; however, a judicious friend, into whose bosom we can pour out our souls, and tell our corruptions as well as our comforts, is a very great privilege. When our corruptions do not drive us from Christ, but drive us to him, it is the greatest blessing to commune with Christ on this side heaven: and, my

brethren,

brethren, if your hearts are right with God, you will fee fuch things as nobody elfe could think of. A good woman, who was charmed with Dr. Manton, faid, O, fir, you have made an excellent fermon to-day, I wifh I had your heart; do you fo, faid he, good woman, you had better not wifh for it, for if you had it, you would wifh for your own again. The beft of men fee themfelves in the worft light.

How many thoufand things are there that make you mourn here below! who can tell the tears that godly parents fhed for ungodly children! O you young folks, you don't know what plague your children may be to you! O they are pretty things while young, like rattle-fnakes and alligators, which I have feen when little, but put them in your bofom and you will find they are dangerous. How many are there in the world that would wifh, if it were lawful, that God had written them childlefs: there is many a poor creature that makes his father's heart ach. I once afked a godly widow, madam, how is your fon; fhe turned afide with tears, and faid, fir, he is no fon to me now. What in the world can come up to that! here, fays one, I have bred up my children, I cannot charge myfelf with educating

them

them wrong, though few parents can say that, for many parents lead them into the paths of death, and so are murderers of their own children, and by their manner of education help to damn them for ever; but if you can say, I have done all I could, and yet, O my God, my children are worse than any other peoples; this is a dreadful state indeed; and the more you mourn, the more they laugh at you; O these are my godly parents. They increase their trouble, like Dr. Horneck's son, who said, *There is not a post in my father's house but stinks of piety.* I once saw a man that was awakened at the Orphan-house, fall down and throw himself on one of their beds, crying out, O, sir, what will become of my poor grey-headed father, who knows nothing of this birth ! It is a difficulty with some to know how to behave towards unconverted relations; if you don't go to them, they will say you are precise; if you do, and are faithful, they will soon show you they have enough of your company : this sends a godly person home mourning; and then there comes a thought, shall I speak to them any more, or let them go to the devil. This is not like parting from your friends by death, but burying them alive :

F f   when

when dead, we know we muſt ſubmit, but to part from friends, thoſe we loved, and thought to have lived with till we came to heaven, is mournful indeed.

Moreover, the poor ſtate of the church makes many a miniſter and cloſe-walker with God to weep over the deſolations of the ſanctuary, and to mourn for thoſe that will not mourn for themſelves: thus our Lord wept over Jeruſalem, *O Jeruſalem, Jeruſalem, how often would I have gathered thy children, as a hen gathereth her chickens,* but it is over with thee now; the decree is gone forth, and Jeruſalem ſhall ſuffer.

Brethren, the time will fail, and therefore I leave it to you to ſupply more caſes; for if I was to preach till to-morrow morning, I doubt not but a thouſand here would ſay, there are many things you have not mentioned yet. You know the ſtate of your own hearts, and the many particular trials in your own caſe; and you may alſo know, though your trial ſeems over, it is only changed: but let it be obſerved, the day of your mourning ſhall be ended; mind, it is but days, though ſometimes made very ſad ones indeed, by the neglect and ingratitude of thoſe who have made

the

the people of God ferve them with rigour, as
though all the world was made for them, as
well as their incapacity to help themfelves, by
poverty, pain, fore fickneffes, and of long con-
tinuance. This has been, and is the lot of many a child of God; blefled be fovereign mercy,
'tis but a few days. An end fhall arrive, and
that end fhall be happy, when death, the believer's friend, fhall come with an angel's face,
to difmifs them from all their fin and forrow.
When I was laft at Briftol, I could not help
remembring good Mr. Middleton, who ufed
you know to have the gout very much, and
in that clofet were kept his crutches: now,
thought I, he needs them no more, the days
of his mourning are ended, and fo fhall ours
by and by too, when we fhall no longer want
our fpiritual crutches or armour, but fhall fay
to the helmet of hope, the fhield of faith, I
have no more need of thee; and the all-pre-
vailing weapon of prayer be changed into
fongs of endlefs praife; when God himfelf
fhall be our everlafting light, a fun that fhall
never go down more, but fhall beam forth
his infinite and eternal love in a beatific ftate
for ever. The profpeᦑ of this made one of
the fathers cry out, O glory! how great! how

great!

great! what art thou? a friend afking him
what he faw? he anfwered, I fee the glory
of the only begotten Son of God. And if a
fight of Chrift on earth is fo great, as could
make good Mr. Wardrobe, an excellent Scotch
minifter fay, after he was given over, ftarting
up in the arms of an excellent friend who told
it me, in a rapture of joy, crowns! crowns!
crowns of glory fhall adorn this head of mine
e're long! and ftretching up, added, ftars!
ftars! ftars fhall e're long fill thefe hands of
mine! and fo fweetly fell afleep in Jefus:
what a pleafing, awful trial is that for an
affectionate friend! So our dear fifter, who is
to be buried to-morrow night at Tottenham-
court, talked with her friends for an hour or
two, and took leave of her hufband and children, and faid, Now come, ye heavenly cha-
riots! We fhall thank God then for all our
loffes, croffes, and difappointments; and I believe thofe things which we mourn for moft,
and puts us moft to the trial, will give us moft
comfort when we come to die: God fhall be
our everlafting light, as well as the days of
our mourning fhall be ended.

Take care, don't be fecure, pray don't
think the day of your mourning to be ended

yet:

yet: you may put off mourning for your friends, but may have freſh cauſe of mourning for your ſouls; whilſt you remember that holy mourning is conſiſtent with holy walking, following the Lord in all his ways. You have often heard me ſpeak of one of our miniſters, who was not one of your fine velvet mouths, that ſaid once in the pulpit, As ſure as you ſee the ſun ſhine on my breaſt, which at that time it did, ſo ſure does the Spirit of God dwell in the ſouls of true believers. How often has he told you, *I am for having you have godly ſorrow, I wiſh your hearts were full of it, becauſe it will end in everlaſting joy.* Comfort, my brethren, one another with theſe things, the day of your mourning ſhall ſoon be ended for ever.

But what am I to ſay? I apprehend I ſhall grow forgetful to-night; — I have ſpoken ſo much to ſaints, I am afraid I ſhall have but little time to ſpeak to ſinners: I mean, I have taken ſo much time up in ſpeaking to you that know God, that I have but little to ſpeak to you that know him not. How different your ſtate, poor hearts! poor hearts! my ſoul mourns for you; my blood, whilſt I am ſpeaking, is ready to curdle in my veins. The ſe-

raphic

raphic Mr. Hervey, when he did me that honour to fojourn under my roof, faid, My dear friend, it is an awful thing when we fee an unconverted man die, and his eyes clofed, to think that that poor foul will never fee one gleam of comfort or life more ; to have a fight of God, of Chrift, and the heavenly angels and faints; but to fee what the rich man faw, a God they want; to fee Lazarus, whom he would not permit to be feen at his door, now taken particular notice of in heaven; and to fee himfelf now a beggar in hell. The Lord help you to think ! O think how foon your fun will go down, and even your bodies will feel damnation, not only in refpect to pain, but lofs.

Bifhop Ufher's opinion was, and I heartily concur in it, that thofe who value themfelves moft on their beauty and drefs, and do not love God on earth, will be moft deformed in hell, and their bodies fuffer proportionally there. There is no dreffing in hell, nothing but fire and brimftone there, and the wrath of God always awaiting on thee, O finner, whoever thou art, man or woman. It was a fine faying of Maclane, who was executed fome years ago, when the cap was pulling over his
eyes,

eyes, Muſt I never ſee the light of yon ſun
any more; Lord Jeſus Chriſt, thou ſun of
righteouſneſs, ariſe with healing under thy
wings on my departing ſoul! May the Lord
Jeſus Chriſt do that for us all! When you are
damned, the days of your mourning will be
but at their beginning; there is no end of
your mourning in hell. There is but one
ſong, if it may be called ſo, in hell, to wit,
that of Dives, which will be always repeating,
How am I tormented in this flame! Conſider
this, ye that forget God; and O that God
may bleſs you to-night with godly ſorrow.
Believers, pray for them: Lord help you,
ſinners, to pray for your vile ſelves. Some
may think, what do you cry for? why, I
cry for you. Perhaps you will ſay as a
wicked one did to a poor woman in Scotland,
when thouſands were awakened there; ſeeing
her weep, he ſaid, what do you weep for?
for this people, ſays ſhe; weep for yourſelf,
ſays he; ſhe replied, I do; but what is my
ſoul, to all theſe poor ſouls! O that miniſters
may never riſe up in judgment againſt you:
O may Moſes, in the hand of the Spirit, make
you mourn! may the love of God make you
cry! may you not go home to-night without

an

an arrow fteeped in the blood of Chrift. It was wonderful what a good woman awaking thought fhe faw written over her head, *O earth, earth, earth, hear the word of the Lord!* May every earthly foul be made to hear it; to awake, arife from their fleep in fin. The fun is going down, and death may put an end to all to-night: the Lord help you to come, though it is the eleventh hour: O that you would fly, fly this night to Chrift, left God deftroy you for ever. Jefus ftands ready with open arms to receive you whom he has firft pricked to the heart, and made you cry out, *What fhall I do to be faved!* he will then make you believe in his name, that you may be faved: God grant this may be the cafe of all here to-night. Amen.

SERMON

SERMON X.

Self - Enquiry concerning the Work of God.

NUMBERS xxiii. ver. 23.

According to this time it shall be said of Jacob and of Israel, what hath God wrought?

WHEN I read you, my dear hearers, these words; when I consider what occasion, and by whom they were originally spoke, I can't help thinking of that triumphant expression of the royal Psalmist, *Why do the Heathen rage?* When Pontius Pilate and the Jews conspire to destroy the cause of God, *he that sitteth in heaven laughs them to scorn; the Lord not only has them in derision,* but over-rules even their malice and violence (no thanks to them) to promote that very cause they attempted to destroy; so that 'tis a very wrong maxim, and argues great ignorance in us, to imagine that God never

G g

brings

brings about his defigns by the means and in-
ftrumentality of wicked men. This is the
Papifts objection againft the reformation: great
pains have been taken to blacken the reformers,
and to make it believed that a reformation
could not be good that was begun by people
of bad character, and a king of an immoral
life. But fo far is this from eclipfing, that it
illuftrates the wifdom and goodnefs of divine
Providence, in obliging the wicked to do what
they never defigned, and over-ruling their
counfels for the fulfilling God's holy, wife,
and fovereign decree. This obfervation naturally arifes from the words of our text, which
were fpoken by, as far as I can judge, one of
the vileft men upon the earth, you doubtlefs
know his name, Balaam, who, though florid
in his expreffions, and high in profeffion of in-
tercourfe with God, and puts on a fine face of
religion, was but a rotten-hearted hypocrite,
for he divined for money, made a trade of
religion; and fo loved the wages of unrigh-
teoufnefs, as to have wifhed to curfe even thofe
whom God had bleffed. I need not inform
you, that this was the end for which Balak
fent for him; and no wonder he was fo willing to go, when he knew he was to be well
                                                    paid

paid for his journey. Achilles, the Græcian hero, is said to be capable of being wounded only in the heel, but bad priests, ministers, and people, have a great deal more dangerous part to be wounded in, that is, the palm of the hand; if you can keep that secure from being wounded with gold, never fear; the devil can't have his end. Balak promised him great preferment, if he would but come and curse the people of God. A prophet, or soothsayer, is one that pretends to have inter- course with God or the devil, and Balak did not care by which of them it was, so that he could but get the Israelites cursed; Balaam catches at the golden bait, pretends to ask counsel of God; and what seems strange, God bids him go, and yet sends an angel to meet him in the way, who stands ready to slay him for going. Does it not seem very strange, that God should bid a man go, and then offer to slay him for going; but people that read this passage, should carefully mind the particulars of it. God said, if the men come and call thee, go; but he did not wait for that, but saddles his ass and goes : this is called by St. Peter, the madness of the prophet: witness his rising early in the morning, not waiting for

G g 2   the

the call of the princes, which shewed how
eager he was to be gone; and though this so-
lution should not be allowed, God was justly
angry for his going with an ill design, that is,
maliciously to curse a people whom he knew
God resolved should be blessed, and that for
the sake of the wages of unrighteousness *.
The king and his nobles wait upon him, in
hopes this foothsayer will answer their purpose; but after all he can do nothing without
God's leave: however, no cost is spared to
obtain the end; so true is it, that the devil's
children are ten thousand times more expensive
in persecuting the people of God, than God's
people are in promoting his glory. This footh-
saying priest pretends to go to God, which is
permitted, but forced to speak what God
would have him; once and again his mouth
is stopped, or rather his curses are stopped,
and turned into a blessing. Balak, enraged
at his repeated disappointment, bids him neither to curse or bless them at all; and thinking,
perhaps, that the sight of the people affected
                              him,

* It is no unusual thing in holy writ, for heaven to resent
and punish even those actions that it has permitted. Witness
Deut. i. 20—35. comp. with Numb. xiii. 2.—Hof. xiii. 11.
comp. with 1 Sam: viii. 7. cap. xv. 23. cap. xvi. 1. Psal.
81. 11, 12. &c. &c.

him, carries him to a place where he would fee but a fmall part of them; he goes, and there God made him confirm the blefling inftead of the curfe, more abundantly than before. Oratory is beautiful, though out of the mouth of the worft of men, *Surely,* faid he, *there is no enchantment againft Jacob, neither is there any divination againft Ifrael. Behold, the people fhall rife up as a great lion, and lift up himfelf as a young lion; he fhall not lie down until he eat of the prey, and drink the blood of the flain;* having faid juft before, *According to this time it fhall be faid of Jacob and Ifrael, what hath God wrought!*

What words are here out of the mouth of a wicked man! and yet I hope it will do no hurt to chufe them as a proper fubject for an evening meditation. Let us leave this prophane diviner, and the king his employer, vexed that they could not get their end of the people of God: let us fnatch the words out of the vile prophet's mouth, and fee if we can ferve him as David did Goliah, take his fword and cut off his head. Some people run to extreams, and becaufe fome have abufed religion, therefore they think there is no religion at all. Perhaps it is for this reafon, that fo many

offences

offences are permitted to happen in the churches, that one of the twelve fhould be a traitor, and that the devil fhould come with his bible under his arm to tempt us to difbelieve or abufe it, by which God ftirs up the people of God to watch, fight, and pray.

How fhould we take the words of our text? by way of interrogation? or admiration? as fpeaking in a prophetic ftrain how God had wrought, and did then work, and would afterwards work for the profperity of his faithful Jacob and his pofterity, the Ifrael of God.

Suppofe we take them in the way of queftion, which, perhaps, is moft agreeable to the context, and it may be moft ferviceable to you and to me; and in order that I may not run into too great a field to-night, I will confine myfelf to what Balaam confines himfelf, *from this time it fhall be faid of Jacob and Ifrael,* in a way of enquiry, *what hath God wrought?*

If we look round the world and furvey the works of creation, *the heavens declare God's glory: and the firmament fheweth his handy work.* If we look further, my brethren, down upon thefe bodies of ours, if we confider the curious form of them, we may cry, *what*
hath

hath God wrought ! furely I am fearfully and
wonderfully made ; and when we confider that
we are made up of the four elements; when
we confider to what cafualties we are expofed,
how wonderfully thefe bodies have been kept
up, when thoufands have dropped into the
grave before us, we may well fay, *what hath
God wrought !* but I rather chufe to confine
myfelf to that better part ; and I am perfuaded
of it, we fhall never go to heaven unlefs God
works powerfully on our fouls : fuppofing you
and I now were to forget all created beings,
fuppofing we were to forget our neighbours
to-night, and to hear only for ourfelves, as the
fhades of the evening are coming on, and as
we are going fhortly to reft, may be to rife
no more in this lower world, what if we fhould
fteal a little time from our fhop, a little time
from our worldly bufinefs, as we know not
but we may be called to judgment to-morrow,
and afk and fay, O my foul, what hath God
wrought in thy heart ? I am glad to hear you
are fo inquifitive. Obferve, what hath God
wrought; now whatever is done in us, is all
done by God; it is all done by an Almighty
power, and it is all the effect of infinite wifdom ; fuppofing then you and I are new creatures,

tures, hath God, O my foul, wrought in thee
a deep, a penitent, a humbling fenfe of thy
tranfgreffions againft his holy law; this is a
moft important queftion, this is the very beginning of religion, this is the very firft letter
of the Chriftian's alphabet, the firft line in his
book; with this Chrift himfelf began to teach
fallen man. *Adam, where art thou*, was the
firft queftion that the Son of God put to his
fallen creatures; what condition art thou in?
how art thou fallen, thou fon of the morning! and when he came to the woman, he
took the fame way, he preached, and minifters fhould preach conviction firft; *what is
this*, faith God, *that thou haft done?* to break
thy hufband, and bring all thy pofterity unto
ruin; and it feems to me that there was a
confcioufnefs in this; and I wonder fometimes,
the Deifts have not run fo far as to do it in jeft.
I don't know that I ever heard of a female
child's name called Eve; probably, we are
afhamed to call a child by that name, becaufe
of the guilt of our mother Eve, that brought
us all into fin. Now hath God wrought in
you? hath he even given this conviction to
you; not a little flight now and then, or a
qualm of thy confcience; the devil and natural

con-

confcience may do this; but when it is wrought
in thy heart by the Spirit of God, it goes to
the bottom, the arrow fticks faft, and a poor
foul fometimes endeavours to pray, endeavours
to pull it out, but in vain. Hath God wrought
this in thy foul? now when God works this
change in the foul, the devil is always bufy in
tempting the poor convicted finner to defpond,
if not defpair. Ignorant formalifts, who are
fome of the worft people under heaven, when
a perfon is under conviction, think the devil
is got into them, whereas the devil is in
themfelves; for the devil hoodwinks people,
and he endeavours to perfuade them, that there
is no harm done to God by finning againft
him. It is God wounds the foul, and it is he
that heals it; has he wrought in thee not only
a deep and humbling fenfe of the outward
acts of fin, but a humbling fenfe of the inward
corruptions of thy heart? has he led thee beyond the ftreams, through the powerful operations of his Spirit, to the fountain-head? when
he has done fo, then are we Chriftians indeed;
and this cannot be the work of the devil, who
never did, nor do I know whether he can,
fhow a perfon the inward corruptions of his
heart; it muft be the Spirit of God: the devil

H h   may

may frighten a perſon, as to outward things, but I very much queſtion whether it is in the power or will of the devil to ſhow a perſon that he is totally depraved, that the whole fountain is corrupt; this cannot be, becauſe this would make the devil omnipotent, of equal power with the Holy Ghoſt, who alone ſhows thee the guilt and corruption of thy heart.   This I have found to be the fact, from thirty years obſervation and experience of thouſands, thouſands, thouſands, with whom I have ſpoken about their hearts.   So it was, I remember, when I went firſt to Georgia, when I was about twenty-five years old, I had them day after day, week after week, and night after night, ſaying, *What ſhall I do to be ſaved?* O my wicked heart, my deceitful heart, from morning to night.   Hath God wrought this in any of you? are you com-plaining of your wicked heart and corrupt nature? have you found out that your hearts are cages of unclean birds, only a lodging for vain thoughts to dwell in? O my friends, my dear hearers, O may you turn the queſtion into a note of admiration, and ſay, *what hath God wrought!* he has not only convinced me of my outward ſins, but powerfully convinced

me

me of the corruptions of my heart. Do afk
yourfelves this queftion, has God wrought in
me a view of the fpirituality of his holy law ?
till this is done, you are as faft in the devil's
arms as he can clafp you. Of all the children
the devil has in the world, I believe he moftly loves his Pharifaical children: I was talking
with one of them fome time ago, and fomebody very innocently afked me where the
Pharifees lived, ·O, faid I, they live every
where. Some people think that they only
lived in the times of the apoftles. Do you
know, vipers and toads have the moft eggs
and moft numerous progeny ? if you was to
fee the eggs of a toad through a microfcope,
you would wonder at the innumerable multitude; and the Pharifees are an increafing
generation of vipers, which hatch and fpread
all over the world: if you want to know what
a Pharifee is, he is one who pretends to endeavour, and talks about keeping the law of
God, and does not know its fpirituality; they
are fome of them very great men in their own
opinion, and always made the greateft figure
in the church: one of them, a gentleman's
fon, becaufe he had not broke the letter of
the law, thought he was right and without

fin; O, fays he, if I have nothing elfe to do
but to keep the commandments, I am fafe; I
have honoured my father and mother; I never
ftole; what need he fteal that had fo good an
eftate? I never committed adultery; no, no,
he loved his character too well: but our
Lord opens to him the law, *this one thing thou
lackeft, go fell all thou haft*; he loved his money more than his God: Chrift brought him
back to the firft commandment, though he
catechized him firft in the fifth. So Paul was
a Pharifee; he fays, *I was alive without the
law once*; *I was, touching the law, blamelefs*;
how can that be, can a man be without the
law, and yet, touching the law, blamelefs;
fays he, *I was without the law*; that is, I was
not brought to fee the fpirituality of it; I
thought myfelf a very good man, no man
could fay of Paul, black is his eye; but, faith
he, when God brought the commandment
with power upon my foul, then I faw my
fpecks, and do now. Pray mind and fay the
commandments, if you go to church you fee
them, and if you go to meeting I hope you
have not forgot them; *thou fhalt not bear falfe
witnefs againft thy neighbour, thou fhalt not
covet*; from repeating the laft commandment,

we

we are taught that God's law is fpiritual, *I fhould not have known fin,* as the apoftle faid, *if the law had not faid, thou fhalt not covet;* now has God wrought in you thefe things? haft thou really feen his law that it is fpiritual? have you been made to fee that the law of God requires perfect, finlefs obedience? have you been made to fee that you are under the curfe, becaufe you have finned, by the inward teaching of the bleffed Spirit of God? for then be affured, as fure as thou art in this place, God has wrought this in thy foul, and thou mayft turn the queftion to admiration, and fay, *what has God wrought!* has he wrought in thee a fenfe of unbelief, that thou canft no more believe than thou canft create a world? I mention this, becaufe I have told you often, and I am in the fame mind; yet there are very few books that talk about unbelief, there is a long catalogue of fins, but not one word about unbelief; why? O becaufe thefe good folks, that have wrote communion books, take it for granted, all folks that go to church are believers; I take it there are more unbelievers in the church than out of it; why, fay you, do not they affent to the gofpel? fo does the devil; do not they affent to all the articles of the

Chriftian

Chriſtian faith? ſo does the devil; the devil is
a ſtronger believer than an Arian; the devil is
a ſtronger believer than a Socinian, he believes
Chriſt is God, for he has felt his power by his
damning him to hell; *we know thee who thou
art, the holy one of God.* But remember
Chriſt ſays, when he is gone the Spirit of God
ſhall come to reprove the world, in the margin it is, convince, and not a tranſient conviction, but a conviction that faſtens, that brings
ſalvation with it; if conviction brings its own
evidence, ſurely faith muſt bring its own evidence along with it too; *now he ſhall convince
the world,* ſaith our Lord, *of ſin*; what ſin?
the ſin of unbelief, *becauſe they believe not in
me.* It is mentioned by the dear Mr. Hervey,
by the dear Mr. Marſhall himſelf, and alſo
by ſomebody elſe, that when complaining
to a miniſter that he could get no eaſe to his
ſoul, and told the miniſter he confeſſed his ſins
every day, he put them all down, (a man
muſt have a good memory that can do that)
the miniſter ſaid to him, I think your catalogue is worth nothing at all, the grand ſin is
not mentioned; what is that? ſir, ſaid he, the
ſin of unbelief, a ſin the poor creature thought
he had never been guilty of. Has God
wrought

wrought in thee a fenfe of thy unbelief? what
bleffed times have I feen in New, as well as
Old England and Scotland, when thoufands
were awakened at Edinburgh, at Glafgow,
and many other places, when I have feen them
taken out of the congregation by fcores, and
afked what is the matter? what do you want?
I can't believe! I can't believe! I can't believe! We think we can believe when we will,
but the Spirit alone can convince us we have
no faith, the Spirit alone can convince us of
our want of faith, and can alone impart it to
the poor awakened finner; confequently, you
may afk yourfelves whether God has wrought
in you, not only a fenfe of your own mifery,
but alfo a fenfe of your remedy; fet you upon hungering and thirfting, fuch a hungering
and thirfting as has never been fatisfied but by
an application of the blood of Chrift imputed
to you. I do not want to difpute upon the
fcriptures with any body: there are a great
many good men have been prejudiced by Antinomian principles and practices, and becaufe
fome people have run to a dangerous extream,
and have not thought proper to make ufe of
the word *imputed* at all. The beft truth may
be fpoiled by bad books; but, for my part, I

am

am more than ever convinced, that the doctrine of imputed righteoufnefs is a doctrine of
the gofpel; and that as Adam's fin is imputed
to me, fo the righteoufnefs of Chrift muft be
imputed alfo: I ftand not only as a pardoned
finner, but as a juftified finner; I ftand before
God juftified, and fo do all whom Jefus Chrift
has purchafed. Now has God wrought this in
thee, O man; in thee, O woman? I am not
going to afk, whether it was wrought in thee
by hearing a fermon or reading a book, God
may make ufe of a minifter, or of a book;
and I don't like people to get above minifters
and books, faying, we do not want thefe.
God draws with the cords of a man, and generally draws us with cords by men fuch as ourfelves. Canft thou fay, there is a book, there
is the minifter, in reading or hearing which,
Chrift's blood was applied, and the Spirit of
God witneffed with my fpirit that I was one
of his children? now this is all God's working,
indeed it is, the devil can't do this, it is out
of his power; he may attempt to perfuade
them that he has done it, when he has not,
and cannot. The magicians turned their rods
into ferpents, but the rod of Jehovah fwallowed them all up. Has the Lord God wrought
a change

a change of heart in thee, and a change of life as a consequence of that; I mention this, but I would have every body that stands up for Chrift's imputed righteoufnefs, efpecially as fome good people are apt to fpeak of it and carry it very high, to be careful in the fame difcourfe to fpeak as highly of obedience too, to Chrift's commandments. I don't like only to mention the word promifes; when people tell me they hang upon the promifes, I always afk them how do you hang upon them? have you got the thing promifed? the promife is, that the Promifer fhould come to my foul; the promife is, what, my brethren? the promife is, for this and that good thing; have I got it? How would you do if you was to take falfe bank notes, if you was to take falfe bills? the people generally afk, is the man that has given me this note worth any thing? if you have a bad note you go to the notary and note it, you fay, I was to have had this note paid ten, twenty, thirty days after fight, or upon fight; where is the notary? they note it and proteft it: let us be careful then to fee that God pays his notes, as we are that man does. Haft thou got the thing promifed? the thing promifed is, all peace and all joy; the thing

promifed

promifed is, a new heart; the thing promifed
is, a new nature; and therefore David goes to
God for the thing promifed, and fays, *Create
in me a clean heart, O God, and renew a
right fpirit within me.* Now is this the cafe
of thy heart? the devil never can make a new
creature; I am fure nothing but an Almighty
power can take away the heart of ftone, and
give a heart of flefh: has God wrought this
in thee? if he has, though it is not come to
fuch a heighth as thou would wifh, yet be
thankful for what he has done, and fay, what
has God wrought in me! Attend to the word,
I do not mean lazily, there is not a thing upon
the face of the earth that I abhor fo much as
idlenefs or idle people; I am fo far from having a love to people that are lazy, that if I had
the dealing with a number that are called
Chriftians, they fhould go to bed fooner, and
get up fooner; there is one thing that will
make people rife fooner in the morning in London, and that is, for merchants to agree to
have the 'Change opened at fix, and that will
make people as much alive in the morning, as
the markets are after people have been travelling all night to prepare for them.

Has

Has God wrought in you a fpirit of zeal and love? has he wrought in you a love to his name, a zeal for his caufe? has he wrought in thy heart a deadnefs to the world, that you can live above it from morning to night, having your converfation in heaven? has he wrought in thee a love to his people, not people that are Calvinifts only; not people that hold univerfal redemption only; O be careful as to that; O what nonfenfe is that, for people to hold univerfal redemption, and yet not love all mankind; what nonfenfe is it to hold election, and not *as the elect of God to put on bowels of mercy, kindnefs, humblenefs of mind, meeknefs and long-fuffering*; as the woman faid, I have a houfe will hold a hundred, a heart ten thoufand. Has he wrought in thee a love to thy enemies, fo that thou doft not only love them that love thee, but them that hate thee? what fay you? muft I put a fnake in my bofom, no, no; I may hate the conduct, and at the fame time pray to God for them. Enmity is, *an eye for an eye, a tooth for a tooth.* Love as archbifhop Cranmer did, that it became a proverb concerning him, that if any man would make him his friend, he muft do him an injury. Has he wrought in thee a defire to go

to heaven? has he wrought in thee fuch a love
to Jefus, that you prefer him to the heaven
he dwells in? We count heaven a fine place,
and we may fay, I am glad to fee the departed
faints and the angels, but all that will be nothing
unlefs I fee the Lamb in the midft of the
throne. Has God wrought in thee a defire to
promote his glory, to be upon the ftretch for
God, to deny thyfelf, to take up the crofs
daily and follow him? if God has wrought
this in thee, and I verily believe from my foul
he has wrought it in fome degree in many of
you, O you may well fay, *what has God
wrought!* efpecially if you confider the manner, and the time in which he wrought it; if
you confider the inftruments he made ufe of,
when, and by which he wrought it; and if
you confider the ineftimable price that was
paid for it, and the Spirit taking poffeffion of
your hearts. One part of our entertaintment
in heaven will be, to count the fteps of the
ladder by which God brought us there; one
will fay, God wrought in me when I was
young; another, when I had grey hairs. Mary
Magdalen will fay, God wrought in me when
I was a finner; the expiring criminal will fay,
God wrought it in me juft as I was turned off,

I was

I was a brand plucked out of the burning. The anthem, as good Mr. Erſkine obſerves, will be in heaven, *what has God wrought!* Curioſity led me to hear the preacher, and God touched my heart; there was a young fellow, called emphatically *wicked Will of Plymouth,* who came, as he ſaid, to pick a hole in the preacher's coat, and the Holy Ghoſt picked a hole in his heart. What has God wrought, to work it in you, and not in your father; you, and not your children; work it in you, and not a fellow-ſervant; work it in one brother and not in another; all theſe things will make us cry, *what has God wrought!* Well, I do not want you to reſt in this by no means; I do not like to hear people talk, and ſpeak againſt inward frames and inward works, nor do I like to hear people legal, let every thing have its proper place. It is about thirty-three years ago, or very near, when a man came to me, after I had preached upon marks and evidences, at Whitechapel I think it was, and ſaid, I am come to tell you, that I don't chuſe any marks at all; then, ſaid I, you muſt be content with the marks of the devil, for you muſt have the one or the other.

Now,

Now, my brethren, if God has wrought this in us, what fhall I fay? why, I pray the Lord Jefus Chrift that your life and mine may be a life of praife. I would have you not only dwell upon particular words of God fet home upon your hearts, but his various providences, the numerous trials he has brought you through: O think how often you have been kept, think how often you would have run away from God if he had not ftopped you; what has God wrought, by preventing me from fin; what has God wrought, by delivering me from blafphemous thoughts; what has God wrought, in fnatching me out of the jaws of ruin; even after converfion, when I was damning my own foul, his grace arrefted me. Have we brought ourfelves into trials, how has he made thefe very trials work for good; made our fcolding hufbands and wives, perfecuting fathers, friends and relations, that you have thought would devour you, made the bulls of Bafhan inftruments of bringing you nearer to God; and eternity will be too fhort to cry perpetually, *what hath God wrought!*

And if God has not wrought this in any of you that are here, which, perhaps, may be the cafe, though I cannot think what fhould

bring

bring any body here if they had not a defire of the falvation of their fouls; if God hath not wrought it in you yet, O that this may be the time; O that God may give us fome parting bleffing; that fome poor creatures that have nothing but the devil's work in them yet, may now feek after the blefled work of the Holy Ghoft. If we may afk what God has wrought, let me afk you what the devil hath wrought in you; O thou unconverted foul, fin has made thee a beaft, made thy body, which ought to be the temple of the living God, a cage of every unclean bird; what hath fatan wrought in thee? but made thee a neft of vile ftinking fwine; and what will he give thee? hell, hell, hell. The wages the devil gives no man can live by; *the wages of fin is death:* and here I come to bring you good news, glad tidings of great joy; O that God may now counter-work the devil, and take thee into his own work-manfhip, create thee anew in Chrift Jefus, give thee to feel a little of his Spirit's work on thy heart, and make thee, of a child of the devil, a child of God! Say not, it cannot be; fay not, it fhall not be; fay not, it is too late; fay not, it is for others but not for me; my brethren, God help you to cry, and to try

to-night,

to-night, if thou canſt turn the text into a
prayer, Lord God, I have felt the devil work
in me, now, good God, let me know what it
is for thee to work in me; make me a new
creature, create a new ſpirit within me, that I
may join with thy dear people in ſinging,
what hath God wrought ! O remember, if this
is not the caſe with you, you muſt have a
dreadful different ditty in hell; the note there
will be, what hath the devil wrought! what
hath ſin wrought! how am I come to this
place of torment! I fold my birthright for a
meſs of pottage! Heaven or hell is ſet before
you to-night; Jeſus grant, that the terrors
of the Lord may awaken you to-night, and
that you may not reſt till you have comfort
and ſupport from God.

You that have this work begun in you, look
ſtill for better things to come, even after death,
when our bodies are made like Chriſt's glorious
body, and our ſouls filled with the fulneſs of
God, we ſhall then cry, Churchmen and Diſ-
ſenters, Methodiſts and Foundery-men, and
the Lock too, we ſhall all then join without
any bickerings, ſaying, *what has God wrought !*

I could enlarge, but I am afraid I have
been too long already; yet as I think the providence

vidence of God calls me, and I fhall give a
particular account of my call to-morrow evening, at the other end of the town, I think if
I fhould keep you a few minutes longer, it
might be excufed. I begin to feel already it
muft be executed in a few days; I feel already
that I fhall foon part from you, and O that
God may awaken many of you poor unawak-
ned fouls; my heart bleeds for you; O may
the oil of the bleffed Spirit foften every hard,
unconverted heart, that we may go away
praifing and bleffing God that we fhall at
laft meet, whether we go by land or by water,
before the throne, where we fhall afcribe
glory, and honour, and power, to him for
evermore. Amen.

K k   SERMON

SERMON XI.

The Burning Bush.

Exodus iii. ver. 2, 3.

Aud he looked, and behold the bush burned with fire, and the bush was not consumed; and Moses said, I will now turn aside, and see this great sight, why the bush is not burnt.

IT is a common saying, and common sayings are generally founded on matter of fact, that it is always darkest before break of day; and I am persuaded, that if we do justice to our own experience, as well as consider God's dealings with his people in preceding ages, we shall find that man's extremity has been usually made God's opportunity, and that *when the enemy has broke in like a flood, the Spirit and providence of God has lifted up a standard against him:* and I believe at the same time, that however we may dream of a

con-

continued scene of prosperity in church or state, either in respect to our bodies, souls, or temporal affairs, we shall find this life to be chequered; that the clouds return after the rain, and the most prosperous state attended with such cloudy days, as may make even the people of God sometimes cry, *all men are liars, and God has forgotten to be gracious.*

The chapter in which is our text, is an instance of this. What a glorious day of the son of man was that when Joseph sent for his father to Egypt; and the good old patriarch, after he had thought his son had been dead many years, agreeably surprized by a message from him to come to him, with all his family, and are by him comfortably settled in Goshen; where the good old patriarch, after many a stormy day, died in peace, and was highly honoured at his funeral by Pharaoh and his servants, and attended to the sepulchre of his fathers in Canaan by all his sons. After which, Joseph continued to live in splendor, lord of all the land of Egypt; and his brethren, doubtless, in the height of prosperity: but how sadly did the scene change at Pharaoh's death, soon after which, *another king arose that knew not Joseph,* verifying the observation, New

K k 2   lords,

lords, new laws, by whom the defcendants of Jacob, inftead of reigning in Gofhen, were made bond-flaves; many, many long years, employed in making bricks, and, in all probability, had what we call their bibles taken from them, by being forced to conform to the idolatry of Egypt, and fo were in a worfe ftate than the unhappy Negroes in America are at this day. No doubt, numbers of them either wondered that ever they had been profpered at all, or that God had forgot them now; but what a mercy it is that *a thoufand years in God's fight are but as one day*, and therefore when God's time is come, the fet time that he has appointed, he will, maugre all the oppofition of men and devils, he will come down and deliver his people, and in fuch a manner, that the enemy fhall know, as well as friends, it is the Lord's doing. A deliverer is born and bred in Pharaoh's court, a Mofes is brought up in all the learning of the Egyptians, for Pharaoh intended him for a high and exalted poft: but when offers of the higheft preferment are made to him, he did not catch at them as fome folks now do, who are very good and humble till fomething occurs to take them from God. Young as he was, he re-

fufed

fufed the higheft dignity, and fpurned at it with an holy contempt; and chufes rather to fuffer affliction with the people of God, than enjoy all the grandeur and pleafures of, perhaps, one of the greateft courts on earth. Forty years continued he in this ftate of obfcurity, in which time he acquired fuch a competent degree, and variety of knowledge, as qualified him for every thing God intended him for: the occafion of this, was his kind attempt to compofe a difference between two of his brethren, one of whom accufed him of murder, on which he that was to be king in Jefhurun, is forced to fly into a ftrange land; there he fubmits to the humble office of a fervant, marries, and lives in a ftate of fubjection for forty years, as was faid before. At length, when he was eighty years old, dreaming of no fuch thing, behold God calls, and commands him to go and deliver his people; as he himfelf informs us, who is the author of this book, ver. 1. *Now Mofes kept the flock of Jethro his father-in-law, prieft of Midian:* he might have faid, what fuch a fcholar as I keep a parcel of fheep! fuch a learned man as I am employed in fuch a menial fervice! fome proud hearts would break firft, but you never knew a truly great

man

man but would stoop; some that are called great men, swell till they burst; like sturdy oaks, they think they can stand every wind, till some dreadful storm comes and blows them up by the roots, while the humble reed bends and rises again. Moses was one of the latter, he keeps the flock of Jethro his father-in-law, and leads them to the mountain of God, even to Horeb. This shows how persons ought to methodize their time; but however the name of a Methodist is despised, they will never be bad servants and masters; you would be only weathercocks, unless you took care to order things in proper seasons: the devotion and business of a Methodist go hand in hand; I will assure you, Moses was a Methodist, a very fine one, a very strong one too; he kept his flock, but that did not hinder his going to Horeb, he took them to the desert, and being thus employed in his lawful business, God met him. Some say, we encourage people in idleness; I deny it; we say, people ought to be industrious; and I defy any one to say, a person is called by God that is negligent in his calling. *The angel of the Lord appeared to him in a flame of fire out of the bush:* some think this angel was Gabriel, but most agree,

and

and I believe with the greateſt probability, that it was Jeſus Chriſt, *the angel of the everlaſting covenant*; and an expoſitor tells you, that the eternal *Logos*, longing to become man, often viſited this earth in that form, as an evidence of his coming by and by, and dying a curſed death for man. The manner of this angel's appearing is taken particular notice of, it was to Moſes when nobody was with him; I do not hear he had ſo much as a boy, or one companion; and I mention this, becauſe I believe we have often found that we are never leſs alone than when with God; we often want this and that companion, but happy they that can ſay, Lord, thy company is enough. Moſes was ſtartled at the ſight, and I don't know that he is to be diſcommended for it, it was not to gratify a bare curioſity, but ſeeing a buſh burning it engaged his attention, and made him think that ſomething was uncommon; *the buſh burned with fire and yet was not conſumed*; this ſtartled him, as it was intended to do; for where God deſigns to ſpeak, he will firſt gain attention from the perſon ſpoken to; Moſes therefore ſays, *I will now turn aſide and ſee this great ſight, why the buſh is not burned*; he did not know but the

buſh

bush might take fire by some accident; he saw no fire come from above, he saw no fire round the bush, yet that did not so much startle him, as to see, though it did burn, it was not consumed, or in the least diminished; it was a strange sight, but it was, my brethren, a glorious one; a sight which, I pray God, you and I may behold with faith and comfort this evening; for, my dear hearers, this bush, and the account of it, was given for our learning; and I will venture to say, could Moses arise from the dead, he would not be angry with me for telling you, this is of no private interpretation, but is intended as a standing lesson, as a significant emblem of the church, and every individual child of God, till time it self shall be no more. I would therefore observe to you, that this bush,

In the first place, is typical of the church of God in all ages; the bush was burning, why might it not be a tall cedar, why might it not be some large or some glorious tree, why should the great God chuse a bush, a little bush of briars and thorns, above any other thing? but because the church of Christ generally consists of poor, mean, despicable creatures: tho' it is all glorious within, yet it is all despicable without.

without. It is obfervable, that when the church came to profper, when Conftantine fmiled on it, it was foon hugged to death; and that great poet, Milton, obferves, that when that emperor gave minifters rich veft-ments, high honours, great livings, and golden pulpits, there was a voice heard from heaven, faying, this day there is poifon come into the church; and I have fometimes faid in difcourfe, I don't doubt but if any one made an experiment, and left 100,000*l.* or 200,000*l.* only among the Methodifts, there would be hundreds and thoufands that would not be reckoned Methodifts now, that would turn Methodifts prefently, that would buy an hymn-book, becaufe a part of the legacy would pay for the hymn-book, and would wifh to have a living into the bargain : but though *not many mighty men, not many noble are called,* yet fome are; if any of you are rich here, and are Chriftians, thank God for it, you ought to be doubly thankful for it ; God's people are but like a little bramble bufh. I remember an eminent minifter faid once, when I heard him preach upon Chriftmas-day, *Chrift perfonal is very rich, but Chrift myftical is very poor ;* and Jefus Chrift does this on purpofe to confound

L l the

the world. When he comes to judgment, millions that have their thoufands now, will be damned and burn to all eternity, and Chrift's church will be rich to all eternity, that is now like a bramble all on fire.

The bufh burned, what is that for ? it fhewed that Chrift's church while in this world, will be a bufh burning with fiery trials and afflictions of various kinds ; this was a lively emblem of the ftate of religion, and liberty of Ifrael at that time : they were bufy making of brick, and there confequently were burning continually ; as though the Lord had faid, this bufh is burning with fire, fo my people are burning with flavery. Ah but, fay you, that was only the cafe of the Ifraelites when they were under Pharaoh ; pray is not that the cafe of the church in all ages ? yes, it has been ; read your bibles, and you may inftantly fee that it is little elfe than an hiftorical account of a burning bufh ; and though there might be fome periods wherein the church had reft, yet thefe periods have been of a fhort date ; and if God's people have *walked in the comforts of the Holy Ghoſt*, it is only like a calm that preceeds an earthquake. If you remember, before the laft earthquake it was a fine morning,

and

and who, when they arofe in the morning, would have thought the earth fhould fhake under them before night; and fo with the church when they are in a calm, and all feems fafe there, then comes a ftorm: God prepare us for it.

But this is not only the cafe with the church of Chrift collected, but alfo it is fo with individual believers, efpecially thofe that God intends to make great ufe of as prophets in his church. I know very well that 'tis faid, that now the cafe is altered: modern commentators therefore, and our great Dr. Young, calls them downy Doctors; they tell us, now we have got a Chriftian king and governor, and are under the toleration act, we fhall have no perfecution; and, bleffed be God, we have had none fince this family has been on the throne: may God continue it till time fhall be no more. Yet, my dear hearers, we fhall find, if God's word is true, whether we are born under a defpotic power, or a free government, that they that will live godly in Chrift Jefus muft fuffer perfecution. You have heard of that faying, *Wonder not at the fiery trial wherewith you are to be tried*; and God faith, *I have chofen thee,* which is appli-

cable

cable to every believer, *in the furnace of affliction.* Now the furnace is a hot place, and they that are tried in the furnace muſt be burnt ſurely. Now what muſt the Chriſtian burn with ? with tribulation and perſecution. I heard a perſon not long ago ſay, I have no enemies. Biſhop Latimer came to a houſe one day, and the man of the houſe ſaid, he had not met with a croſs in all his life; give me my horſe, ſays the good biſhop, I am ſure God is not here where no croſs is. But ſup-poſe we are not perſecuted by the world, is there one Chriſtian but is perſecuted by his friends; if there is an Iſaac in the family, I warrant there is an Iſhmael to mock at him, *Woe is me,* ſays David, *that I muſt dwell with Meſheck, and in Kedar :* and in one's own family, one's own brothers and ſiſters, one's own dependants, though they wait for our death, and, perhaps, long to have us gone, that they may run away with our ſubſtance, to have theſe perſons mock at us, and if they dare not ſpeak out, yet let us ſee they hate the God we worſhip; if this is thy caſe, why, God knows, poor ſoul, thou art a burning buſh ; but if we have no ſuch thing as mock-ing, yet if we are ſurrounded with afflictions,

domeſtic

domeftic trials, the lofs of dear and near friends, the bad conduct of our children, the dreadful mifconduct of thofe that are dependant upon us; O there is many a parent here that is a burning bufh; burning with what? with family afflictions; fome don't care what becomes of their children; O, I thank God, I have left my boy fo much, and my daughter a coach, perhaps; ah! well your fon and daughter may ride in that coach poft to the devil: but the godly man fays, I want an eternal inheritance for my fon; I want God's bleffing for him; this is the poor man's prayer, while the poor deluded youth mocks him: or, fuppofing this is not the cafe, a perfon may burn with inward temptation; you have heard of the fiery darts of the devil, and was you to feel them, I believe you would find them fiery darts indeed! and you have great reafon to fufpect your experience, your having any intereft in the love of the Son of God at all, if you never found the fiery darts of the devil. O, fays one, I never felt the devil; I am fure thou mayft feel him now; thou art dadda's own child; thou art fpeaking the very language of the devil, and he is teaching thee to deny thy own father; therefore, gracelefs child of the

devil,

devil, you never felt the devil's fiery darts, it
is becaufe the devil is fure of thee ; he has got
thee into a damnable flumber; may the God
of love wake thee before real damnation comes !
The fiery darts of fatan are poifoned, and
wherever they ftick they fill the perfon with
tormenting pain like fire ; this I mention, becaufe there are fome poor fouls perhaps here
to-night, whom the devil tells, thou haft committed the unpardonable fin; you are afraid to
come to facrament, you are afraid to go to
prayer, becaufe at thefe feafons the devil difturbs thee moft, and tempts you to leave thefe
feafons; and there are fome go on thus burning a great while. My brethren, the time
would fail, and I fhall draw this difcourfe to
too great a length, and hinder you from your
families, if I was to mention but a few more
of thofe thoufands that the believer burns with,
the trials without, and, what is ftill worfe,
their trials within. Why, fays one, it is very
ftrange you talk thus to-night; I am forry it
is ftrange to any of you; fure you are not
much acquainted with your bibles, and lefs
with your hearts, if you know not this. Why
fure, fay fome, you make God a tyrant ; no,
but having made ourfelves devil's incarnate,

we

we are now in a state of preparation, and these
various trials are intended by the great God to
train us up for heaven ; and therefore, that
you may not think I am drawing a picture
without any life, give me leave to observe,
that it is particularly remarkable, that though
the bush burned, it was not consumed : it was
this struck Moses, he looked to see why the
bush was not consumed. But the burning I
have been here painting forth to you, is not
a consuming, but a purifying fire ; is not that
enough to answer the shade that has been already drawn ; it is true the bush burns, the
Christian is persecuted, the Christian is op-
pressed, the Christian is burned with inward
trials, he is perplexed at times, he is *cast
down, but,* blessed be God, *he is not destroyed,*
he is not in despair. Who is that, that says
he has got into such an estate that nothing difturbs him ? vain man ! he discovers an ignorance of Christ ; are you greater then than the
apostle Paul ? some people think that the apostles had no trials ; so they think, perhaps, of
some ministers, that they are always on the
mount, while, perhaps, they have been in the
burning to get that sermon for them. We
that are to speak for others, must expect to
be

be tempted in all things like to our brethren, or we fhould be only poor whip-fyllabub preachers, and not reach mens hearts. But whether minifters or people burn, the great God, the angel of the everlafting covenant, fpoke to Mofes out of the bufh; he did not ftand at a diftance from the bufh, he did not fpeak to him fo much as one yard or foot from the bufh, but he fpoke to him out of the bufh; he faid, Mofes, Mofes, my people fhall burn in this bufh to the end of time, but be not afraid, I will fuccour them; when they burn, I will burn too. There is a fcripture vaftly ftrong to this purpofe, in which it is not faid, *the good will of him that* was *in the bufh,* but *the good will of him that* dwelt *in the bufh.* Amazing! I thought God dwelt in heaven; but as a poor woman who was once in dark- nefs fourteen years, before fhe was brought out of it, faid, God has two homes, one in heaven, the other in the loweft heart. He dwells in the bufh, and I am fure if he did not, the devil and their own curfed hearts would burn the bufh to afhes. How is it that it is not confumed? why, it is becaufe God has declared it fhall not be confumed; he has made an everlafting covenant, and I pity thofe

that

that are not acquainted with an interest in
God's covenant; and it would be better that
people would pity them, than dispute with
them: I really believe a disputing devil is one
of the worst devils that can be brought into
God's church, for he comes with his gown
and book in his hand, and I should always
suspect the devil when he comes in his gown
and band, and this is the cause they agree and
disagree. Some, who it's to be hoped are God's
children, if you tell them that God has loved
them with an everlasting love, they are afraid
to suck it in, and especially if you pop out the
word election, or that hard word predestina-
tion, they will be quite frightned; but talk
to them in another way, their dear hearts will
rejoice. God has said, *As the waters of Noah*
shall ceafe for ever, so he will not forget the
covenant of his peace; nothing shall pluck them
out of his hand. Ah! say some, the apostle
has said, *that neither things present, nor things*
to come, shall separate us from the love of
Christ; but he has not said an evil heart shall
not; I fancy that is one of the *present things.*
The bush is not consumed, because if the devil
is in the bush, God is in the bush too; if the
devil acts one way, the Lord, the Spirit, acts

M m another

another to balance it, and the Spirit of God
is engaged to train up the fouls of his people;
and God has determined the bufh fhall not be
confumed; his Spirit ftands near believers to
fupport and guide, and make them more than
conquerors: all that are given to Jefus Chrift
fhall come, he will not lofe one of them; this
is food for the children of God; a bad mind
will turn every thing to poifon; and if it was
not for this, that God had promifed to keep
them, my foul within thefe thirty years would
have funk a thoufand times over. Come then,
O fuffering faints, to you the word of this
falvation is fent. I don't know who of you
are the followers of the Lamb; may the Spirit
of the living God point them out, may every
one be enabled to fay, I am the man. O,
fays one, I have been watching and very attentive to-night, but you have not mentioned
my burnings; what do you think of my burning lufts? what do you think of my burning
corruptions? what do you think of my burning pride? O, perhaps fome of you will fay,
thank God, I have no pride at all; like the
bifhop of Cambray, as mentioned by Dr.
Watts, who faid, he had received many fins
from his father Adam, but, thank God, he

had

had no pride. Alas! alas! we are all as proud as the devil. Pray what do you think of paffion, that burns not only themfelves but all around them? what do you think of enmity? what do you think of jealoufy, is not this fomething that burns the bufh? and there are fome people that pride themfelves, they have not got fo much of the beaft about them, they never got drunk, fcorn to commit murder, and at the fame time are as full of enmity, of envy, malice, and pride, as the devil: the Lord God help fuch to fee their condition. Happy is it Chrift can dwell in the bufh when we cannot dwell ourfelves there: there are few Chriftians can live together, very few relations can live together under one roof; we can take that from other people that we can't bear from our own flefh and blood; and if God did not bear with us more than we bear with one another, we fhould all have been deftroyed every day. Does the devil make you fay, that you will give all up; I will go to the Tabernacle no more; I will lay upon my couch and take my eafe; Oh! if this is the cafe of any tonight, thus tempted by fatan, may God refcue their fouls. O poor dear foul, you never will have fuch fweet words from God as when you

are in the bush; our suffering times will be
our best times. I know we had more comfort
in Moorfields, on Kennington-Common, and
especially when the rotten eggs, the cats and
dogs were thrown upon me, and my gown
was filled with clods of dirt that I could scarce
move it; I have had more comfort in this
burning bush than when I have been in ease.
I remember when I was preaching at Exeter,
a stone came and made my forehead bleed, I
found at that very time the word came with
double power to a labourer that was gazing at
me, who was wounded at the same time by
another stone, I felt for the lad more than for
myself, went to a friend, and the lad came to
me, Sir, says he, the man gave me a wound,
but Jesus healed me; I never had my bonds
broke till I had my head broke. I appeal to
you, whether you were not better when it was
colder than now, because your nerves were
braced up; you have a day like a dog-day,
now you are weak, and are obliged to fan
yourselves: thus it is prosperity lulls the soul,
and I fear Christians are spoiled by it.

Whatever your trials are, let this be your
prayer, Lord, though the bush is burning,
let it not be consumed. I think that is too
low,

low, let it be thus; Lord, when the bush is burning, let me not burn lower as the fire does, but let me burn higher and higher: I thank thee, my God, for trouble; I thank thee, my God, for putting me into these afflictions one after another; I thought I could sing a requiem to myself, that I should have a little rest, but trouble came from that very quarter where I might reasonably expect the greatest comfort: I thank thee for knocking my hands off from the creature; Lord, I believe, help my unbelief; and thus you will go on blessing God to all eternity: by and by the bush shall be translated to the paradise of God; no burning bush in heaven, except the fire of love, wonder, and gratitude; no trials there, troubles are limited to this earth, above our enemies can't reach us.

Perhaps there are some of you here are saying, *burning bush, a bush burnt and not consumed!* I don't know what to make of this nonsense: come, come, go on, I am used to it, and I guess what are the thoughts of your hearts: I pray God, that every one of you here may be afraid of comfort, lest they should be tossed about by the devil. What is it I have said? how have I talked in such an unintelligible
gible

gible manner? why, fay you, what do you mean by a burning bufh? why, thou art the very man, how fo? why, you are burning with the devil in your hearts; you are burning with foppery, with nonfenfe, with *the luft of the flefh*, with *the luft of the eye, and pride of life*; and if you do not get out of this ftate, as Lot faid to his fons-in-law, e're long you fhall be burning in hell, and not confumed: the fame angel of the covenant who fpake to Mofes out of the bufh, he fhall e're long defcend, furrounded with millions of the heavenly hofts, and fentence you to everlafting burnings. O you frighten me! did you think I did not intend to frighten you? would to God I might frighten you enough! I believe it will be no harm for you to be frightned out of hell, to be frightned out of an unconverted ftate: O go and tell your companions that the madman faid, that wicked men are as firebrands of hell: God pluck you as brands out of that burning. Bleffed be God, that there is yet a day of grace; Oh! that this might prove *the accepted time;* Oh! that this might prove *the day of falvation;* Oh! angel of the everlafting covenant, come down; thou bleffed, dear comforter, have mercy, mercy, mercy upon the unconverted,

upon

upon our unconverted friends, upon the unconverted part of this auditory; *speak, and it
shall be done; command, O Lord, and it shall
come to pass*; turn the burning bushes of the
devil into burning bushes of the Son of God:
who knows but God may hear our prayer,
who knows but God may hear this cry, *I have
seen, I have seen the afflictions of my people;
the cry of the children of Israel is come up to
me, and I am come down to deliver them*: God
grant this may be his word to you under all
your trouble; God grant he may be your
comforter. The Lord awaken you that are
dead in sin, and though on the precipice of
hell, God keep you from tumbling in: and
you that are God's burning bushes, God help
you to stand to keep this coat of arms, to say
when you go home, blessed be God, *the bush
is burning, but not consumed.* Amen! even so,
Lord Jesus. Amen!

SERMON

SERMON XII.

Soul Dejection.

PSALM xlii. ver. 5.

*Why art thou caſt down, O my ſoul, and why
art thou diſquieted within me? hope thou in
God, for I ſhall yet praiſe him, for the help
of his countenance.*

I HAVE often told you, in my plain way
of ſpeaking, that grace is very frequently
grafted on a crab-ſtock; that the Lord
Jeſus picks out perſons of the moſt peeviſh,
churliſh diſpoſition, and imparts to them the
largeſt meaſure of grace, but for want of a
better natural temper, a great deal of grace
does not ſhine ſo bright in them, as a ſmall
degree in thoſe that are conſtitutionally good-
natured: perſons of this diſpoſition are generally complaining, and are not only tormen-
tors of themſelves, but are great plagues to thoſe
that are about them; you will hear them
always

always complaining fomething or other is the matter. What a pity it is we cannot all agree in one thing, to leave off chiding others to chide our own felves, till we can find nothing in ourfelves to chide for; this we fhall find will be a good way to grow in the divine life, when, by conftant application to the Lamb of God, we get a maftery over thofe things which hitherto have had the maftery over us; but are thefe the only people that complain? are people of a melancholy difpofition only fub- ject to a difquietude of heart? I will venture to affirm, that the greateft, the deareft chil- dren of God, have got their complaining, and their dreary hours. Thofe who have been favoured with large meafures of grace, even thofe that have been wrapped up as it were to the third heavens, bafking on the mount in the funfhine of redeeming grace, and in raptures of love crying out, *It is good for us to be here*, even thefe muft go down to Gethfemane; and if they would not be fcorched with a ftrong burning fever from the fun of profperity, fhall find clouds from time to time overfhadowing them, not to burn, but to keep them low. It is on this account, that you fee good men in different frames at different times: our Lord

himfelf

himfelf was fo, he rejoiced fometimes in fpirit, but at other times you find him, efpecially near the laft, crying out, *My foul is exceeding forrowful even unto death, tarry you here and watch.* And I am going to tell you of one tonight, who had the honour of being called, *the man after God's own heart ;* and who, though an Old Teftament faint, was greatly bleffed with a New Teftament fpirit, and had the honour of compofing Pfalms, which in all paft ages of the church have been, and in future ones will be a rich magazine, and ftorehoufe of fpiritual experience, from which the children of God may draw fpiritual armour for fighting the good fight of faith, until God fhall call them to life eternal : may this be your happy lot. What frame was this good man in when he compofed this forty-fecond Pfalm ? the Pfalm itfelf can beft tell. It feems compofed when he was either perfecuted by Saul, or driven from his own court by his fondling, beloved fon, Abfalom ; then David appeared truly great ; I honour him when I fee him yonder, attending a few fheep ; but I admire the young ftripling, when I fee him come out with his fling and ftone, and aiming it at the head of Goliah, the ene-

my

my of God; or, when exalted and filling the
feat of juſtice; but to me he never appears
greater, than when he is bowed down in low
circumſtances, befet on every ſide, ſtruggling
between fenfe and faith; and, as the fun after
an eclipfe, breaking forth with greater luſtre
to all the ſpectators. In this view we muſt
confider this great, this good man, David,
when he cries out, *Why art thou caſt down,*
O my foul, why art thou difquieted within me?
hope thou in God.

Suppofing you underſtand the words as a
queſtion, *Why art thou caſt down, O my foul,*
though thou art in fuch circumſtances? pray
now what is the caufe of thy being fo dejected?
The word implies, that he was finking under
the weight of his prefent burden, like a perfon
ſtooping under a load that lies upon his ſhoul-
ders; and the confequence of this preſſure
without was difquietude, uneafineſs and
anxiety within; for, fay what you will to the
contrary, there is fuch a connection between
foul and body, that when one is difordered,
the other muſt fympathize with its ever-loving
friend.

Or, you may underſtand it as chiding himfelf, *Why art thou caſt down, O my foul, why*
　　　　　　　　　　art

art thou difquieted within me, how foolifh is
it to be thus drooping and dejected; how
improper for one favoured of God with fo
many providences, and fpecial particular privileges, for fuch a one as thou art thus to
ftoop, and be made fubject to every temptation; why doft thou give thy enemies fuch
room to find fault with thy religion on account of thy gloomy looks, and the difquietude of thy heart? a yoke which thou wilt
find to be lined with love, and God will keep
it from galling thy fhoulders. You fee, he
fpeaks not to others but to himfelf; would to
God we did thus learn that charity begins at
home. Then he goes to God with his cafe,
O my God, fays he, *my foul is caft down within
me.* O that we could learn, when in thefe
moods to go more to God, and lefs to man,
we fhould find more relief, and religion would
be lefs difhonoured. But fee how faith triumphs in the midft of all, no fooner does
unbelief pop up its head, but faith immediately
knocks it down. A never-failing maxim is
here propofed, *hope thou in God,* truft in God,
believe in God; for I am fure, and all of you
that know Jefus Chrift are perfuaded of it
too, that all our troubles arife from our unbelief:

belief: O unbelief, injurious bar to comfort, fource of tormenting fear! on the contrary, faith bears every thing. *Put thy truft in God,* as in the old tranflation; *hope in God,* as in the new, *I fhall yet praife him.* The devil tells me my trouble is fo great, I fhall never lift up my head again; but unbelief and the devil are liars; *I fhall yet praife him*; my God will carry me through all; I fhall yet praife him, even for cafting me down; I fhall praife him even for that which is the caufe of all my dif-quietude; he will be *the health of my counte-nance*; though my afflictions have now made my body low, fuck up my fpirits, and hurt my animal frame, *he will be the help of my counte-nance*; I fhall by and by fee him again, and be favoured with thofe transforming views, which my God has favoured me with in times paft; *he is the health of my countenance, and my God:* though the devil tempts me, and my evil neighbours fay, *where is now thy God?* Doft thou think thou art a child of God, and thy Father fuffers thee to be caft down? I tell thee, I tell thee, O fatan, that God who I have been fo vilely tempted as to believe has forfaken me, will come over the mountains of my guilt, will forgive my backflidings againft himfelf,

himſelf, my unbelief ſhall not make his promiſes of none effect; I ſhall praiſe him even
while I live, I ſhall praiſe him before I die, I
ſhall praiſe him for ever in heaven, where he
will be, after death, *the health of my countenance, and my God*; thus faith will get the
better in a ſaint.   David was ſometimes left to
ſay, in effect, all things are againſt me; yet
ſtill in moſt of the Pſalms, in this, the next,
the cxiiith, and many of the reſt, he triumphs
in God; and he compoſed but very few without praiſing at the end, though he complains
at the beginning: God help us thus to do!

But it is time to leave off ſpeaking particularly of David, and to turn to you to whom
theſe words, I pray God, may prove ſalutary
and uſeful.   I have had a great ſtruggle in my
mind this afternoon what I ſhould preach from;
I have been praying and looking up to God,
and could not preach for my life on any other
text, which has often been the caſe before,
and whenever it was, ſome poor ſoul has been
comforted and raiſed up; and among ſuch a
mixed multitude, there are ſome, no doubt,
come to this poor deſpiſed place caſt down and
diſquieted within; I ſhall endeavour to enquire
what you are caſt down for, and then I ſhall

                                        propoſe

propofe a great cure for you, namely, truft in God; and I pray, that what was David's comfort may be yours. Why fhould not we expect an anfwer when we pray, that God before you go home may make you whether you will or no, leave your burdens behind you? and God keep you from taking them up as you go home.

Probably, there may be fome of you that are real believers; perhaps, I ought to afk your pardon: where am I preaching, in the Tabernacle! the moft defpifed place in London! fo fcandalous a place, that many of the children of God would rather go elfewhere! God help us to keep up our fcandal! But yet I believe there are many King's daughters here, many of you whom God enabled in this place firft to fay, *My Lord, and my God.* When you put your fingers, as it were, on the print of Chrift's nails, and put your hands into his fide, and were no longer faithlefs, but believing, you thought you fhould never be caft down any more, but now you have found yourfelves miftaken; and I fhall endeavour, in the profecution of this text, to fpeak to all that are caft down, whether before or after converfion, and then to fuch that were never caft

down

down at all; and if you was never caſt down
before, God caſt you down now.

What are perſons caſt down for? what are
ſome of you diſquieted within for? I have reaſon to believe, from the notes put up at both
ends of the town, that there are many of you
that have arrows of conviction ſtuck faſt in
your ſouls; I have taken in near two hundred
at the other end of the town, within a fort-
night; if this be the caſe, ·that God is thus at
work, let the devil roar, and we will go on in
the name of the Lord. And what are you
caſt down for? ſome poor ſoul will ſay, with
a ſenſe of ſin, the guilt of it, the enmity of
it, the very aggravated circumſtances that attend it, appear and ſet themſelves as in battle-
array before me : once I thought I had no ſin,
at leaſt, I thought that ſin was not ſo exceeding ſinful; but I now find it ſuch a burden, I
could almoſt ſay with Cain, *it is greater than
I can bear.* And, perhaps, ſome of you are
ſo caſt down, as in your haſte to ſay as colonel Gardiner, that great man of God, told me
himſelf had ſaid when under conviction, " I
" believe God cannot be juſt, unleſs he damns
" my wicked ſoul." Is this thy caſe? art
thou wicked, art thou ſo caſt down, ſo diſ-

quieted,

quieted, that thou canst not reft night nor day, fhall I fend thee away without any comfort ? fhall I fend thee away as the legal preachers do ? as a minifter fome time ago did, when a man told him how wicked he had been ; O, fays he, if you are fo wicked you are damn'd to be fure, I fhall not trouble myfelf with you. When a poor negro was taken up for thieving, another went to him and faid, you are fo bad I muft turn my back to you ; that is the law, but the gofpel is turn thy face to God ; think not that God is dealing with thee as an abfolute God, a God out of Chrift. I would have nothing to do, fays Luther, with an abfolute God ; as fuch he is a confuming fire. Truft God in Chrift, throw thyfelf upon him, throw thyfelf on the Son of God ; cry with thy brother, and now thou art in that temper, thou wilt not be afhamed to call the thief thy brother ; fay with him, *Lord, remember me when thou art in thy kingdom :* thou fhalt yet praife him, thou fhalt yet have the forgivenefs of thy fins ; thy pardon fhall not only be fealed in heaven, but thou fhalt have it in thy heart : thefe are only the pangs of the new birth, the firft ftrugglings of the foul immerfing into the divine life ; he fhall yet be the health of thy

O o   coun-

countenance: thefe poor cheeks, though be-
dewed with tears, fhall by and by have a fine
blufh, when a pardoning God comes with his
love ; it fhall even make a change in thy
countenance, for as a heavy heart makes a
man's countenance fad, fo a chearful heart
makes the countenance pleafant: thou fhalt
know him to be thy God, thou fhalt fay, *my
Lord, and my God:* Lord Jefus grant this may
be the happy moment. Was Jefus here, was
the Redeemer now in this metropolis, I am
fure he would go about the ftreets, he would
be a field-preacher, he would go out into the
highways and hedges, he would invite, he
would run after them ; Lord Jefus, take the
veil from our hearts, and let us fee to-night
thy loving heart as the Son of God! Truft in
God, you will fay, it is very eafy for you to fay
fo, but I cannot truft in God ; can't you, who
told you that ? that is the work of God , you
are not far from the kingdom of God. Who
convinced thee of thy inability to believe, do
you think the devil did ? no, it was the Spirit
of God procured by the blood of the Lamb,
that was to come to convince the world of fin.
If thou canft not truft as thou wouldft, fay,
Lord, I believe, help my unbelief ; ftretch out
thy

thy poor hand. I am thinking of Sunday laft, when I was giving the facrament, I obferved there was one blind communicant that could not fee, but he thruft out his hand; I obferved feveral lame perfons, but there were enough to give it to them; I faw alfo a poor barrow-woman, and I took particular care to give the cup to her; fo I put it up to the mouth of the poor blind man: if that is the cafe, what love muft there be in God to the poor foul!

But, methinks, I hear fome poor foul fay, that is not my cafe, I am not caft down for that, but I am caft down becaufe after that I knew God to be my God, after I knew Jefus to be my King, and after I had mounted upon my high places, the devil and my un-believing heart threw me down again; would you not have me caft down? would you not have me difquieted? a perfon of an Antino-mian fpirit would fay, don't tell me of your frames, I have learned to live by faith, I don't care whether Chrift manifefts himfelf to me or no, I have got the word and the promife, I am content with a promife now; fo thefe poor creatures go on without any frame, be-caufe they will not live in it: from fuch An-tinomianifm, good God, deliver me. How! O o 2   how!

how! how! not caft down at an abfent God,
not difquieted when God withdraws? where
are you gone? you are gone far from your father's houfe; if nothing elfe will do, may your
father whip you home again. But tender
hearts when they reflect how it was once, are
caft down; David fays, *My tears have been
my meat day and night, for I had gone with a
multitude to the houfe of God.* Here he looks
back upon his former enjoyments, his fpiritual
profperity, (as Job looks back upon his temporal) and fays, *Why art thou caft down, O my
foul;* it is becaufe I don't meet God in his
ordinances as I ufed to do; poor deferted,
panting foul! poor difquieted foul! he muft
be the help of thy countenance, he will yet
be thy God. Who was it fought Jefus for-
rowing? what would you have thought of the
Virgin Mary if fhe had faid, I don't care whether I fee my fon or not; fhe fought him, and
found him in the temple: God grant every
poor deferted foul may find him to-night; I
mean, in the temple of his heart. And in the
cafe of Mary, fhe fays, *They have taken away
my Lord, and I know not where they have laid
him;* if they had not taken away her Lord,
Mary would have been rich: fo you may fay
your

your corruptions, your backflidings and ingratitude, have taken away your Lord: Lord grant thou mayft find him to-night. He that faid, *Mary*, can call thee to-night, and can make thee fay, My dear Lord, I come to-night; he can call thee by thy name.

But, fay you, I am caft down becaufe I am wearied with temptation ; not only my God is departed from me, but an evil fpirit is come upon me to torment me ; I am haunted with this and that evil fuggeftion, that I am a terror to myfelf. Come, come, hear what David faith in the beginning of the Pfalm, *As the hart panteth after the water-brooks, fo panteth my foul after thee, O God.* What fay you to that? if you have a mind to fee the beauty of this verfe, read Mr. Hervey's Theron and Afpafio, which will live when its defpifers are dead ; and thofe that have endeavoured to difparage him will be obliged to own, that he was one of the greateft luminaries we ever had, and one that has laid down the doctrines of the gofpel, in a manner to charm and allure the great and noble. Well, is it thy cafe that unbelief dogs thee go where thou will? well, ftill truft in God, *thou fhalt yet praife him for the help of his countenance ; he will command his loving-kindnefs in the day,*

and his song shall be with thee in the night.
Though it be night, there is some moon,
blessed be God, or some stars; and if there is
a fog that you cannot see, God can quiet his
people in the dark, he will make the enemy
flee; fear him not, God will comfort thee,
and punish the devil for tempting thee, if thou
trust in him.

But, say you, I am cast down and disquieted within me; why? because I have one
affliction after another, no sooner is one trial
gone, but another succeeds; now I think I
shall have a little rest, the tormentor will not
come nigh me to-day, but no sooner has the
Christian so said, but another storm comes,
and the clouds return after the rain; then we
think we must be cast down, and that we
ought to be disquieted; this was David's case;
what does he say? *All thy waves and thy bil-
lows are gone over me.* I believe he found
after that, there were more waves to come
than he had yet felt; why? says a poor dif-
tressed foul, because I have been so long in
Christ, and have got these cursed corruptions
yet within. I thought to have been rid of
them all long ago; I thought I had no corruptions left thirty-three years ago, and that
the

the Canaanites were all rooted out of the land, that Pharaoh and his hoft were all drowned in the red-fea; but I find the old man is ftrong in me, I look upon myfelf to be lefs than the leaft of all faints, God knows; and you that walk near God, and have made greater advances in the divine life, if you are honeft muft fay, O this body of fin and death, if I fhut this old man out at the fore-door, he comes in at the back-door. Come, come, come foul, truft in God, he will give power to the faint, he will give ftrength, and in due time deliver thee: go to God, tell him of them; beg thy Redeemer to take his whip into his hand, either of fmall or large cords, and ufe it, rather than your corruptions fhould get head again.

Time would fail to mention all that are caft down on thefe accounts, but I muft mention one more; perhaps, fome of you may be caft down with the fear not of death only, but of judgment. I believe there are thoufands of people die a thoufand times, for fear of dying once. Dr. Mather and Mr. Pemberton, of New-England, were always afraid of dying, but when they came to die; one or both of them faid to fome that were intimate with

them,

them, *Is this all, I can bear this very well:*
and I have generally found that a poor foul,
that cannot act that faith on God it once did,
or in old age when the body grows infirm, as
they ufed to do, yet they go off rejoicing in
God, as a good foul that was buried at the
Chapel the other day, faid, *I am going over
Jordan.* Therefore, O poor foul, leave this
to God, he will take care of thy dying hour.
If any of you are poor here, and I was to
promife to give you a coffin and a fhroud you
would be eafy; now can you truft the word
of a man, and not that of a God? Well, the
Lord help you to truft in him; *having loved
his own, he loves them to the end*; he is a faithful, unchangeable friend, that fticketh clofer
than a brother.

Who would not be a Chriftian, who would
but be a believer, my brethren; fee the pre-
cioufnefs of a believer's faith; the quacks will
fay, here buy this packet, which is good for
all difeafes, and is really worth nothing; but
this will never fail the foul. Now I wifh I
could make you all angry; I am a fad mif-
chief-maker; but I will affure you, I don't
want to make you angry with one another:
fome people that profefs to have grace in their

hearts,

hearts, feem refolved to fet all God's people at variance; they are like Sampfon's foxes with firebrands in their tails, fetting fire to all about them. Are any of you come from the Foundery, or any other place to-night? I do not care where you come from, I pray God you may all quarrel to-night; I want you to fall out with your own hearts; if we were employed as we ought to be, we fhould have lefs time to talk about the vain things that are the fubjects of converfation : God grant your croffes may be left at the crofs of the Lamb of God this night.

And if there be any of you here, as no doubt there are many, that are crying what nonfenfe he is preaching to-night, I fhould not wonder if they were to mimick me when they go home; if they fhould fay, I thank God, I was never caft down; you take God's name in vain ; you thank God you was never caft down, the very anfwer you have given makes me caft down for you; why fo? why, as the Lord liveth, I fpeak out of compaffion, there is but one ftep between thee and death. Don't you know the feffions began at the Old-Bailey to-day, if there were any capitally convicted, what would you think to fee them

playing

p'aying at cards, o. go on rattling and drinking, and swearing? would not you yourself
cry, and if it were a child of your own, would
it not break your heart? but yet thou art that
wretch; I must weep for thee, my brother-
sinner; we had both one father and mother,
Adam and Eve; this was our sad original.

Dear Christians, pray for me to-night. I
remember once I was preaching in Scotland,
and saw ten thousand affected in a moment,
some with joy, others crying I cannot believe;
others, God has given me faith, some faint-
ing in their friends arms: seeing two stout
creatures upon a tomb-stone, hardened indeed,
I cried out, you rebels come down, and down
they fell directly, and cried before they went
away, *What shall we do to be saved?* Have
any of you got apprentices, whom you have
brought from time to time to the Tabernacle,
but now will not let them come, because you
think they grow worse and worse, and you
will be tempted to leave off praying for them?
don't do that; who knows but this may be the
happy time. Children of godly parents, apprentices of godly people, servants of people
who fear the Lord, that hear gospel-preachers,
that are on the watch for every infirmity, that

go

go to their fellow-fervants and fay, thefe faints love good eating and drinking, they are only gofpel-goffips; is this the cafe of any of you, if it is, you are in a deplorable condition, under the gofpel and not convinced thereby: O may God bring down you rebels to-night; may this be the happy hour you may be caft down and difquieted within you. What can I fay more? I would fpeak till I burft, I would fpeak till I could fay no more. O poor foul, that haft been never yet caft down, I will tell you, if you die without being caft down, however you may die and have no pangs in your death, and your carnal relations may thank God that you died like lambs, but no fooner will your fouls be out of your bodies, but God will caft you down to hell, you will be lifting up your eyes in yonder place of torment, you will be difquieted, but there will be nobody there to fay, *hope thou in God, for I fhall yet praife him*, &c. O my God, when I think of this, I could go to the very gates of hell to preach. I thought the other day, O if I had my health, I would ftand on the top of every hackney coach, and preach Chrift to thofe poor creatures. Unconverted old people, unconverted young people, will you have no

com-

compaffion on your own fouls: if you will damn yourfelves, remember I am free from the blood of you all. O if it be thy bleffed will, Lord moft holy, O God moft mighty, take the hearts of thefe finners into thy hand. Methinks I fee the heavens opened, the Judge fitting on his throne, the fea boiling like a pot, and the Lord Jefus coming to judge the world; well, if you are damned, it fhall not be for want of calling after. O come, come, God help you to come, whilft Jefus is ftanding ready to receive you. O fly to the Saviour this night for refuge; remember if you die in an unconverted ftate you muft be damned for ever.

O that I could but perfuade one poor foul to fly to Jefus Chrift, make him your refuge; and then, however you may be caft down, *hope in God, and you fhall yet praife him.* God help thofe that have believed, to hope more and more in his falvation, till faith be turned into vifion, and hope into fruition. Even fo, Lord Jefus. Amen and Amen.

SERMON

SERMON XIII.

Spiritual Baptifm.

ROMANS vi. ver. 3, 4.

*Know ye not, that fo many of us as were bap-
tized into Jefus Chrift, were baptized into
his death? Therefore we are buried with him
by baptifm into death : that like as Chrift was
raifed up from the dead by the glory of the
Father, even fo we alfo fhould walk in newnefs of life.*

I BELEIVE, my dear hearers, I may venture to tell you, that the longer you live,
the more you will find that the royal
preacher fpoke truth when he faid, *There is
nothing new under the fun* ; for as God is always the fame, fo the world, the flefh, and
the devil will be always the fame, frail, vile,
inimical and deceitful. New fcenes furprize
us, not becaufe they are really new, but be-

caufe

caufe they are new to us: our lives are moftly
taken up with viewing only the prefent appearance of things; we have neither time or leifure
to look back as we ought, or might, upon
the events of Providence, or the effects of the
doctrines of grace. I will not fay, my thoughts
always run in a religious channel, but I will
fay, I wifh they did. The words in our text,
as connected with what preceeds and follows,
contain the unchangeable truths of God: nor
am I any ways ftaggered by oppofition to the
vindication of what the good old Puritans, and
the Diffenters of the prefent age, call evangelical doctrine. I do not know a man that has
wrote in a legal ftrain, or that reads, or talks
in common converfation in a legal ftrain, but
difcovers his ignorance of, if not his enmity
to the doctrine of juftification by faith alone,
by charging it with very bad confequences,
and endeavouring to explode it as a dangerous
doctrine, deftructive of holinefs, which they
would feem to patronize; though if one were
always to judge of them by their calumniating
practice, one would imagine they had never
read with proper attention, either the preceeding or following chapters, nor that wherein is
our text, which proves it to be a doctrine
                                        according

according to godlinefs, and therefore properly
begins, *What fhall we fay then, fhall we continue in fin that grace may abound?* You will
fay, I have been infifting upon the univerfal
depravity of nature, I have been bringing all
down upon an equal level; that I have not
only mentioned the dreadful ftate of Heathens,
but the equally dreadful ftate of the haughty
Jews, and ignorant Gentiles, one only finning
againft the light of nature, and the other finning againft the light of revelation, by which
both, in one fenfe, ftand on an equal footing,
though the laft, who thinks he ftands upon
higher ground, appears to be only fuperior in
fin; why then, how muft either or both be
faved, fince they have nothing to recommend
them, nothing to plead as an atonement for
their fins? Here comes in the bleffed doctrine
of juftification, by the glorious imputed righteoufnefs of Jefus Chrift, to be received by
faith as an inftrument by the poor convicted
finner. If this be the cafe, *fhall we fin that
grace may abound?* this ferves as a foil, to fet
off the riches of grace with a greater luftre.
Is it not a very unfair deduction, to fay never
mind holinefs, but fin that grace may abound,
that God's grace may be more confpicuous?

Pray

Pray how does the apoftle treat this? with the utmoft abhorrence; *God forbid,* fays he; how dare you charge the doctrine of grace with fuch a horrid confequence? God forbid that it fhould enter into our hearts; for *how fhall we that are dead to fin live any longer therein? Know ye not,* faith he, *that as many of us as were baptized into Chrift, are baptized into his death:* therefore, faith he, fo far from finning that grace may abound, we look upon ourfelves as *being buried with Chrift by baptifm into death, that like as Chrift was raifed from the dead by the glory of the Father, even fo we alfo fhould walk in newnefs of life.* This I thought a proper fupplement to fome difcourfes I have endeavoured to deliver you for fome days laft paft, when treating on the credibility and authenticity of our bleffed Lord's refurrection.

I cannot make fport for the devil by railing againft infant or adult baptifm; it is a ftrange thing how bigots can fet the world on fire by throwing water at one another, and that people cannot be baptized, or fprinkled, as the others call it, without befpattering one another, and fhow that the chief thing they have been baptized into, are the waters of ftrife; this is catching at fhadows, and making fport

for

for the devil, while the combatants on both
fides, being thus engaged in throwing the fha-
dowy water at one another, lofe the fubftan-
tials of religion, while they are defending the
outfide of it. For my part, I do not enter
into the debate about infant or adult baptifm;
there has been a difpute about the mode, as
well as the fubjects of baptifm; perfons equally
fkilled in language, pretend to bring various
texts from the original, to prove that the word
baptizo, fignifies either fprinkling or plunging;
and I believe you and I might as well attempt
to draw two parallel lines, and bring them to
meet at fome certain place, as to bring thefe
learned combatants together; for of all difputants, religious difputants are the moft fiery
and obftinate; therefore, I am for thofe that
have learned to throw water upon bigotted
fire, *to think, and let think,* about the mode,
and confider what it imports.

It is certain, that in the words of our text,
there is an allufion to the manner of baptifm,
which was by immerfion, which our own
church allows, and infifts upon it, that children fhould be immerfed in water, unlefs thofe
that bring the children to be baptized affure
the minifter that they cannot bear the plunging.

We will allow this then, that one was plunged
when he was young, another plunged when
he was old ; and, in fact, when adults are
plunged as they ought, it is backwards at
once : but whether I am plunged in a great
deal, or *buried* with a little water, as a body
is when it is faid, *Earth to earth, afhes to afhes,
duft to duft,* what fignifies it, if I go in and
come out, and continue juft the fame as before,
unlefs you can fay, *in Heathen and out Chriftian*; but we fee very often they are not one
bit the better, they have not one grain of
Chriftianity more. Suppofing a child when
young grows up to a man, is fprinkled, or
dipped as the children I faw at Lifbon, or in
our font, as they are made large enough to
dip in, though now they fprinkle; fuppofe
one of thefe grows up a child of the devil, and
fays, I don't look upon what was done in my
infancy to be baptifm, I will be baptized really ;
and yet fuppofe alfo, that perfon takes up only
the outward fign, and both of them die and go
to the devil, would it give either of them
fatisfaction to fay, I am in hell, but I was baptized when an infant, or adult ? both of them
would have to lament they were tormented in
the flame. Would it not be better for us to
take

take care not to offend our brethren, not to
raife one anothers fpirits and corruptions, but
rather, when we come together, talk of the
heart, and enquire whether, when we received
the outward fign by fprinkling or dipping, we
really received the thing fignified in our hearts,
and exemplify that thing fignified, in our lives.

Now pray what is the thing fignified? we
need not go farther for an anfwer than our
text, *As many of them as were baptized into
Jefus Chrift, were baptized into his death :* and
it is worthy remarking, that our Lord told his
difciples, that they were *to baptize all nations
in the name of the Father, and of the Son, and
of the Holy Ghoft.* Now I believe all perfons
that have but a little fkill in fcripture interpretation, muft allow that the word name fignifies Chrift; my name is in him, fpeaking in
the Old Teftament of Chrift's name; and
when we fay, *in or by the name,* it has a peculiar reference to every thing that belongs to
God : and I verily believe that when the Redeemer faid, *baptize them in the name of Father, Son, and Holy Ghoft,* he not only intended to eftablifh the doctrine of three perfons in
one God, but alfo to point out the nature of
true baptifm, namely, to be baptized into the

nature

nature of the Father, into the nature of the
Son, and into the nature of the Holy Ghoft,
and this feems to be the meaning of our text,
Know ye not that fo many as were baptiʒed;
if we have been baptized aright, have been
baptized not only in the name of Chrift, but
have been baptized into Chrift; that is, we
have not only put on Chrift in an outward profeffion, but have been fo baptized by the Holy
Ghoft, as to be made members of Chrift's
myftical body, united to him by the bleffed
Spirit; fo that in a degree, though not in every
fenfe, we are one with Chrift, and the Father,
through him. This is religion common to all,
whether we are Baptift or Pœdo-baptift; for
we may call one another by this and that name,
it is no matter what we are called, the grand
matter is, what God looks upon us to be;
whether we are become by baptifm, and with
the powerful operations of the Spirit of God
accompanying that ordinance, branches of
Jefus Chrift, the true vine. It has been always
an argument with me, and I may plead for
the fame liberty that I give, that I think infant-baptifm is an ordinance of Chrift, becaufe
if our children are not to be baptized, they are
left inferior in their privileges to the Jews,

their

their children were circumcifed to God, and
why fhould not our children be as foon initiated
into Chrift as they? The apoftle faith, *He is*
not a Jew that is one outwardly, neither is that
circumcifion which is outwardly in the flefh,
but circumcifion is *that of the heart and of the*
fpirit, whofe praife is not of men but of God;
fo it may be faid of outward baptifm, he is
not a Chriftian who is baptized only outwardly, but he that is baptized inwardly of the
Spirit, *whofe praife is not of men but of God.*
When we get a profelite, we are fo fond of
them that we hug them to death: I have got
the praife of men efpecially when religion
walks in filver flippers; when a perfon fays, I
may get bufinefs if I get into fuch a church,
into fuch a fociety; a man may become religious as he may go to 'Change for trade, but
he is a Chriftian who is one inwardly, who
has no worldly views, no defigns but what are
fubordinate to the glory of God. The primitive Chriftians gave great proof of their fincerity,
they were baptized over the dead; *what fhall*
they do who are baptized for, or over, *the dead?*
notwithftanding they faw their fellow-creatures
murdered, they dared to go openly to be baptized; though they knew very well foon after,

that

that for their baptifm with water, they fhould be baptized with fire, and yet they dared openly to avow their profeffion of Chrift. This is being baptized into Chrift; well, what then? why, then we are baptized into his death. Can you tell me what that is? I cannot fully, I don't know that myfelf; and we fhould preach according to our experience, (a man of little true grace, he will give you a little, little, little practical application; very little, becaufe he has but little himfelf; a man that has a good deal of it in his heart, he will not neglect his principles, but he will give the people a good found meal of practical religion) though I am but a babe in Chrift, though I have been in Chrift four or five and thirty years, and know but little of Chrift, yet I think I can tell you a little what it is to be baptized into Chrift, to be baptized into his death. Am I immediately to die in the body? that does not always follow, but we are to die daily, we are to be conformed to Chrift's death, which we never can till we have been baptized into Chrift; we can never die till we have been enabled by his power to die. When we talk of dying the death of Chrift, we mean being crucified to the world with him.

I live,

I live, fays Paul, *yet not I, but Chrift lives in me; and the world is crucified to me, and I unto the world.* Now we all come into the world alive to the world, the flefh, and the devil. Some people fay, a child muft cry in order to prove itfelf an heir; what do you think it cries for? I believe fome people think 'tis becaufe it is in pain, but I am afraid the child cries becaufe he is hurt; I believe he finds the air too cool for him; and the firft thing he does, is giving a proof of original fin to his parents, and all the attendants about him: this is called in fcripture, the old man; and however fome may find fault with the Church of England, and its forms (perhaps they may be mended, but I queftion whether we have men capable of mending them now-a-days, either for zeal or fpiritual knowledge) yet I am fure there is fomething in it very good, particularly there is that prayer to be put up by a child, deferves to be written in letters of gold, *Grant, O Lord, that all things belonging to the old man may die in me;* and then follows (what I fhall fpeak of by and by*) and all belonging to the new man may live and grow in me.* There is the whole fum and fubftance of religion, the Alpha and Omega, the beginning,

ginning, the middle, and the end, as Mr.
Ambrofe's works are intitled. We want nothing but all things belonging to the old man
to die in us, and all things belonging to the
new to live, to make us fit for the kingdom
of Chrift; and if we can find this in us, God
grant we may not quarrel one with another,
though I verily believe young men think the
old man is very troublefome. There is one
does not live very far from hence, who is a
very worthy man, I remember a few years
ago he came in, in his firft love, faying, " he
had got on the mount; the fire burnt upwards,
though there was a good deal of fmoak. Pray,
fays I, is the old man dead yet? no, faid he,
he is not quite dead, but fpoke as if he thought
he was expiring; fays I, I will fpeak to you
three or four years hence. Some time after
that, meeting him, I afked him concerning
the old man, he faid, he thought he was alive
and worfe than ever, and that he was a fly
creature, would lie down as if he was afleep,
that he may attack you when off your guard
the better." I heard of a good man in the country, who faid, he found his corruptions were
a monfter of a thoufand heads; now this is
called a crucifixion, which is a painful and a
gradual

gradual death, but a certain death : God forbid any of you now fhould turn the food into
poifon, faying, this is a very good doctrine, I
like it ; the minifter fays the old man dies flow,
fo I will not crucify him ; they tell me he will
die by and by, but not yet, fo I will not trouble myfelf much about him ; why then, my
dear hearer, whoever thou art, thou talkeft
like a ftinking hypocrite, or a rank, vile Antinomian ; how, how, is the old man fuch a
pleafant companion, that you love to have him
dwelling under your roof? would you chufe
to have a parcel of whores and rogues to live
in your houfes? would you like, if you lived
by letting of lodgings, two or three rooms
fuppofe, to have a parcel of thieves and rob-
bers, and pickpockets, come and tell you
their profeffion, would it not be foolifh for
you to let fuch people in, would it not? and
juft fuch fools you are to let pickpockets,
ftreet-robbers, God-robbers, vile proftitutes in
your wicked hearts, the lufts of the flefh, the
lufts of the eye, and the pride of life, ftay not
only till quarter-day, but long after : before
you turn them out, you may be dead; no,
no, it is not an inftantaneous, but a gradual,
progreffive work.

R r   Then

Then we are baptized into Chriſt, when we ſtudy to glorify Chriſt; that is the reaſon that God Almighty ſends you ſo many trials, that you may be baptized into his death; and generally you will find, when you have had moſt communications from God, that ſome croſs trials ſoon follow. Haſt thou been praying for reſignation? perhaps God takes away a beloved child; you have been praying for great patience, perhaps a croſs wife, a Nabal of a huſband, bad ſervants, undutiful children, or ſomething or other, and the devil at the head of them, making you uneaſy, ſo that you find you have not ſo much patience as you thought you had; you never was upon the mount in your lives, but when you came down, you were tempted to break the tables: was it not ſo with Moſes after forty days communion with God? down he came, and ſeeing the people dancing round the calf, down he throws the tables, and breaks them all to pieces; and if God was not to keep us, after all our communion with him, we ſhould break the tables to pieces and be damned. After all that perſon then is dying every day, who looks upon himſelf every morning as one that is to be crucified afreſh, that looks for

croſſes,

croffes, and at the fame time walks fo inof-
fenfively as to bring no crofs upon himfelf. I
fpoke to a perfon yefterday about the crofs;
pray fir, fays he, would you have me bring a
crofs upon myfelf; no, faid I, only be honeft,
and you will find croffes enough.

Then we muft be raifed to newnefs of life,
as Chrift was raifed from the dead by the glory
of the Father; this points out to us in what
fenfe Jefus Chrift is the refurrection and the
life, and fhews us that every thing Jefus Chrift
did and fuffered, muft be fpiritually experienced in our hearts. You have often heard
me fay, as he was born in the Virgin's womb,
he muft be born in our hearts, and as he died
for fin, we muft die to fin, as he rofe again,
we muft rife to newnefs of heart and life.
What is the new birth? fays a great doctor:
fuppofe any of thefe doctors were to come to
any woman when her travelling pains were
upon her, and fhe was crying out, and labour
pains came on fafter and fafter, and they fhould
ftand preaching at the door, and fay, good
woman, thefe are only metaphorical pains,
this is only a bold expreffion of the Eafterns,
it is only metaphorical, I queftion whether the
woman would not wifh the doctors fome of

thefe

thefe metaphorical pains for talking fo, which
they would find real ones ; though fhe could
not read fhe might feel.   But notwithftanding
the reality of the new birth, and the pains that
attend it, yet they fay it is only a metaphorical
thing.   I am of an odd temper, and of fuch a
temper, that I heartily wifh they may be put
under the pangs of the new birth, and know
what it is by their own experience, know there
is nothing in nature more real than the new
birth.   The apoftle Paul faid, *I travel in
birth till Chrift be formed in you* : now don't
you think the apoftle had this metaphorical
expreffion of fomething real ; the apoftle's
travelling in birth muft be fomething analogous
to the natural birth ; muft I fay there is no
fuch thing as pangs becaufe I don't feel them :
I am fearfully and wonderfully made, that my
foul knows right well ; and in refpect to the
new birth we may fay, I am fearfully and
wonderfully redeemed by Chrift, and renewed
by the Holy Ghoft ; the new life imparts new
principles, a new underftanding, a new will
and new affections, a renewed confcience, a
renewed memory, nay, a renewed body, by
making it the temple of the living God, an
habitation of God through the Spirit, and
walking

walking in newnefs of life; if I am not miftaken, it implies a progreffive motion, going
from ftrength to ftrength, from one degree of
grace to another, paffing from glory to glory,
for grace is only glory in the bud, till grace is
fwallowed up in endlefs glory. A perfon that
walks, though he may not walk equally faft
as others, yet may get ground : hence, *not t_0
go forward is to go backward.* Enoch walked
with God; it befpoke the habitual tendency
of his heart, the actual exercife of grace, that
he was kept in a lively frame, walked with
God among a very wicked generation, dared
to be good when all were wicked around him,
and he was fo favoured, as to be tranflated to
heaven; this was the cafe with Elijah. *Mofes,*
fays the Lord, *go up to the mount and die:*
God made him undrefs himfelf, and put on
his own grave cloaths, gives him a fight of
Canaan, but to let him know that he even to
the very laft would chaftife his people, when
he is even taking them to heaven; tells him,
thou fhalt not go into the earthly Canaan, but
I will take thee to the heavenly one, which is
far better. Being baptized into the death of
Chrift, befpeaks the habitual tendency and
practice of the heart and life; the old man muft
die,

die, hence the new man muſt live ; it muſt
be emptied of ſelf, that there may be more
and more room for God : now I appeal to
your hearts, how far you have experienced
this. I believe the world pretty well knows
the temper of my mind, both in reſpeƈt to
politics and church-government, and church-
principles : I am a profeſſed avower of moderation, and I heartily wiſh that all who are
concerned in church and ſtate, may particularly
take care to let their moderation be known to
all men, for if we quarrel with one another,
we ſhall only make ſport for the devil, and
occaſion deſtruƈtion. I don't care whether
you go to church or meeting ; I am, I profeſs, a member of the church of England, and
if they will not let me preach in the church,
I will preach any where ; all the world is my
pariſh, and I will preach wherever God gives
me an opportunity, but you will never find me
diſputing about the outward appendages of
religion ; don't tell me you are a Baptiſt, an
Independant, a Preſbyterian, a Diſſenter, tell
me you are a Chriſtian, that is all I want ; this
is the religion of heaven, and muſt be ours
upon earth ; I ſay, are there any of you under
the gallery, or in the green-ſeat, or any where,
                                    I will

I will try to find you out before I have done my fermon, though you are come in the dark.

But I will juft at prefent fpeak to you who underftand the gofpel, to you that are my brethren, though, in all probability, my elder brethren in the gofpel. Methinks there is fomething folemn in meeting in the evening, fomething folemn in coming to worfhip after we have been in the labours of the day; and I verily believe, that when weekly preaching is banifhed from London, that all Chriftianity will be banifhed, it cannot be very long after it, there have been fuch inftances, you may die before to-morrow. I think a good tradefman, whether he deals largely or not, will take care to keep his day-book well; if a man will not keep his day-book well, it is ten to one but he lofes a good deal when he comes to count up his things at Chriftmas; now I take it for granted, a good fpiritual tradefman will keep his fpiritual day-book well: can you fay, this day I hope I have died a little more to the world than yefterday, this day I hope I have been a little more alive to God than I was yefterday; and yet when I look upon my family, whether a man trades wholefale or retail, when he finds he has done but

little

little bufinefs that day, great going out, and little coming in. I hope when you die but little daily, that you go to bed begging pardon, and begging grace, that you may die more to yourfelves and the world, and live more to God to-morrow; for I am fure I can call you to witnefs, that you never lived fo comfortably as when you lived near to God; you may as well pretend to fay, that a perfon in a cold winter's day is warmeft when he keeps from the fire, as to fay, a foul can live near to God when he does not die daily to fin. O, fays one, don't tell me of your frames, don't mind them; I will tell you of them, *don't mind your frames,* I don't in refpect to juftification, but I will to the well-being and comfort of my foul: a man that has got but very little fpirits may be alive, but there is a wide difference between having a diforder that one can hardly fpeak, having no fpirits at all, or but very few, and having folid health: God grant we may be healthy Chriftians; the more you live to God, the more you will have health; be not angry with me; affure yourfelves a lukewarm Chriftian does more hurt to religion, than all the open infidels in the kingdom; we have God himfelf afferting this, *Thou art neither*

hot

hot nor cold, I would thou waft either cold or hot, but becaufe thou art neither cold nor hot, but lukewarm, I will fpew thee out of my mouth; what an expreffion is that! what a naufeous thing is lukewarm water to a fick ftomach! *I will come and remove my candleftick from you.* Therefore, I believe, it is the opinion of all judicious men, that if we fhould have a fevere rod of correction to ftir us up, it is becaufe of the lukewarmnefs of moft Chriftians: my brethren, God make us all alive to Chrift to-night; come, come, if your foul is for Chrift, to arms, to arms, put on your cockades, you that have them in your pockets, for fear you fhould be known to be Chrift's. O you cowards; many foldiers put off their cockades, as if they were not foldiers; as many of our clergy affect to drefs like the laity, that they may go to the plays, that the orange-women may not know them, and they don't care whether God fees them or no. I defire you will all appear in your proper dreffes, let us fee it is painted on the breaft-plates of your hearts, by the bleffed monitor, the eternal Spirit of God; I don't want you to wear them as the Papifts, upon your faces, no; you that are for infant-baptifm, were figned with the fign of the

S f   crofs,

crofs, for what ? that you might, when you came of age, *prove Chriſt's faithful ſoldiers to the end :* God grant, the nearer we come to the end the bolder we may be for Chriſt.

If there be any of you here that are formaliſts, *that have a name to live and are dead,* the Lord grant, that our Lord Jeſus Chriſt, who was raiſed from the dead by the glory of his Father, cauſe a ſtirring among theſe dry bones. Think what it will be to go to hell to-night, to want a drop of water, wherewith you was ſprinkled, to cool your tongues in hell; think what it will be to go to hell by the way of heaven, which is the worſt way you can take; think what it will be to be juſt at the threſhold, and not have religion enough to take you over; my heart bleeds for you. Had you a ſon, a father, a mother, a relation, to be tried at the Old-Bailey this feſſions, how would you be concerned, how carefully would you enquire when your relation would be tried, how anxious would you be to hear whether he is condemned or no; and if ſomebody was to come to tell you, now he is about to be tried and caſt, and now the judge is going to put his cap on, to paſs ſentence on him; how would you bear it ? I believe ſome of you would drop a tear, and

ſay,

fay, O that this poor creature fhould be born
for this; and can you blame a poor minifter of
Chrift, a poor finner that has been redeemed
by the blood of Chrift, and I humbly believe
and hope, has been made a partaker of the
Spirit, will you blame me for being concerned
for you, my brethren and my fifters, for you
and I fprung from one father and mother,
Adam and Eve, the common parents of us all;
can you blame me for pouring out my foul,
can you blame me for fpeaking a little home,
when the Judge is juft ready to mount the
throne, when the books are open, when I fee
the elements melting with fervent heat, when
I fee all nature concurring to ufher in the awful
coming of the Son of God. Sinners in Zion,
baptized heathens, profeffors but not poffeffors,
formalifts, believing unbelievers, talking of
Chrift, talking of grace, orthodox in your
creeds, but heterodox in your lives, turn ye,
turn ye, Lord help you to turn to him, turn
ye to Jefus Chrift, and may God turn you
infide out to-night; may the power of the
higheft overfhadow you, and may that glorious
Father that raifed Chrift from the dead, raife
your dead fouls. Turn the text into a prayer,
go home and fay, for what purpofe have I

lived? into what have I been baptized? I
have not fo much as yet been baptized into
Jordan; I have never led a life one day of reformation but when I was obliged to it: blefs
God that you are not now among the damned;
blefs God that you are not now howling in
hell; blefs the Lord that Jefus ftands with
pitying eyes, and outftretched arms to receive
you now; will you go with the man? will
you accept of Chrift? will you begin to live
now? may God fay, Amen; may God pafs
by, not in anger but in love; may he, as he
hath hitherto feen you in your blood, has faid
to you, live, and has preferved you in your
natural ftate, may that fame God of love, mercy, and life, pafs by you, and caft the fkirts
of his love over you, and fay to you dead finners, come forth, live a life of faith on earth,
live a life of vifion in heaven; even fo, Lord
Jefus. Amen.

SERMON

SERMON XIV.

Neglect of Chrift the killing Sin.

J OHN v. ver. 40.

And ye will not come to me that ye may have life.

THE great apoftle of the Gentiles, after he had fet before the Hebrews the great cloud of witneffes of Old Tefta-ment believers, exhorts them to look higher, even to Jefus the common Saviour, and that not tranfiently, but earneftly and conftantly, in his mediatorial character of humiliation, as enduring unheard of, unparalleled contradic-tion of finners againft himfelf; *leaft,* fays he, *ye be weary, and faint in your minds.* If we had not fuch an example fet before us, and brought to us by the Holy Ghoft in a fuffering hour, we fhould never hold out to the end: this was not the contradiction of the openly profane and fcandalous, thofe that were with-

out,

out, fo much as from thofe that were within the pale of the church, even thofe to whom were committed the lively oracles of God, who had not only the very bible in their own hands, but were fet apart to explain it to others. That the words of our text were fpoken to them, appears from thè preceeding verfe, in which he bids them *fearch the fcriptures*; as a perfon digs for a mine, or fearches for fome hidden treafure. The word bible, or book which I have in my hand, is well applied to the holy fcriptures, becaufe it is the book of God, written by him, that is, by his order, and by thofe who were infpired by him for that end; and yet, of all writings in the world, thefe are moft neglected! God has condefcended to become an author, and yet people will not read his writings. There are very few that ever gave this book of God, the grand charter of falvation, one fair reading through : though we profefs to have affented to the truth of fcripture, as our Lord faid, *in them we think we have eternal life*, yet moft read them as they would a proclamation, a romance, a play, or novels, that help only to bring them to the devil, but chufe not to read God's book, which is to be our guide to glory ; *they are they*, fays Chrift,

which

which teſtify of me: Lord God convert and change our hearts.

However, this was ſpoken in reference to the Old Teſtament, and certainly ſhows us, that Chriſt is the treaſure hid in that field, yet as there are equal proofs of the divinity of the New Teſtament, the word Holy Scriptures include both, eſpecially as Chriſt is the anti-type of all the types, the Alpha and Omega, the beginning and the end of all divine revela-tion: would to God he was your Alpha and Omega too! Now, faith Chriſt, you pretend to reverence the ſcriptures; you that are ſet apart as perſons learned in the ſcriptures, ye Scribes, ye lawyers, ſuch as were mentioned in the goſpel to-day. I fancy ſome people think, that when we read of lawyers in the ſcriptures, that we mean ſuch lawyers as ours, who deal only in the civil and common law, but they were thoſe that opened and explained the law to the people; theſe were the perſons who thought and profeſſed, that in them they had eternal life, that they teſtify of Chriſt the great Prophet that was promiſed in the ſcrip-tures to come into the world; yet, faith our divine maſter, to theſe very profeſſors, theſe maſters in Iſrael, *ye will not come to me that*

ye

ye may have life: though I am now prefent with you, though I am now come to explain the fcriptures, and fulfil them, am now come to proclaim to you that life, that eternal life, which the fcriptures declare were to be pub- lifhed and proclaimed by me, yet *ye will not come unto me that ye may have life.*

By eternal life we are to underftand, all the bleffings of a converted ftate, particularly the pardon of 'fins, not only before converfion but after. It is impoffible but there fhould be fin every day and every hour in every profeffing perfon. My dear hearers, as I fhall not have an opportunity for fome time to fpeak to you, I don't chufe, efpecially when I am about to take my leave of you, to fpeak any thing that is fevere, but I affure you without attempting to offend, with a broken heart I affure you, that this was the treatment Jefus Chrift met with of old, and, God knows, this is the treat- ment Jefus Chrift meets with now : *ye will not come to me that ye may have eternal life.*

If I am not miftaken, and I think I am not, the words fuppofe, that they and we are all dead in fin, for if we are not, I do not know why we need come to have life; and I mention this, becaufe for want of believing and know-

ing

ing this, some that pretend to know Chrift and to preach him, forget to lay the proper foundation, original fin; and that there is no ability or inclination in the heart of a natural man, so much as to do any thing spiritual; he is stupid and dead. But if we have eyes to see, if we have ears to hear, and if our hearts are not waxed hard, doubtlefs it would appear as clear to us as the fun shining in its meridian brightnefs, that man was dead till God breathed into him the breath of life, and then he became a living foul. I know some people believe that the words mean this, that God breathed into man, and he became a natural living foul; like other animals, but then they don't confider what a life God did breath into the foul, he breathed into it the life of God, a spiritual life was breathed into the foul; it is exprefsed in the strongeft, but at the same time in the moft concife terms that is poffible, none but God, none but a man infpired by God, could fay fo much in fo few words; it fhows great fkill in men to fay fo much in a little; what uninfpired man ever wrote fo as Mofes did? Now Mofes when he penned the fcriptures, faid, *God made man after his own image,* and you know ten thoufand volumes

T t

could

could not have faid more than that. How
long do you think it was that man continued in
his original purity? I don't know that I ever
yet heard, that any one thought he continued
in his bleffed ftate fo long as from Saturday to
Saturday. Mr. Bofton, who, perhaps, is one
of the beft writers that ever Scotland produced,
fays, that there is an allufion in one of the
Pfalms to man's fudden fall, *Man being* born
in honour, continued not; i.e. but a night before he fell. O much good may do thofe that
boaft of their free-will, that think they can
ftand by a power of their own, when father
Adam, who had no corruption, did not ftand
a week, perhaps not two days; and how can
we pretend to ftand, let us have what grace
we will, when that grace has fo much corruption to oppofe it? if Jefus Chrift did not
take care to fecure our ftanding, we fhould
fall to our ruin. Adam fell, and being our
federal head, we fell in him. Why, fays a
Deift, and too many profeffors alfo, pray what
bufinefs had God Almighty to make our fall
or our ftanding depend on another? you will
not object to this you church of England men,
will you? then why have you god-fathers and
god-mothers to promife for you? why have

we

we members of parliament to be the heads of
the people, and what the parliament does, the
people do, you have conftituted them your
heads and reprefentatives, you muft ftand and
fall by them; fo if you are bound for a perfon,
you muft ftand and fall with him, muft not
you? I remember one of the minifters that
preached the morning exercifes, when moft,
if not all the churches in this city, were filled
with gofpel-preachers, till on Bartholomew-
day near 2,500 of them in the whole were
turned out, and the other minifters that did
not preach the gofpel continued till the plague
came, and then they ran away, and left the
pulpits to thofe that were turned out, who
were willing to go into them, though they
expected the plague would feize them in
preaching Chrift there; one of thofe minifters
fays, fuppofe God had chofe all that were to
be created, and to proceed from the loins of
Adam, had been prefent, and that he fhould
have faid to them, I have been feven days employed in preparing the whole creation; I
have made a garden, and will have one chofe
by you to dwell in it, as my vicegerent and
your reprefentative here below; here is Adam,
the father of you all, whom I have bleffed

with a partner, that is bone of his bone, and
flesh of his flesh, a creature like himself; all
that I desire of your head and representative is,
that he abstains from yonder tree, of every
other tree in the garden he may freely eat
except that; this I ordain as a test of his obedience, to see whether it is fulfilled, and you
shall all stand or fall by this; who shall be the
man? would they not all say, our first parent
to be sure. O there is not a single man but
would have chosen Adam to be their representative, they would rather stand and fall by
him than by any body else; now pray why
should we quarrel with him for acting in the
manner we ourselves should have done, had
we been in his situation? *God*, saith the apostle, *included all under sin.* What is sin but a
breach, that is, a transgression of the law; *the
wages of sin is death*; every transgression of the
law incurs damnation. Have we eaten of the
forbidden fruit? we must die, we are legally
dead; and there is not a little child in the
world that is not. It is enough to make the
parents pray night and day for their children;
there is not a child born but, to use the words
of our own church, brings in with it corruption, which renders it liable to the wrath of

God

God forever. Then, fay fome, it is true what
I have heard fay of you, that there are little
children in hell a fpan long; I never had fuch
a thought in my life; I never believed that any
infants, black or white, were damned in hell.
I think a poor child, though it is born in a ftate
of original fin, and I have ofren thought *that*
is the reafon why little children are feized with
fuch terrible diforders as often carry them
out of the world, with ten times more agony
than parents feel; a great proof of man's
offence. We fee a poor little infant foon after
it is born, in two or three months taken with
fits, lie fcreaming and ftruggling, while the
diftreffed parents are breaking their hearts, and
wifhing, though they love it dearly, that God
would take it out of its pain. Is not this a
ftrong proof that man is fallen from God? elfe
who can tell what God defigns hereby: however, I verily believe that by his grace he fits
them for heaven. We have broken God's
law, and are liable to eternal condemnation,
we are therefore legally dead, every one of us
without diftinction; we are all upon a level,
from the greateft king in the world, who has
it in his power to write death or life upon the
poor condemned malefactors; bring him to
the

the bar of God's holy law, and it will tell
him there, thou art the malefactor in the
fight of God, thou thyfelf, and thus God is
glorified.   It is not greatnefs of ftation, nor
external differences, that make a difference in
the internal ftate of the foul.   A nobleman
may come with his ftar and garter to the king's
bar, and be tried by his peers at Weftminfter-
hall, and may be attended from the Tower by
fome of the king's officers, but whether a nobleman be tried at Weftminfter-hall, or a criminal in rags at the Old-Bailey, the law muft
be executed upon both: this is our ftate towards God, we have lived in trefpaffes and
fins, are legally dead now; is that all? Dr.
Taylor, of Norwich, fays, that all the lofs
we have had by the fall is, that our mifery is
temporary.   Alas! alas! when Arminians talk
of the fall, you will find very few of them have
courage enough to ftab themfelves. Confcience
makes them cowards; they have loft all by
Adam's fall.   What death have we fuffered,
not only legally but fpiritually dead; what
do I mean by that? why, that we are deprived
of that life of God in which we originally
ftood.   Have you ever feen any body die? I
have.   Have you ever feen one of your friends
die?

die? have you ever ftole into the room, and
looked but once at the dear object of your love,
the partner of your life, but wait till the next
day, and efpecially in the fummer feafon, and
fee how changed! the laft object I faw, put
me in mind of the fall I faw nature in. O what
a change! the glory is departed!

But befides this legal death, there is a fpiritual death, and the confequence of that is
eternal death; if I die in that ftate I muft die
for ever; that is, I muft be a creature living
eternally banifhed from God: if I be annihi-
lated when I die, then, indeed, temporal death
is all; but it is not fo, I am to live in another
world; the wifeft man upon earth tells us,
that there is a future ftate; and therefore by
legal and fpiritual death, I am liable to death
eternal. I have the longer infifted on this,
becaufe it is impoffible to know, or to value
that life that Jefus Chrift came into the world
to impart to us and procure for us, without
confidering the nature of the death he delivers
us from.

Now let us attend to what our Lord fays,
Ye will not come to me that ye may have life;
in the tenth chapter he fays, *I am come that
they might have life, and that they might have it*
more

more abundantly; now what life is that? to be fure, the life which a malefactor wants, who is tried by a Jury; why, he wants to have the chain taken off; what do you and I want? for we may want to eternity if we plead our innocence; there is not one of us but muft plead guilty before God; well, what muft I do? why, if ever I have life, I muft be acquitted, fomething muft pronounce me not guilty; my confcience fays, guilty; why, then Jefus Chrift came that we might have a legal life, that we might be acquitted from all that condemnation which we are under by our breaking his law; fo far the remedy anfwers to the difeafe; but the remedy would not be extenfive enough if that was all; therefore, it was an excellent anfwer a poor woman made at the Old-Bailey, I heard of it twenty years ago: fhe was brought fick to the bar to receive a pardon; the judge faid, Woman, his majefty has given you a pardon: My lord, fays fhe, I thank his majefty for a pardon, and you for pronouncing it, but that is not all I want; what my poor foul wants is, a pardon from Jefus Chrift; what fignifies a pardon from a judge, if I have a difeafe in me that will kill me? whether I am pardoned or not, I muft have my difeafe cured,

cured, that the pardon may do me good. I thought it a ſtrange plea of a man, a captain of a ſhip, that I heard tried ſome years ago for throwing a poor negro overboard; he aſked the ſurgeon, do you think that the child will die? Sir, ſaid he, it will not live above an hour; then, ſays he, you may let it down now: O, ſays the judge, you have murdered the child. I muſt have a pardon from my God, or I am damned; and if I have loſt the divine image, which was the original dignity of man, I ſhall never get to glory without the reſtoration of that image I have loſt by my ſin. Spiritual life in the heart, is that which comes from Jeſus Chriſt, and this is the life of God in the ſoul of man; it is not a metaphorical but a real thing, a reſurrection to life by the power of Chriſt, *who is the reſur-rection and the life,* ſo there is a connection between a legal and a ſpiritual life; the type and antitype anſwers as face anſwers to face in water: thus as all in Adam have died, ſo all in Jeſus Chriſt, the ſecond Adam, are made alive. We are apt to think that ſuch a one, and ſuch a one, were found Chriſtians and gone to heaven, but there is a great deal of falſe charity in the world; without this life we are all undone.   U u   Now,

Now, my brethren, if this is the cafe, how muft I have my life in glory? how muft a dead creature be a Chriftian? how muft a finner that is fpiritually dead have divine life? and how muft a creature, every moment liable to death eternal, be made eternally alive? can any body anfwer that queftion? will reafon tell me? no; will philofophy help me? no; for if *the world by wifdom knew not God,* furely, the world by wifdom knows not how to turn to God; therefore, you will find the greateft fcholars the greateft fools, proudeft deifts, and moft fcornful atheifts; for knowledge puffeth up; and if bare knowledge makes a Chriftian, the devil muft be very good, he is the moft knowing, and yet the moft wicked. The only way to get this life reftored, is to come to Jefus Chrift; *ye will not come unto me,* faith our text, *that ye may have life;* implying, that without coming to him they cannot have life: *there is no other name given under heaven whereby we can be faved, but that of Jefus Chrift. I am the way, the truth, and the life. I am the refurrection and the life,* faith the Lord. In order to have this life, we muft come to Chrift for it: I hope you don't think coming to Chrift, means coming to fee his perfon, that can never be;

be: for our Lord talks of coming to him
when he himfelf was the preacher, and they
were all about him; though fo many round
him, yet there was but one that touched him.
A great many people fay, dear, if Chrift was
here, how would I carefs him! I would let
him in! when, perhaps, at the fame time
turn out one of his members. Would you
like to fee Jefus Chrift with a parcel of boys
and girls running before him, a parcel of poor
fifhermen with him, and Mary Magdalen,
with a mob of poor people and publicans following him? we have got the fame fpirit the
people had then, we fhould hoot at him and
defpife him, as the Pharifees did. A great
many people think coming to Chrift is to come
to the facrament; you know very well I love
that privilege; and one of the greateft afflictions I have is, that my health will not permit
me to attend all the ordinances; but thoufands
come to ordinances, that have no view of the
God of ordinances in them, therefore you will
find, that in all our public places it is as much
the fafhion to go to public worfhip about eleven
o'clock, as any where elfe. They are not up
time enough to their mattins; they go and
fay, we thank God, who has brought us to

the beginning of this day, and that when perhaps the clock ftrikes twelve, and they juft
up; thus people go to church as to a play,
to fee and be feen, and as foon as they go out
of church, they afk where they are to go
to next, and what party? Thoufands go to
church, or to meeting, and facrament, and
don't come to Chrift: come and like this
preaching, and numbers who are called fools
for following us, eat the fragments that are
left, that hear preaching, eat the fifh and the
loaves, and are only feafting upon fhadows
and not upon Chrift: this fhould make us
extremely careful to examine whether we ever
came to Chrift or no. A great moral preacher
fays of our preaching, when all their ftock is
out, then they cry come, come, come, and
that is the burden of their fong, fay they; and
I hope that will be the burden of our fong till
Chrift fays, *Come ye bleffed of my Father*;
what would you have us fay? O, fay you, bid
a man do and live, fo we will; and in the fame
fenfe Chrift in the gofpel fays, thou art dead;
what fhall I do, fays the man, to inherit eternal life? thou knoweft our Lord faid to him,
Keep the law. Our Lord always fpoke to the
people in their own language; that is, thou
fhalt

ſhalt love the Lord thy God with all thy heart ;
he began with morality at the right place, we
begin at the fifth commandment. The great
morality, ſays Dr. Young, is beginning with
the love of God. *Thou ſhalt love thy neighbour
as thyſelf* ; *thou haſt anſwered right,* ſays he,
do this, and thou ſhalt live. Whoever loves
the Lord God as he ought to do, with all his
ſoul and ſtrength, ſhall certainly live ; but our
Lord takes pains to convince him of his ignorance and folly ; ſays he, *who is my neighbour ?*
as to the love of God, he had no thought of
that. Thus we deceive our own ſouls, till
Jeſus Chriſt opens our eyes. What muſt we
come to Chriſt for ? to be acquitted ; come to
his blood to be pardoned ; you muſt believe on
him, not only with a bare ſpeculative belief,
that the devil has, and all the damned in hell,
but to have his blood applied and brought home
to the ſoul ; we muſt come to him as the author and finiſher of our faith. Did not you
juſt now ſay, I believe in the Holy Ghoſt,
the Lord and giver of life ; and the form of
baptiſm is in the name of the Father, Son, and
Holy Ghoſt ; it means, baptize them into the
nature of the Father, Son, and Holy Ghoſt :
and I remember about three or four and thirty

years

years ago, a friend mentioned that word in private converſation to me, we tranſlate it, we believe in God ; ſaid he, we ſhould tranſlate it, *we believe it in God,* for we never do till God has put his faith in us, then we have in our ſouls a new life in Chriſt, then we live a life of faith ; *the life I now live is by faith in the Son of God. I live, yet not I, but Chriſt liveth in me.* In order to this I muſt come to Jeſus Chriſt, and believe on him for life eternal, the earneſt of which eternal life I muſt have in my heart before I can be aſſured I do believe on him. O, my dear hearers, do we think of this, this is no new doctrine; I ſet out, bleſſed be God, with this doctrine. The ſecond ſermon I ever made, the ſecond ſermon I ever preached, was on theſe words, *He that is in Chriſt is a new creature :* I was then about twenty years and a half old. The next ſermon I preached was upon, *Ye are juſtified*; the next ſermon, *Ye are glorified* ; which ſhows, that though I am near fifty-five years old, yet, I thank my God, I am ſo far from changing my principles, which I am ſure I was taught by God's word and Spirit, that I am more and more confirmed, that if I was to die this moment, I hope I ſhould have

ſtrength

ſtrength and courage given me to ſay, I am more convinced of the efficacy and the power of thoſe truths which I preached when I was twenty years old, when I firſt preached them.

Now, my dear hearers, what could enter into the heart of any perſon in the world, to rejeċt ſuch a ſalvation as this? can you think that when a king ſaith to a priſoner, let him go, he would refuſe it? there are ſome perſons that refuſe Chriſt. I remember when, by the bounty of the people here, we begged for the poor, one man went to the turnpike and ſaid, this is Dr. Whitefield's bread and be damned. Human nature, what is it without Chriſt, the bread of life! We will not come to him that we may have life, though we may have it for aſking; no, not for life eternal, as a free gift: we will not come to Chriſt and accept it at his hand; we *will* not: it is not ſaid, we *ſhall* not, but we *will* not. Pray why will not people come to Chriſt to have life? becauſe they do not think that they are dead, and do not want it; remember when you ſay, *you are rich and increaſed in goods,* that you know not, ſaith Chriſt, that *ye are poor and miſerable, and blind and naked.* We do not ſee ourſelves fallen creatures, we do

not

not know that: God give thee to know and feel, that *there is no name given under heaven whereby we can be faved, but Jefus Chrift.* What, faith one, muft I have inward feeling? what would the polite world do without feeling? do you think they would go to the playhoufe and places of public diverfion without feeling? if I can feel other things that do not concern religion, how can I come to God till I feel a need of him. We don't chufe to come to Chrift, becaufe we don't chufe to have him as a free gift; we don't like to come to him as poor and needy. I remember I heard an excellent minifter of Chrift in Scotland, one Mr. Wallis, of Dundee, preaching upon thefe words, *Behold I ftand at the door and knock,* fays he. Chrift comes knocking at the door to come into your houfes, but you will not come down to accept of his mercy. When the prodigal faid, *I will arife and go to my Father, and will fay unto him, I have finned againft heaven and in thy fight, and am no more worthy to be called thy fon, make me as one of thy hired fervants:* now you think that it was very humble in him, he who was a fon of the head of the houfe, to be willing to be a fervant. 'Tis true he fays, I will go to my fa-

ther's

ther's houfe, but at the fame time he fays, I
will work for my living, he fhall not maintain
me for nothing; but when he comes to his
father, he is quite brought down, he fays, *I
have finned againft heaven and in thy fight*; the
joyful father clafps him in his withered arms,
and takes the poor ragged wanderer home.
The lawyers and other Jews thought they
were righteous, and therefore they would not
come to Jefus Chrift. Our Lord fpoke of the
Pharifees, who trufted in themfelves that they
were righteous, and would not come to him
that they might have life; and if we truft in
ourfelves, neither fhall we. Our Lord fays,
*I receive not honour from men. How can you
come to him, that receive honour one of another?
Honour to whom honour is due.* To fuch as
are in power, whether in church or ftate,
refpect is due to their outward fituation. I am
for no levelling principles at all; but, my brethren, at the fame time there is a fault, that
we love to be applauded. There is no going
to heaven, faith Mr. Gurnal, without wearing a fool's cap and a fool's coat, and there is
no going to heaven without being accounted
fools: fo you fee many profeffors follow the
world, they have not courage enough to live

in

in holy non-conformity to the world; and many people are frightned from Chrift, becaufe they would not be counted Methodifts; the fear of man has damned thoufands. You will not come to him, becaufe you cannot truft God, and then we love the world more than Chrift. *If any man love the world, the love of the Father is not in him.* If I had the management of people, their fhops would be open three or four hours before they are now; I do not want to hinder mens bufinefs; thofe that have moft money and moft power, if they acted as they ought to do, would be the greateft flaves to their fellow-creatures. When I talk of loving the world, I mean an inordinate love: I may live in the world, and not live upon it; my heart may be towards God: the love of the world is to be renounced, and therefore they will not come to Jefus Chrift they think, till they are going out of the world. If you are one of thofe who hate Chrift, why you are the man that will not come to him: why, fay you, does any body hate Chrift? pray hold your tongue, for fear of difcovering your ignorance: O, fay you, God forbid I fhould hate him. But, my dear foul, learn from this time forward, that every

one

one of us by nature hates Jefus Chrift: we fent
this meffage to him ; we will not have this
man to reign over us, we hate him becaufe he
is defpifed, we hate him becaufe of the appearance of the people that are his followers, we
hate him becaufe of the narrownefs of the way
we are to pafs in to him, becaufe we muft part
with our lufts ; we hate him becaufe we muft
be non-conformifts: I hate that rag of the
whore of Babylon, O that form of prayer, O
all that ftuff, I thank God I was born a Diffenter, I love to be a Puritan, I don't love
rites and ceremonies, no not in the church,
and yet, perhaps, are more conformed to the
world than numbers of the church, and have
nothing but rites and ceremonies about their
houfes and families.   What do we more than
others ? a churchman fhould prove himfelf a
churchman, by having his articles, and keeping up the practice of religion ; and a Diffenter
fhould prove himfelf one, not by diffenting
from the church, but from the *lufts of the
flefh, the luft of the eye, and the pride of life,*
and then we fhall agree very well together,
though one went to a place called a church,
and another to a place called a meeting.: would
to God every foul now prefent would put this

X x 2   queftion

queſtion to himſelf, Am I come to Chriſt, or am I not ? There is a great number of perſons here, you have heard of Providence calling me abroad, no doubt curioſity brings many of you here, to hear what the poor babler ſays: I tell you what I will ſay to you, that without you have an intereſt in the Son of God, you muſt be damned. *Examine yourſelves whether you are in the faith*, whether your religion reaches any further than the church-door, whe-ther you are the inward court worſhippers: conſcience, conſcience, conſcience, thou faith-ful monitor, God help thee to give a proper verdict. When I had the honour of opening lady Huntingdon's chapel, as I turned about I obſerved over my head were theſe words, *Earth, earth, earth, hear the word of the Lord:* O that every earthly ſoul may hear God's word this day. Don't be angry with me, I am now upon the decline of life, going toward threeſcore, ſurely now I may claim leave to ſpeak to you freely; after next Sun-day, perhaps, you may never hear me any more, though I do not intend to live abroad, but return, if pleaſe God, in a proper time, but long before that thou mayſt be in hell or heaven. As the Lord lives, in whoſe name I

ſpeak,

fpeak, if you will not come to Chrift to have
life, you muft come to his bar to hear him pronounce you damned to all eternity. If you
come to him that you may have life, *Come, ye
bleſſed*, will be the fentence there, but if you
refufe now, *Depart, ye curfed*, will be your
fentence then from the Lord, for in a little
while he that fhall come will come, and will
not tarry. Hark! hark! don't you hear him,
don't you hear him, don't you hear him yonder; hark! methinks I hear him, what does
he fay? fee yonder, don't you fee, good people, that yonder fun is darkened, and the moon
turned into blood. *O, who can abide the day
of his coming?* O, to think of his coming,
may the finner fay, when I know his coming
is only to damn my foul! How do the murderers dread the affizes, but pardoned finners,
pardoned criminals, are glad when they hear
the high-fheriff coming: O, fay they, I long
to go to the bar, becaufe I am going there
only to plead the king's pardon. Happy,
happy, happy you, that have come to this Jefus Chrift that you might have life, that you
might walk becoming him in your life and
converfation. O, Chrift will come, and come
to you as his children; but God grant this life
may

may be displayed in you and me more and
more! If we are helped to know that Christ
came that we might have life, and might
have it more abundantly, O, pray that others
may come, bring your children to Christ. I
was pleased one day after I had been preaching
on *Moses lifting up the serpent in the wilder-*
ness, I think it was in New-England, I was
taken up into a room to repose myself, there
was a mantle-piece, representing the children
brought in the arms of their parents to look at
the brazen serpent: O may God help you to
bring your children and your relations to view
Christ. O Lord help my mother, my father,
my child, my servant, to come to Jesus Christ
that they may have life. The Lord help you
to come, come young people. O I was
charmed this morning, and every morning I
give the sacrament, to see so many young men
there crouding to the table; may the Spirit of
God keep you near to Jesus Christ; and you
young women, may God draw you nearer unto Christ. I remember when God touched
my heart, and sent me down to see my friends
in the country, I prayed God to bless me to
those to whom I was called to dance and to
play at cards with, and, blessed be God, he
                                     blessed

bleffed me to them all before I was twenty
years of age, and after that he fent me to a
prifon, I there preached to a murderer, and
fome others, and, bleffed be God, they came
to Jefus Chrift, and one of them went off moft
triumphantly. A poor creature, fourfcore years
of age, who has made it a practice to go and
read to poor people, and to the prifoners,
faid, " Sir, I began late, but, by the help of
God, I now work the harder for Jefus Chrift."
May he incline you to come, O young women and young men. There was a good woman who died fometime ago, whofe laft word
I think was, I now go to my God. Will you
come and go too, you old grey-headed finners,
that have one foot in the grave, God help you
to go, God remove every obftacle; God grant
that every mountain may be brought low, and
a highway made into your hearts for Jefus
Chrift. Don't be angry with me; in a week
or two I fhall be toffing on the ocean, while
you are hearing God's word here; while I am
amidft ftorms and tempefts, you will be upon
the earth. Paul could ftand the whipping,
but it is not a whipping, but weeping, that
breaks my heart; my greateft trial is, what if
this fermon fhould help to fink thefe people

deeper

deeper in the pit, that makes my blood run cold. O that my fermon may never rife in judgment againſt you, my poor dear fouls. I believe you find it hard when any of you are forced to be witneſſes againſt your own children, your own friends, and whoever deals with the word with a diſintereſted ſpirit, muſt do it; the only way to prevent it, is to come to Chriſt; and if you cannot come, if you are fenfible of it, God be praiſed; he will come to you if you cannot come to Chriſt, he will come and make you willing in the day of his power; that this may be the happy cafe, God grant to us all, for his name's fake.　Amen.

SERMON

SERMON XV.

All Mens Place.

ECCLESIASTES vi. ver. 6.

Do not all go to one place?

I Remember an ingenious writer, who had been very copious in his publications, obſerved, that the beſt and moſt profitable were written after he was fifty years of age : it is ſuppoſed, then the judgment is ripened, and the genius is as it were advanced to maturity and knowledge ; and experiences gathered when young, will be more uſeful in the decline of life, when grey hairs are ſeen here and there upon them. It is ſaid indeed, that old men are twice children ; but there are ſome whoſe geniuſſes are ſo very low that they cannot be twice children, becauſe they are no better than children from their cradle to their grave ; but this is not the caſe with God's

Y y

children,

children, for upon a reflection of the wrong
steps they have taken, if it proceeds from the
sanctified sense of afflictions, they serve to make
them more instructive in their latter day. This
was the case of Solomon, though highly favoured when young, for the Lord appeared
unto him twice, yet he fell most awfully, and
had we not read of his recovery again, the
doctrine of the final perseverance of the saints,
must seem to fall to the ground, but we have
reason to think that he was restored, and gave
evidence of his recovery by writing in such a
manner, that none could but one that knew
much of God and himself; witness the book
of Ecclesiastes, which in all ages of the church
has been received with a peculiar respect. Ecclesiastes signifies a preacher, such Solomon
was from his own experience, and exceeded
by none but him *who spake as no man ever did.*

The chapter in which is the text, describes
the vanity and misery of our present state, if
unsanctified. *There is an evil,* saith he, *that
I have seen under the sun, and it is common
among men :* though he is going about to de-
scribe a monster, yet it is a monster that walks
and stalks abroad, a man to whom God hath
given riches, wealth, and honour, so that he
wanteth

wanteth nothing for his foul of all that he de-
fireth, though God gives him not power to
eat, this is vanity and a great difeafe. Was
there ever a more ftriking defcription of an
old covetous mifer, who leaves his wealth to
fome perfon that fpends it fafter than the poor
wretch got it ? He goes on and fays, *If a man
beget an hundred children, and live many years,
fo that the days of his years be many, and his
foul be not filled with good, and alfo that he have
no burial, I fay, that an untimely birth is better than he, for he cometh in with vanity, and
departeth in darknefs, and his name fhall be co-
vered with darknefs. Moreover, he hath not
feen the fun, nor known any thing; this hath
more reft than the other.* And then though
this creature fhould be fuppofed to live a thoufand years twice told, why, faith he, yet hath
he feen no good, he has never been poffeffed
of real good to make him happy here or hereafter, for, adds he, do not all go, both the
abortive and the aged, young and old, high
and low, rich and poor, whether bleffed with
children, or have no children, whether like
Lazarus, that beg their bread, or Dives,
cloathed in purple and fine linen, and fare
fumptuoufly every day, *Do not all go to one
place ?*   Y y 2   An

An important queſtion! ſhall I propoſe it
to you to-night? do you know what the wiſe
man, means when he offers this queſtion to
your conſideration, *Do not all go to one place?*
what can be the deſign of this? the thing, no
doubt, here ſpoken of is death, the place here
ſpoken of, no doubt, is the grave. An amazing conſideration! part of the firſt ſentence
that the great and holy God ever denounced
againſt fallen man, to one and all, *Duſt thou
art, and unto duſt thou ſhalt return.* On account of our firſt parent's tranſgreſſion, it is
appointed unto all men, all ſorts of men, all
the inhabitants under heaven, once to die;
and therefore the apoſtle ſaith, *Death hath
paſſed upon all men, even upon thoſe who have
not ſinned after the ſimilitude of the tranſgreſſion of Adam,* that is, who have not been
guilty of actual ſin. Can there be a ſtronger
proof of the imputation of Adam's guilt, of
original ſin, or a more cutting trial that a tender father and nurſing mother can undergo,
than to ſee a dear little child juſt born, or but
lent to the loving parents for a few months,
taken away often in the greateſt agonies that
we can conceive? and if God, my dear hearers, has ever ſuffered your dear children ſud-
denly

denly to be feized with convulfions, and continue in anguifh and agonizing pains for many days together, you have had fufficient proof of it. A friend of mine in London, about thirty-two years ago, that was dotingly fond of every child he had, to whom I wrote a letter from Georgia, beginning with thefe words, Is your idol dead yet? for I thought it was fuch an idol that would foon go. The account he gave me the firft time I faw him was, that the day before my letter was received, the child died in fuch agony and torture, that its excrements came out of its mou th, whic made the fond and too indulgent parent wifh to have rather died a thoufand deaths himfelf, than that his child fhould die in fuch a way ; and added, I was obliged to go to God, and defire him to take my darling away. What an awful proof are their fufferings, that children come into the world with a corruption that renders them liable to God's wrath and damnation, but the blood, the precious blood of Jefus Chrift, it is to be hoped, cleanfes them from the guilt and filth of fin. So any of you that have got children dead in infancy, O may you improve what I fhall fay by and by from the text, and pray and endeavour to go to that

place,

place, where I hope you will fee your children making a bleffed conftellation in the firmament of heaven: in this refpect all go to the fame place, fome at the beginning of life, fome at the middle, and fome at the decline; and happy, happy they who go to bed fooneft, if their fouls are faved!

But, my dear hearers, in another cafe we may venture to contradict even Solomon; for if we confider the words of our text in another view, all do not go to one place; it is true, all are buried in the grave either of earth or water, but then after death comes judgment; death gives the decifive, the feparating blow. Suppofe then in our enlarging on the text, we fhould confine the word all to the unregenerate, and to thofe who are not born of God, thefe indeed, die when they will, all go to one place. If you fhould afk me, for I love dearly to have an inquifitive auditory, who I mean by unregenerate? who I mean by thofe that are not born of God? I anfwer, I do not mean all that only bear the name of Jefus Chrift; I mention this, becaufe a great many people think that all that are baptized, either when they are adult or when they are young, whether fprinkled or put under water, I believe

lieve a great many people think that all thefe
go to heaven. I remember when I began to
fpeak againft baptifmal regeneration in my firft
fermon, printed when I was about twenty-
two years old, or a little more; the firft quarrel many had with me was, becaufe I did not
fay that all people who were baptized were
born again; I would as foon believe the doctrine of tranfubftantiation. Can I believe that
a perfon who gives no evidence of being a
faint, from the time of his baptifm to the time
perhaps of his death, that never fights againft
the world, the flefh, and the devil, and never
minds one word of what his god-fathers and
god-mothers promifed for him, can I believe
that perfon is a real Chriftian? no, I can as
foon believe, that a little wafer in the prieft's
hand, about a quarter of an inch long, is the
very blood and bones of Jefus Chrift, who was
hung upon the crofs without the gates of Jerufalem. I do believe baptifm to be an ordinance of Chrift, but at the fame time, no can-
did perfon can be angry for my afferting, that
there are numbers that have been baptized
when grown up, or when very young, that
are not regenerated by God's Spirit, who
will all go to one place, and that place is where
                                        there

there will be no water to quench that dreadful fire that will parch them with thirſt. I am ſpeaking out of a book which contains the lively oracles of God, and in the name of one who is truth itſelf, who knowing very well what he ſpoke, is pleaſed in the moſt ſolemn and awful manner to ſay, and that to a maſter in Iſrael, that *if a man be not born again of water and the Spirit, he cannot ſee the kingdom of God*; he can have no idea, no proper, no adequate notion of it, much leſs is he to expect to be happy eternally with God hereafter; and therefore as our Lord ſpoke to this man, give me leave to obſerve to you. I don't mean the Deiſts only by unregenerate ſinners; I don't mean the profane mocker, who is advanced to the ſcorner's chair, nor your open profligate, adulterers, fornicators, abuſers of themſelves with mankind, theſe have damnation as it were written upon their foreheads with a ſun-beam; and they may know that God is not mocked, for if they die without repenting of theſe things, they ſhow they are in an unregenerate ſtate, and will all go to one place: if any of you are going thither, may God ſtop you this night. But, my brethren, I will come cloſer; there are more unbelievers

within

within the pale than without the pale of the church ; let me repeat it again, you may think of it when I am tofling upon the mighty waters, there are more unbelievers within the pale of the church than without: all are not poffeffors that are profeffors, all have not got the thing promifed, all are not partakers of the promife, that talk and blefs God they have got the promifed Saviour ; I may have him in my mouth and upon my tongue, without having the thing promifed, or the bleffed promife in my heart. A moral man that can walk touching the law blamelefs, a perfon that thinks he is righteous, becaufe he does not know why a perfon who has got no other religion but to go to a particular place of worfhip, values himfelf upon being a churchman or a diffenter ; he is fuch a bigot, that he thinks no man will go to heaven but himfelf; thefe, however they may think themfelves fafe, will e'er long go to one place, whether they think fo or no ; they will be foon fummoned to one bar, and the voice of the archangel founding, *Arife, ye dead, and come to judgment,* will be the great alarm ; the dead fhall arife and appear before the Son of God, as Judge of all mankind ; thefe, as well as the infidels, would gladly be

Z z excufed;

excufed; and as they once faid, I pray to have me excufed from coming to Chrift, fo they will fain be excufed from appearing before, and being condemned by him, but they muft all go to one place: and as they know not God, and are unacquainted with the divine life, they muft hear and fuffer the dreadful fentence, *Depart, ye curfed, into everlafting fire, prepared for the devil and his angels.* This is a thought, that if our hearts, my dear hearers, were properly awakened, would make our blood run cold: to be in a place of abfence from God, a place where damned fouls will be for ever curfing God and one another: give me leave to dwell upon it a little, and may it be bleffed, under God, to awaken fome carelefs perfon, who, perhaps, may be taking a walk to-night, and juft ftep in to hear what the babler has to fay while he is about to take his leave of the people. When I faw you from my ftudy crowding to come in, when I faw you pufhing forward, fome to go up to the Tabernacle, or into the veftry, fome to fill the area, and others to ftand at the door, I thought how fhall I manage with myfelf to-night, fhall I endeavour to make thefe weep and cry, fhall I not earneftly addrefs fo many

precious

precious fouls in a practical way, to bring
them not to the preacher, but the preacher's
mafter; knowing the terrors of the Lord, we
would fain perfuade all to flee from this wrath
to come. O awful thought! and yet it is a
certain truth, all on earth muft go to one
place; if we live like, and are devils here,
we muft go to and be with them when we die
for ever! A bleffed minifter of Chrift, in
Scotland, told me a ftory he knew for truth, of
a dreadful anfwer a poor creature gave on her
death-bed, for the Scotch, except the people
of New-England, are the moft knowing people
in religious matters, perhaps any where; this
perfon when dying was afked by a minifter,
where do you hope to go when you die? fays
fhe, I don't care where I go; what, fays he,
don't you care whether you go to heaven or
hell? no, fays fhe, I don't care whither I go;
but, fays he, if you was put to your choice
where would you go? fays fhe, to hell; to
that he replied, are you mad, will you go to
hell? yes, fays fhe, I will; why fo? fays
he; why, fays fhe, all my relations are there.
The dear minifter of Chrift preached after her
death, told the ftory, and afked, is it not
fhocking to hear a woman fay fhe would go

to hell becaufe her relations were there : why, you that are unregenerate muft go to hell for all your unregenerate relations are there ; your father the devil is there, all damned angels and damned fpirits ; your brothers and fifters are there ; as they went one way here, fo they muft be banifhed from Jefus Chrift to one place hereafter.

But I muft clofe this mournful theme, it is too gloomy to dwell upon ; bleffed be God, I have another place to tell you of, and another fort of people to fpeak of, who fhall all, as well as thofe I have fpoken of, go to one place ; perhaps, here are fome of them ; bleffed is it to live in God. When death clofes the eyes an actual feparation is made, and inftead of hearing, *Depart, ye curfed,* they will hear, *Come, ye bleffed of my Father, inherit the king-dom prepared for you from the foundation of the world.* Our bleffed mafter, and who fpeaks like him, gives us an awful view of Dives and Lazarus, the one feafting and fattening his body to the grave, not keeping one faft-day in a year, and the other ftarving at his gate, per-haps buried in the ditch, denied a grave by the parifh, while this vile wretch, who died alfo, had a pompous funeral ; there he was

carried

carried to one place; he was, perhaps, laid in ſtate, two mutes attending round the coffin, while damned devils were gnawing his ſoul; he lift up his eyes in torment. Hark! don't you hear him, I will ſtop a little that you may: you ungodly ones, do not you hear your brother cry? he would not pray while alive, but hell makes him pray, not to God but to Abraham; *Father Abraham*, ſays he, *ſend Lazarus to dip the tip of his finger in water, and cool my tongue*; and I verily believe, the damned will have a ſight of thoſe that are in heaven, to let them know what a heaven, what a Chriſt, what a glory they have loſt: God grant this may be none of your caſe, it will not be if you are of the number of thoſe who are born from above, that are made new creatures in Chriſt Jeſus; for by being born again from above, I mean receiving a principle of new life, imparted to our hearts by the Holy Ghoſt, changing you, giving you new thoughts, new words, new actions, new views, ſo that old things paſs away, and all things become new in our ſouls. I know very well, that the doctrine of a divine influence is exploded: I have often told you, and I tell you again, now I am about going to another clime

for

for a-while, that the grand quarrel that our
Lord Jefus Chrift has with England, and I do
not fpeak it as a prophet, or the fon of a prophet, but as the Lord God liveth, in whofe
name I fpeak, for whofe glory I am going
abroad, and in whofe fear I defire to die, if
the Spirit of God and his divine influence is
not more regarded in this land than it has
been, wo, wo, wo to thofe that defpife it,
they may by and by, one day or other, wonder and perifh. Blefled be God, there are a
happy few who do regard it; and I am perfuaded in my very foul, that the number in
England, in Scotland, in Ireland, in Wales,
and in America, does, and I pray it may, ftill
greatly increafe. Yet, notwithftanding the
word of God does run and is glorified, how
many are there at this day, that wilfully do
defpite to the Spirit of God, that hate the
doctrine of the Spirit's divine influences; that
if it were in their power, but we live under
revolution principles, and are blefled with toleration, which is the bulwark of liberty of
confcience, otherwife the ftreet would run
with the blood of both churchmen and diffen-
ters, but whether the world will hear or for-
bear, blefled be God, when we fpeak of the

new

new birth, we do not fpeak of a cunningly
devifed fable; what our eyes have feen, what
our hands have handled, and what our hearts
have felt of the word of life, that declare we
unto you. When I was fixteen years of age
I began to faft twice a week for thirty-fix
hours together, prayed many times a-day,
received the facrament every Lord's-day, fafting myfelf almoft to death all the forty days
of Lent, during which, I made it a point of
duty never to go lefs than three times a-day
to public worfhip, befides feven times a-day
to my private prayers, yet I knew no more
that I was to be born again in God, born a
new creature in Chrift Jefus, than if I was
never born at all. I had a mind to be upon
the ftage, but then I had a qualm of confcience; I ufed to afk people, pray can I be
a player, and yet go to the facrament and be a
Chriftian? O, fay they, fuch a one, who is a
player, goes to the facrament; though, according to the law of the land, no player
fhould receive the facrament, unlefs they give
proof that they repent; that was archbifhop
Tillotfon's doctrine: well then, if that be the
cafe, faid I, I will be a player, and I thought
to act my part for the devil as well as any
body;

body; but, bleſſed be God, he ſtopped me
in my journey. I muſt bear teſtimony to my
old friend, Mr. Charles Weſley, he put a book
into my hands, called, the Life of God in
the Soul of Man, whereby God ſhewed me,
that I muſt be born again or be damned. I
know the place; it may be ſuperſtitious, perhaps, but whenever I go to Oxford, I cannot
help running to that place where Jeſus Chriſt
firſt revealed himſelf to me, and gave me the
new birth. As a good writer ſays, a man
may go to church, ſay his prayers, receive the
ſacrament, and yet, my brethren, not be a
Chriſtian. How did my heart riſe, how did
my heart ſhudder, like a poor man that is
afraid to look into his account-books, leſt he
ſhould find himſelf a bankrupt; yet ſhall I
burn that book, ſhall I throw it down, ſhall
I put it by, or ſhall I ſearch into it? I did,
and holding the book in my hand, thus ad-
dreſſed the God of heaven and earth: Lord, if
I am not a Chriſtian, if I am not a real one,
God, for Jeſus Chriſt's ſake, ſhow me what
Chriſtianity is, that I may not be damned at
laſt. I read a little further, and the cheat was
diſcovered; O, ſays the author, they that
know any thing of religion, know it is a vital
union

union with the Son of God, Chrift formed in
the heart; O what a ray of divine life did
then break in upon my poor foul, I fell a writing to all my brethren, to my fifters, talked
to the ftudents as they came in my room, put
off all trifling converfation, put all trifling
books away, and was determined to ftudy to
be a faint, and then to be a fcholar; and from
that moment God has been carrying on his
bleffed work in my foul; and as I am now
fifty-five years of age, going towards fixty, I
tell you, my brethren, as I fhall leave you in
a few days, I am more and more convinced
that this is the truth of God, and without it
you never can be faved by Jefus Chrift: all
thofe born of God, whether when young or
old, at the fixth, ninth, or eleventh hour,
however feparated from one another, through
the grace of God, they fhall all go to one
place.

If you afk where that place is? I anfwer,
bleffed be God, to heaven; if you afk to
whom they fhall go? I anfwer, to the fpirits
of juft men made perfect; and, what will be
beft of all, to Jefus Chrift, the heavenly inheritance. If we were not to go to him, what
would heaven be? if we were not to fee him,

what would glory be? I know fome people think heaven is a fine place, fo it is; but what makes it fo, but the prefence and joy of the God of glory? I would rather die a thoufand deaths, than facrifice my affections as I have done: after I had taken leave of all my friends fome years ago at Deptford, I burft out into tears and faid, Lord, I would not fuffer all I feel for my friends but for thee, then returned to my friends and faid, Now the bitternefs of death is paffed, I am going to be executed, God's will be done. Bleffed be God, after death there are no feparations, we fhall all go to one place; minifters that could not preach in one pulpit, and Chriftians that could not agree with one another, bleffed be God, fhall by and by go to one heaven; whether they go to one place or no in this world, does not fignify: fays one, I go to the Diffenters; another, I go to church; and a great many Chriftians judge of one another as infidels, becaufe they are not of one fentiment. A good woman came to me fome years ago juft as I had done preaching, fome people love to be impertinent, what do you think, fays fhe, of Cotton Mather and another minifter, one faid, I ought to receive the facrament before my

expe-

experience was given in, the other faid not, and I believe the angels were glad to carry them both to heaven. I faid, good woman, I believe they have not talked about it fince, for they will no more talk about thefe things. We have but one Father, one Holy Ghoft, we have lived in one communion of faith; bleffed be the living God, e'er long the angels fhall come and call the elect from the eaft, the weft, the north, and the fouth, to be at home with the Lord.

If this be the cafe, my brethren, it may fupport us under all the changes and partings of this mortal ftate. As I have been in a public character, I fuppofe I may venture to fay, that no one has been called to fuch frequent partings from God's people as I have: I am going now the thirteenth time over the water; yes, I find what is faid of St. Paul is true, he could bear a whipping, not a weeping: what mean you, fays he, to weep and break my heart; he never faid, whip me and break my back, no, no. All get to one place: what a bleffed ftate! to fee one's fpiritual father, to fee one's fpiritual children, and hear them fay, fuch and fuch a time God begat me to himfelf by your miniftry! what a bleffing will it

be to hear them fay, bleffed be God, next to
the Spirit I owe my coming here to that fervant of thine ! and with what ravifhment will
the minifter fay, behold me and the children
thou haft given me ! with what holy triumph
will they all then caft their crowns at the foot
of the Lamb ! with what joy will they cry,
grace, grace, when the top-ftone is brought
forth, and how will they then try who fhall
praife redeeming love and rich free grace in
the higheft ftrain ! The difference here is you
know, that we fing in parts, fome fing treble,
fome tenor, and fome bafe ; what then ? each
part helps the other, were all to fing alike the
harmony would not be compleat; however
fhocking it is in this world, all the differences
that have been among the people of God, will
only make us fing and unite us the better in a
future ftate.

Well, my dear hearers, by this time then I
hope you have began to afk, to what place
am I going ? Suppofe now you reafon thus ;
I have heard to-night that all unregenerate
perfons go to hell, and dwell among the
damned ; I have heard that all that are born
again of God, and all that believe in Jefus
Chrift, whether Jew or Gentile, whether

bond

bond or free, all go to dwell with God, with
angels, and the fpirits of juft men made perfect; I have heard the minifter fay, though
he feems fometimes to ramble in his difcourfe,
that we all go to one place, that is, the grave:
I am haftening there, autumn is coming on,
the fall of the leaf is approaching, a blaft,
occafioned by the fudden change of weather,
or a furfeit, by feafting too luxuriantly on the
fruits of God's bounty; another illnefs may
take me to my long home. I hear of fuch-a-
one's dying, and of fuch-a-one, perhaps in an
apople&ic, perhaps in a paralytic fit: I am
lufty and ftrong, I am glorying in my ftrength,
but who knows but that may be only making
me food for a fever; one would ftand it better
that was more emaciated than I am. If I
fhould be taken this night, am I going the
way to hell, or the way to heaven. Adrian,
the emperor, cried out upon a time, *My trembling, dear departing foul, whither art thou
going?* thefe were his words. Won't you
hear an emperor preach, preach on his dying
bed, when the filver cords of life are loofed?
Confcience, confcience, confcience, thou can-
dle of the Lord, may he help thee to light a
poor finner into a knowledge of himfelf. I

charge

charge thee in the name of our Lord Jefus
Chrift, in the name of that Saviour, in whofe
name and by whofe power, 1 truft, I now
preach; O confcience! thou faithful monitor,
let every one hear their own. Come, if confcience was to fpeak what would it fay? why,
that if you are not acquainted with yourfelf and
Chrift, you are loft for ever. The Ameri-
cans are the moft hofpitable people under
heaven, they love to entertain ftrangers, who
may be hereby kindly provided for without
going to an inn: I always endeavoured to
drop a word for Chrift when I came to their
houfes. I remember Mr. Seeward, and fome
other good friends were with me; when I firft
got into the houfe, I began to talk of Chrift;
the mafter of it faid, Sir, I believe you are
right; I can't open a leaf in my bible, but I
find I am no Chriftian: would to God all here
minded the fame leaf! May be, many here
fay, fir, I fcorn your words; well, don't I?
don't God tell you that won't do? you are
a moral man, but don't love God; you don't
get drunk, becaufe it will make your head
ach; you don't commit fornication and adultery, which is common among the great, and
therefore they think God will not punifh them

for

for it; perhaps you are not a fornicator, left you fhould ftand in a fheet, though we have no difcipline among us now; you don't do thefe things for fear of maintaining the baftard, or being taken up; but does your obedience proceed from love to God, to Chrift; if not, may God convince you of your miferable ftate before you go hence.

But, bleffed be God, there are numbers of dear fouls here, that I hope e'er long to live in one place and to eternal ages with. All hail, my fellow Chriftians; all hail, my dear brethren and friends; all hail, ye that are children of one parent, born of one Spirit, and bring forth the fruits of the Holy Ghoft in your converfation; yet a little while, and we muft part; whether I die, or you die, bleffed be God, one place fhall e'er long hold us; in yonder bleffed world we fhall e'er long meet, and praife free grace; my brethren, we fhall be then for ever with the Lord, for ever one with Chrift; and if this be the cafe, let us comfort one another with thefe things; and if we are all going to one place, God, of his infinite mercy, keep us from falling out by the way. Don't fay, I am of the Foundery; don't fay, I am of the Tabernacle; don't

fpend

spend your time in talking againſt John Weſley and George Whitefield; don't ſay, you go to the Tabernacle, I'll go to the chapel; no, don't ſpeak of Paul and Cephas; God unite us more and more to Jeſus Chriſt; and if you are going to heaven, God help you to travel a little faſter than we do. My brethren, let us preſs forward toward the mark of the prize of our high calling in Chriſt Jeſus. O that the God of love may fill us with ſuch peace and ſuch joy, that every ſtorm, every trial, every temptation we meet with, may be over-ruled to good for us; all our afflictions, all our temptations, are to make heaven more deſirable, and earth more loathſome.

If this is not the caſe with ſome of you, God convert you to-night. Help me, my dear Tabernacle and London hearers, help me, help me, help me for Jeſus Chriſt's ſake. You was once going to hell yourſelves, for God's ſake endeavour to ſtop thoſe that are going there : pray for your unconverted friends. Young people, young people, that are going to hell giddily, may God ſtop you this night : was I to talk to you ſeriouſly, you would ſay as a young gentleman did, when I deſired he would not ſwear; he turned to me and ſaid,

Doctor,

Doctor, (I was no more a doctor then than now, and but young too) it is very hard you will not let a man go to hell his own way; if any of you are of this ſtamp, God grant he may not let you go to hell your own way, but go to heaven in God's way, in Chriſt's way. I am ſure you are not happy; the devil never had a happy child in the world: O that God may turn your feet into the way of peace to-night: O that it may be with you as with a young man one night formerly: I remember I had about two hundred notes then; I came into moorfields this morning at ſix o'clock, ſays he, to meet my ſweetheart, but, bleſſed be God, I met with Jeſus Chriſt, my ſweetheart: would to God you may do ſo, young men, to-night: when you have gone on to that place, O that it may be with you as it was with good Mr. Crane, who is appointed ſteward of the Orphan-houſe; he went once to ſee a play at Drury-lane, but that being full he went to Covent-garden, and that was ſo full he could not put his head in; well, ſays he, he told it me himſelf, and he is an Iſraelite indeed, one of the moſt honeſt men, perhaps, in the world, I will go and hear doctor Whitefield; there God reached his

B b b

heart,

heart, and now he ſhines. I had letters yeſter-day or the day before from Georgia, that made my heart leap for joy ; honeſt Mr. Wright, that ingenious, indefatigable man, and Mr. Crane, have gone on ſo well, and have managed the Orphan-houſe ſo well, that all letters from all parts give me a pleaſure : would to God, one ſays, you could ſend ten thouſand ſuch people as Mr. Wright and Mr. Crane ; would to God you could ſend a thou-ſand ſuch over, and an hundred preachers to preach Chriſt among us. O that curioſity may be over-ruled for good to ſome of you to-night : but I forgot myſelf, and can you blame me if I ſhould detain you a little, tho' I am really afraid of unfitting myſelf for my voyage, if I tire myſelf before I go : to-mor-row I am to go to ſee where I am to ſleep. I intend, God willing, to have a ſacrament here to-morrow, and another next Sabbath-day morning. I intend, God willing, to give you a parting word on Sunday evening, and give you notice of taking my laſt farewel in the week, for I muſt get a day or two to diſ-patch my private buſineſs, and be ready to go where my God calleth me.

I ſhall,

I fhall, I think, be called to do fomething which I would, if poffible, have avoided, and that is, as this place has been repaired, you fee 'tis frefh done, which is expenfive, and I am willing to leave every thing clear before I go, a collection muft be made for defraying the charge. The world thinks I am very rich; a man, the other day, was fo perfuaded of my riches, that he fent me word, if I did not lay thirty pounds in fuch a place, I fhould be killed as fure as I am alive; but, bleffed be God, I am alive yet; I do not fear dying fuddenly, or being difpatched by a poignard, or a piftol to make a paffage for my foul to flee to God. You may think, perhaps, I get a great deal by preaching here; and now I am going away, what do you think my ftated allowance is for preaching at the Tabernacle? I have no more from this place than one hundred pounds a year; and I afked but laft night how it ftood, and inftead of having a fingle fixpence, I was told there were fifty pounds arrears; well, faid I, ungrateful as it is to me, I will make a collection to-night that all may be left free; and if others are left to make an advantage of it, may God make it a bleffing. There are not fix people in this place that I

have

have had the value of a guinea of from Janu-
ary to Auguſt ; nor have I had a guinea from
all theſe ordinances towards bearing the expen-
ces of my voyage. When I come, my brethren, to heaven, you ſhall then know with
what a ſpirit I have ſerved you; you ſhall
then know that all I have done is to build
places for others, where I hope God will
meet you and your children when I am dead
and gone. O that we may meet in one place,
when God calls me hence: the Lord quicken
you, the Lord ſtrengthen you, the Lord Jeſus Chriſt be with you, and grant that e'er
long we may be where there ſhall be no more
ſorrow, but we ſhall dwell with God and one
another for ever; even ſo, Lord Jeſus Chriſt.
Amen.

SERMON

✥✥✥✥✥✥✥✥✥✥✥✥✥✥✥✥✥✥✥✥✥✥✥✥✥

SERMON XVI.

God a Believer's Glory.

Isaiah lx. ver. 19.

And thy God thy Glory.

I LATELY had occasion to speak on the verse immediately following that of our text ; but when I am reading God's word, I often find it is like being in a tempting garden, when we pluck a little fruit and find it good, we are apt to look after and pluck a little more, only with this difference, the fruit we gather below often hurts the body at the same time that it pleases the appetite, but when we walk in God's garden, when we gather fruit of the Redeemer's plants, the more we eat the more we are delighted, and the freer we are the more welcome ; if any chapter in the bible deserves this character and description of an evangelical Eden, this does.

It

It is very remarkable, and I have often told you of it, that all the apoftles preach firft the law, and then the gofpel, which finds man in a ftate of death, points out to him how he is to get life, and then fweetly conducts him to it. Great and glorious things are fpoken of the church of God in this chapter ; and it ftruck me very much this evening ever fince I came into the pulpit, that the great God fpeaks of the church in the fingular number: how can that be, when the church is compofed of fo many millions gathered out of all nations, languages, and tongues ? how is it, that God fays thy maker and not your maker, that he fpeaks of the church as though it confifted only of one individual perfon ? the reafon of it is this, and is very obvious, that though the church is compofed of many members, they have but one Head, and they are united by the bond of one Spirit, by whom they have the fame vital union of the foul with God ; and therefore it teaches Chriftians not to fay to one another, *I am of Paul, I am of Apollos, or Cephas,* but to behave and live fo, that the world may know that we all belong to one common Chrift : God revive, continue, and increafe this true Chriftian love among us!

Of

Of this church, thus collectively confidered, united under one head, the bleffed evangelical prophet thus fpeaks, *Violence fhall no more be heard in thy land, wafting nor deftruction within thy borders, but thou fhalt call thy walls falvation, and thy gates,* where the magif- trates affemble, and the people go in and out, *praife.* From this text, a great many good and great men have gathered what they call the Millenium, that Jefus Chrift is to come and reign a thoufand years on earth, but I muft acknowledge that I have always rejected a great many good mens pofitive opinion about the feafon when this ftate commences, and I would warn you all againft fixing any time; for what fignifies whether Chrift comes to reign a thoufand years, or when he comes, fince you and I are to die very foon; and therefore inftead of puzzling our heads about it, God grant we may live fo that we may reign with him for ever; and it feems to me, that whatfoever is faid of this ftate on earth, that the millenium is to be underftood in a fpiritual fenfe, as an emblem of a glorious, eternal, beatific ftate in the kingdom of heaven. *The fun fhall no more be thy light by day, nor for brightnefs fhall the moon give light unto thee,*

but

but the Lord shall be unto thee an everlasting light; and in order to prepare us for that light, and show us the nature of it, while we speak of it may it come with light and power to our souls. He adds in our text, *and thy God shall be thy glory:* this is spoken to all believers in general, but it is spoken to all fearful believers in particular ; and I don't know that I can possibly close my poor, feeble ministration among you here, better than with these words; though, God willing, I intend, if he shall strengthen me this week, to give you a parting word next Wednesday morning; and O that what has been my comfort this day in the meditation on this passage, may be yours and mine to all eternity. He that hath an ear to hear let him hear what the evangelic prophet saith, *thy God thy glory.*

The Holy Ghost seems, as it were, particularly fond of this expression ; when God published the ten commandments upon mount Sinai, he prefaced it thus, *I am the Lord,* and not content with that, he adds, *thy God;* and the frequency of it, I suppose, made Luther say, that *the gospel deals much in pronouns, in which consists a believer's comfort ;* but if there were no other argument than this,

it

it would cut up that deſtructive principle by
the very root that pretends to tell us that there
is no ſuch thing as appropriation in the Bible ;
that our faith is only to be a rational aſſent to
the word of God, without a particular application of that word made to our ſouls : this is
as contrary to the goſpel, and to experience of
every real ſaint, as light is contrary to darkneſs,
and heaven to hell. My brethren, I appeal to
any of you, what good would it do you, if you
had ten thouſand notes wrote in large characters
by the fineſt hand that can write in London ;
ſuppoſe you have got them, as many men have,
and it is a very convenient way, that they were
put into your little pockets made on the inſide
of your coat ; ſuppoſe you ſhould ſay, my coat
is buttoned, I have all theſe here next my
heart : when I come to look at them, I find
there is not one note payable to me, they are
all either forged, or payable to ſome body elſe,
and therefore are good for nothing to me. All
the promiſes of the goſpel, all that is ſaid of
God and Chriſt, can do us no good, except
that God and Chriſt is ours. The great queſtion
therefore is, whether the God we profeſs to
believe in, is our God ? not only, whether he
is ſo in general, that the devils may ſay ; but

C c c

whether

whether he is our God in particular. The devils can say, O God; but the devils cannot say, my God: that is a privilege peculiar to God's chosen people, who really believe on the Lord Jesus Christ: and therefore, my brethren, a deist cannot say, my God, my Christ, because he does not believe on that medium by which God becomes our God. That was a noble saying of Luther, " I will have nothing to do with an absolute God;" that is, I will have nothing to do with a God out of Christ. Now this is a deist's glory: Lord Bolingbroke values himself upon it, I am astonished at that man's infidelity and cowardice. I don't like those men that leave their writings to be published after their death: I love to see men bold in their writings: I like an honest man that will put out his writings while alive, that he may see what men can say against him, and then answer them; but it is meer cowardice to leave it to the world to answer for it, to set us a cavelling after they are got into the grave: says he, I will have nothing to do with the God of Moses; and I suppose the principles of that deist made one pretty near to him ask as soon as his breath was out of his body, where do you think he is gone to? another

other replies, where do you think but to hell. God grant that may not be the portion of any here!

The queſtion then is, how God is our God; *thy God.* My brethren, our all depends upon it; what ſignifies ſaying, this is mine, and that is mine, if you cannot ſay, God is mine. The beſt thing that God has left in the New Teſtament, is himſelf: *I will be their God,* that is one of the legacies; and *a new heart alſo will I give them,* that is another; *I will put my laws in their mind, and write them in their hearts,* that is another: but all that is good for nothing, comparatively ſpeaking, unleſs God has ſaid at the ſame time, for they are all inſeparable, *I will be their God, and they ſhall be my people.* Now how ſhall I know that God is my God? I am afraid, ſome people think there is no knowing; well then, if you think ſo, you ſet up a worſhip, and go and erect an altar, and inſtead of receiving God in the ſacrament as yours, go and worſhip an unknown God. I am ſo far from believing, that we cannot know that God is ours, that I am fully perſuaded of it, and would ſpeak it with humility, and I would not chuſe to leave you with a lie in my mouth, that I have known

it for about thirty-five years as clear as the fun
is in the meridian, that God is my God. And
how fhall I know it, my brethren? I would
afk you this queftion, didft thou ever feel the
want of God to be thy God? No body knows
God to be their God that did not feel him to
be his God in Chrift: out of Chrift, God is a
confuming fire. I know there are a great variety of ways in peoples converfions, but ftill,
my brethren, we muft all feel our mifery,
we muft all feel our diftance from God, all
feel that we are eftranged from God, that we
bring into the world with us a nature that is
not agreeable to the law of God, nor poffibly
can be; we cannot be faid to believe that God
is our God, till we are brought to be reconciled to him through his Son. Can I fay, a
perfon is my friend, till I am reconciled to
him? and therefore the gofpel only is the
miniftration of reconciliation. Paul faith, *We
befeech you as ambaffadors of Chrift, that you
would be reconciled unto God:* this is to be the
grand topic of our preaching; we are to befeech them, and God himfelf turns beggar to
his own creatures to be reconciled to him:
now this reconciliation is brought about by a
poor finner's being brought to Jefus Chrift;

and

and when once he fees his enmity and hatred
to God, feeling the mifery of departing from
him, and being confcious that he is obnoxious
to eternal wrath, flies to Jefus as to a place of
refuge, and expects only a reconciliation thro'
the blood of the Lamb; without this, neither
you nor I can fay, God is my God: *there is
no peace, faith my God, to the wicked.* The
minifters of Chrift muft take care they don't
preach an unknown God, and we muft take
care we don't pretend to live upon an unknown God, a God that is not appropriated
and brought home to our fouls by the efficacy
of the Spirit. But, my brethren, we cannot fay,
God is our God, unlefs we are in Jefus Chrift.
Can you fay, fuch a one is your father, unlefs
you can give proof of it? You may be baftards,
there are many baftards laid at Chrift's door.
Now, God cannot be my God, at leaft I cannot know him to be fo, unlefs he is pleafed to
fend into my heart the fpirit of adoption, and
to admit me to enjoy familiarity with Chrift.

My brethren, I told you the other night
that the grand controverfy God has with England is for the flight put on the Holy Ghoft. As
foon as a perfon begins to talk of the work of
the Holy Ghoft, they cry, you are a methodift:

as

as foon as you fpeak about the divine influences
of the Holy Ghoft, O! fay they, you are an
enthufiaft. May the Lord keep thefe methodiftical enthufiafts amongft us to the lateft
pofterity. Ignatius, fuppofed to have been one
of the children that Jefus took up in his arms,
in his firft Epiftle (pray read it) wrote foon
after St. John's death, and we value nothing fo
authentic as what was wrote in the three firft
centuries, bears a noble teftimony to this truth.
When I was performing my firft exercifes at
Oxford, I ufed to take delight to walk and
read it, and could not help noting and putting
down from time to time feveral remarkable
paffages. In the fuperfcription of all his
Epiftles, I remember, he ftiles himfelf *Theo-*
phoros, i. e. Bearer of God *, and believed
that thofe he wrote to, were fo too. Some
body went and told Trajan, that one Ignatius
was an enthufiaft, that he carried God about
him : being brought before the emperor, who,
though in other refpects a good prince, was
a cruel enemy to the Chriftians : but many a
good prince does bad things by the influence
of wicked counfellors, like our king Henry the
Vth, who was brought in to perfecute the poor
Lollards,

* Deum ferens, *infpired, divine, holy.*

Lollards, for affembling in St. Giles's fields to
hear the pure gofpel, by falfe accufation of
being rebels againft him. Before fuch a prince
was Ignatius brought; fays Trajan, who is this
that calls himfelf a *bearer of God?* fays Ignatius, I am he, for which he quotes this paffage, *I will dwell in them, and will walk in*
them, and they fhall be my fons and daughters,
fays the Lord almighty. The emperor was fo
enraged that, in order to cure him of his enthufiafm, he ordered him to be devoured by
lions; at which Ignatius laughed for joy: O!
fays he, am I going to be devoured? and when
his friends came about him, he almoft danced
for gladnefs; when they carried him to execution he fmiled, and turning about, faid, now I
begin to be a martyr of Jefus Chrift! I have
heard that the lions have leaped from the martyrs, but when they come to me, I will encourage them to fall on me with all their violence. God give you fuch enthufiafm in a
trying hour! This is to have God for our God:
he that believeth hath the witnefs in himfelf, as
it is written in this bleffed word of God, and
I hope it will be the laft book that I fhall
read. Farewel father, farewel mother, farewel
fun, moon, and ftars! was the language of one

of the Scotch martyrs in king Charles's time,
and it is amazing to me that even Mr. Hume
(I believe) a profeffed deift, in his Hiftory of
England mentions this as a grand exit, and
alfo that feraphic foul Mr. Hervey, now with
God, that the laft words of the martyr were,
Farewel thou precious Bible, thou bleffed book
of God. This is my rock, this is my foundation, it is now about thirty-five years fince I
have begun to read the Bible upon my pillow.
I love to read this book, but the book is nothing but an account of the promifes which it
contains, and almoft every word from the beginning to the end of it fpeaks of a fpiritual
difpenfation, and the Holy Ghoft, that unites
our fouls to God, and helps a believer to fay,
my Lord and my God! If you content yourfelves with that, the devil will let you talk of
doctrines enough : O you fhall turn from Armi-
nianifm to Calvinifm ; O you fhall be orthodox
enough, if you will be content to live without
Chrift's living in you. Now when you have
got the Spirit, then you may fay, God is mine.
O this is very fine, fay fome, every body pretends to the Spirit: and then you may go on
as a bifhop once told a nobleman, My Lord,
thefe methodifts, fay they, do all by the Spirit,

fo

fo if the devil bids them murder any body, they will fay, the Spirit bid them do it; and that very bifhop died, how? why horrid! the laft words he fpoke were thefe, *The battle is fought, the battle is fought, the battle is fought, but the victory is loft for ever.* God grant, you and I may not die with fuch words as thefe. I hope you and I fhall die and fay, *The battle is fought, the battle is fought, the battle is fought, I have fought the good fight; and the victory is gained for ever.* Thus died Mr. Ralph Erfkine, his laft words were, Victory, victory, victory! and they that can call God their God, fhall by and by cry, Victory, victory! and that for ever. God grant, we may all be of that happy number.

If we can call God our God, we fhall endeavour by the Holy Ghoft to be like God, we fhall have his divine image ftamped upon our fouls, and endeavour to be followers of that God who is our Father: and this brings in the other part of the text, *thy God, thy Glory.* What is that? The greateft honor that a poor believer thinks he can have on earth, is to boaft that God is his God. When it was propofed to David, that if he killed an hundred Philiftines, he fhould have the king's daughter for his

wife,

wife, and a very forry wife fhe was, no great
gain turned out to him : fays he, *do you think
it is a fmall thing to be the fon-in-law to a
king?* a poor ftrippling as I am here come
with my fhepherd's crook, what ! to be married to a king's daughter, do you think that is a
fmall thing ? and if David thought it no fmall
thing to be allied to a king by his daughter,
what a great thing muft it be to be allied to
the Lord by one Spirit ? I am afraid there are
fome people that were once poor that are
now rich, that think it a great thing, that wifh,
O that my family had a coat of arms ; fome
people would give a thoufand pounds, I believe,
for one. Coats of arms are very proper to make
diftinction in life, a great many people wear
coats of arms that their anceftors got honourably, but they are a difgrace to them as they
wear them on their coaches. But this is our
glory, whether we walk or ride, whatever our
pedigree may be in life, this is our honor that
our God may be our glory. *O what manner
of love is this,* faith one, *that the Lord doth
beftow on us, that we fhould be called the fons of
God!* born not of the will of man, born not
of flefh, but born from above. O God grant
that this may be your glory and mine !

My

My brethren, if God is our God and our glory, I'll tell you what we fhall prove it by: whether we eat or drink, or whatever we do, we fhould do all to the glory of God. Religion, as I have often told you, turns our whole life into one continued facrifice of love to God. As a needle, when once touched by a loadftone, turns to a particular pole, fo the heart that is touched by the love of God, turns to his God again. I fhall have occafion to take notice of it by and by, when I am aboard a fhip: for as foon as I get on board, I generally place myfelf in one particular place under the compafs that hangs over my head, I often look at it by night and by day; when I rife the needle turns to one point, when I go to bed I find it turns to the fame point; and often, while I have been looking at it, my heart has been turned to God, faying, Lord Jefu, as that needle touched by the loadftone, turns to one point, O may my heart touched by the magnet of God's love, turn to him! A great many people think, they never worfhip God but when at church; and a great many are very demure on Lord's days, though many begin to leave that off. I know of no place upon the face of the earth where the Sabbath is kept

as

as it is at Bofton: if a fingle perfon was to
walk in Bofton ftreets in time of worfhip, he
would be taken up ; it is not trufted to poor
infignificant men, but the juftices go out in
time of worfhip, they walk with a white wand,
and if they catch any perfon walking in the
ftreets, they put them under a black rod. O !
the great mifchiefs the poor pious people have
fuffered lately thro' the town's being difturbed
by the foldiers ! When the drums were
beating before the houfe of Dr. Sawell, one of
the holieft men that ever was, when he was fick
and dying, on the fabbath day, by his meeting,
where the noife of a fingle perfon was never
heard before, and he begged that for Chrift's
fake they would not beat the drum ; they
damned and faid, that they would beat to
make him worfe: this is not acting for the
glory of God ; but when a foul is turned to
God, every day is a fabbath, every meal is a
fpiritual refrefhment, and every fentence he
fpeaks, fhould be a fermon ; and whether he
ftays abroad or at home, whether he is on the
exchange, or locked up in a clofet, he can fay,
O God, thou art my God !

Now, my dear friends, can you, dare you
fay, that your God is your glory, and do you
aim

aim at glorifying the Lord your God : if your God is your glory, then fay, *O God forbid that I fhould glory fave in the crofs of our Lord Je-fus Chrift, by whom the world is crucified to me, and 1 am crucified to the world.* What fay you to that now? don't talk of God's be-ing your glory, if you don't love his crofs. If God is our glory, we fhall glory not only in doing, but in fuffering for him; we fhall glory in tribulation, and count ourfelves moft highly honoured when we are called to fuffer moft for his great name fake. I might enlarge, but you may eafily judge by my poor feeble voice this laft week, that neither my ftrength of voice, or body, will permit me to be long to-night, and yet I will venture to give you your laft parting falutation; and though I have been diffuaded from getting up to preach this night, yet I thought as my God was my glo-ry, I fhould glory in preaching till I died. O that God may be all our glory! All our own glory fades away, there is nothing will be valuable at the great day but this, Thou art my God, and thou art my glory. It was a glo-rious turn that good Mr. Shepherd of Bradford mentions in one of his fermons, where he repre-fents Jefus Chrift as coming to judgment feated

upon

upon his throne, in a fermon preached before
fome minifters.   Chrift calls one minifter to
him, Pray what brought you into the church ?
O, fays he, Lord, there was a living in the
family, and I was prefented to it becaufe it was
a family living : ftand thou by, fays Chrift.   A
fecond comes, What didft thou enter into the
church for ?   O Lord, fays he, I had a fine
elocution, I had pretty parts, and I went into
the church to fhew my oratory and my parts :
ftand thou by, thou haft thy reward.   A third
was called, And what brought you into the
church ?   Lord, fays he, thou knoweft all things,
thou knoweft that I am a poor creature, vile
and miferable, and unworthy, and helplefs, but
I appeal to thee my glory, thou fitteft upon
the throne, that thy glory and the good of
fouls brought me there : Chrift immediately
fays, Make room, men, make room, angels,
and bring up that foul to fit near me on my
throne.   Thus fhall it be done to all that
make God their glory here below.   Glorify God
on earth, and he will glorify you in heaven.
*Come, ye bleffed of my Father, receive the king-
dom prepared for you from the foundation of
the world,* fhall be your portion : and if fo,
Lord God almighty make us content to be
                                                      vilified

vilified whilft here,   make us content to be
defpifed while below,   make us content to have
evil things fpoken of us,   all for Chrift's fake,
yet a little while, and Chrift will roll away the
ftone: and the more we are honoured by his
grace to fuffer,   the more we fhall be honoured
in the kingdom of heaven.   O that thought!
O that bleffed thought!   O that foul tranfport-
ing thought!   it is enough to make us leap into
a fiery furnace;   in this fpirit, in this temper,
may God put every one of us.

If there be any of you that have not yet
called God your God, may God help you to
do fo to-night.   When I was reafoning within
myfelf, whether I fhould come up, or whether
it was my duty or not?   I could not help
thinking, who knows but God will blefs a
poor feeble worm to-night.   I remember, a
dear friend fent me word after I was gone to
Georgia, " Your laft fermon at the Tabernacle
" was bleffed to a particular perfon;" I heard
from that perfon to-day: and who knows but
fome may come to-day, and fay, I will go
and hear what the babler has to fay?   who
knows but curiofity may be over-ruled for
good?   who knows but thofe that have ferved
the luft of the flefh and the pride of life for

their

their god, may now take the Lord to be their
God? O! if I could but fee this, I think I
could drop down dead for you.

My dear Chriftians, will you not help me
to-night, you that can go and call God your
God? go and beg of God for me, pray to
heaven for me, do pray for thofe that are in
the gall of bitternefs, that have no God, no
Chrift to go to, and if they were to die to-
night, would be damned for ever. O poor
finner, where is your glory then? where is
your purple and fine linnen then? your purple
robes will be turned into purple fire, and inftead of calling God your God, will be damn'd
with the devil : O think of your danger! *O*
earth, earth, earth, hear the word of the Lord !
If you never was awakened before, may the
arrows of God, fteep'd in the blood of Jefus
Chrift, reach your hearts now! Think how
you live at enmity with God, think of your
danger every day and every hour, your danger
of dropping into hell; think how your friends
in glory will leave you, and may this confideration, under the influences of the Holy Ghoft,
excite you to chufe God for your God! Tho'
the fun is going down, tho' the fhadow of the
evening is coming on, God is willing, O man,
God

God is willing, O woman, to be a finner's God, he has found out a way whereby he can be reconciled to you. I remember, when I faw a nobleman condemned to be hanged, the Lord High Steward told him, that however he was obliged to pafs fentence on him, and did not know that juftice would be fatisfied but by the execution of the law in this world, yet there might be a way whereby juftice might be fatisfied and mercy take place in another: when I heard his Lordfhip fpeak, I wifhed that he had not only faid, there might be a way, but that he had found out the way wherein God could be juft, and yet a poor murderer coming to Jefus Chrift fhould be pardoned.

You that can call God yours, God help you from this moment to glorify him more and more: and if God be your God and your glory, I am perfuaded, if the love of God abounds in your hearts, you will be willing on every occafion to do every thing to promote his honor and glory, and therefore you will be willing at all times to affift and help as far as lies in your power to keep up places of worfhip, to promote his glory in the falvation and converfion of finners; and I mention this becaufe there is to be a collection this night; I would

E e e   have

have chofe, if poffible, to have evaded this point, but as this Tabernacle has been repaired, and as the expence is pretty large, and as I would chufe to leave every thing unincumbered, I told my friends, 1 would undertake to make a collection, that every thing might be left quite clear: remember, it is not for me, but for yourfelves, I told you on Wednefday how matters were; I am now going a thirteenth time over the water on my own expence, and you fhall know at the great day what little, very little affiftance I have had from thofe who owed, under God, their fouls to my being here: but this is for the place where you are to meet, and where I hope God will meet you, when I am toffing on the water, when I am in a foreign clime. I think I can fay thy glory, O God, calls me away, and as I am going towards fixty years of age, I fhall make what difpatch I can, and I hope, if I am fpared to come back, that I fhall hear that fome of you are gone to heaven, or are nearer heaven than you were. I find there is near 70l. arrears; I hope you will not run away, if you can fay God is my glory, you will not pufh one upon another, as though you would loofe yourfelves in the croud, and fay no body fees

me;

me; but does not God Almighty fee you? I hope you will be ready to communicate, and when I am gone that God will be with you; as many of you will not hear me on Wednefday morning. O may this be your prayer, O for Jefus Chrift's fake, in whofe name I preach, in whofe ftrength I defire to come up, and for whofe honor I defire to be fpent, O do put up a word for me, it will not coft you much time, it will not keep you a moment from your bufinefs; O Lord Jefus Chrift thou art his God! and, Lord Jefus Chrift let him be thy glory! If I die in the waters, I fhall go by water to heaven; if I land at the Orphan Houfe, I hope it will be a means to fettle a foundation for ten thoufand perfons to be inftructed; and if I go by the continent, as I intend to do, I hope God will enable me to preach Chrift; and if I return again, my life will be devoted to your fervice. You muft excufe me, I cannot fay much more, affection works; and I could heartily wifh, and I beg it as a favour, when I come to leave you, that you will excufe me from a particular parting with you; take my public farewell; I will pray for you when in the cabin, I will pray for you when ftorms and tempefts are about

me;

me ; and this fhall be my prayer for the dear
people of the Tabernale, for the dear people
of the Chapel, for the dear people of London,
O God, be thou their God! and grant, that
their God may be their glory. Even fo, Lord
Jefus! Amen.

SERMON

SERMON XVII.

Jacob's Ladder.

A FAREWEL SERMON.

GENESIS xxviii. ver. 12, &c.

And he dreamed, and behold, a ladder set upon the earth, and the top of it reached to heaven: and behold, the angels of God ascending and descending on it. And behold, the Lord stood above it, and said, I am the Lord God of Abraham thy father, and the God of Isaac: the land whereon thou liest, to thee will I give it, and to thy seed. And thy seed shall be as the dust of the earth; and thou shalt spread abroad to the west, and to the east, and to the north, and to the south: and in thee, and in thy seed shall all the families of the earth be blessed. And behold, I am with thee, and will keep thee in all places, whither thou goest, and will bring thee again into this land:

land: for I will not leave thee, until I have done that which I have spoken to thee of.

THE wife man obferves, that *in the multitude of dreams there is many vanities*, being often the effects of a peculiar diforder of body, or owing to fome difturbance of the mind. They whofe nervous fyftem has been long relaxed, who have had fevere domeftic trials, or have been greatly affected by extraordinary occurrences, know this to be true by their own experience; but however this may be, there have been, and poffibly may be ftill, dreams that have no manner of dependance on the indifpofition of the body, or other natural caufe, but feem to bring a divine fanction with them, and make peculiar impreffions on the party, though this was more frequent before the canon of fcripture was clofed, than now. God fpoke to his people in a dream, in a vifion of the night; witnefs, the fubject of our prefent meditation, a dream of the patriarch Jacob's, when going forth as a poor pilgrim with a ftaff in his hand, from his father's houfe, deprived of his mother's company and inftruction, perfecuted by an elder brother, without attendants or ne-

ceffaries,

ceffaries, only leaning on an invifible power.
I need not inform you in how extraordinary
a way he got the bleffing, which provoked
his brother to fuch a degree, as determined
him to be the death of Jacob, as foon as ever
his aged father dropp'd : to what a height did
this wicked man's envy rife when he faid, *the*
days of mourning for my father will foon come,
and what then ? why, though I have fome
compaffion for the old man, and therefore
will not lay violent hands upon my brother
while my father is alive, yet I am refolved to
kill him before my father is cold in his grave.
This is the very fpirit of Cain, who talked to
his brother, and then flew him : this coming
to the ears of his mother, fhe tells the good
old patriarch her hufband, who loving peace
and quietnefs, takes the good advice of the
weaker veffel, and orders Jacob to go to his
mother's brother, Laban, and ftay a little while
out of Efau's fight, (perhaps out of fight out
of mind) and by and by probably, faid he,
thou mayft come to thy father and mother
again in peace and fafety. Jacob, though
fure of the bleffing in the end, by his father's
confirmation of it, yet prudently makes ufe
of proper means ; therefore he obeyed his
parents :

parents: and wo, wo be to thofe who think a parent's blefsing not worth their afking for ! Having had his mother's blefsing, as well as his father's, without faying, I will try it out with my brother, I will let him know that I am not afraid of him, he views it as the call of God, and like an honeft, fimple pilgrim, went out from Beerfheba towards Haran, Was it not a little unkind in his parents not to furnifh him with fome necefsaries and conveniencies ? When the fervant was fent to fetch a wife for Ifaac, he had a great deal of attendance, why fhould not Jacob have it now; his father might have fent him away with great parade; but I am apt to believe this did not fuit Jacob's real, pilgrim fpirit; he was a plain man, and dwelt in tents, when, perhaps, he might have dwelt under cedar roofs; he chofe a pilgrim's life, and prudence directed him to go thus in a private manner, to prevent increafing Efau's envy, and giving the fatal blow.

Methinks, I fee the young pilgrim weeping when he took his leave of his father and mother; he went on foot, and they that are acquainted with the geography of the place, fay, that the firft day of his journey he walked

not

not lefs than forty Englifh miles; what exercife muft he have had all that way! no wonder, therefore, that by the time the fun was
going down, poor Jacob felt himfelf very
weary, for we are told, ver. 11, *that he lighted
on a certain place, and tarried there all night,
becaufe the fun was fet.* There is a particular
emphafis to be put upon this term, *a certain
place*; he faw the fun going down, he was
a ftranger in a ftrange land. (You that are born
in England can have very little idea of it, but
perfons that travel in the American woods can
form a more proper idea, for you may there
travel a hundred and a thoufand miles, and
go through one continued tract of tall green
trees, like the tall cedars of Lebanon; and
the gentlemen of America, from one end to
the other, are of fuch an hofpitable temper,
as I have not only been told, but have found
among them upwards of thirty years, that they
would not let public houfes be licenfed, that
they may have an opportunity of entertaining
Englifh friends : may God, of his infinite
mercy, grant this union may never be diffol-
ved.)

Well, Jacob got to a certain place, and
perhaps he faw a good tree that would ferve
F f f him

him for a canopy; however, this we are told,
he tarried there all night becaufe the fun was
fet, and he took of the ftones of that place
and put them for his pillow, and laid down in
that place to fleep; hard lodgings for him who
was ufed to lie otherwife at home: I don't
hear him fay, I wifh I was got back to my
mother again, I wifh I had not fet out; but
upon the hard ground and hard pillow he lies
down; I believe never poor man flept fweeter
in his life, for it is certainly fweet fleep when
God is near us; he did not know but his
brother might follow and kill him while he was
afleep, or that the wild beafts might devour
him; (in America, when they fleep in the
woods, and I expect to have fome fuch fleeping times in them before a twelvemonth is
over, we are obliged to make a fire to keep the
beafts from us: I have often faid then, and I
hope I fhall never forget it, when I rife in the
morning, this fire in the woods that keeps the
wild beafts from hurting us, is like the fire of
God's love that keeps the devil from hurting
us:) thus weary and folitary he falls afleep,
and fweetly dreams, *and behold*; I don't remember many paffages of fcripture where the word,
behold, is repeated fo many times in fo fhort
a fpace

a fpace as in the paffage before us, doubtlefs, the Lord would have us particularly take notice of it, even us upon whom the ends of the world are come: Behold, *a ladder fet upon the earth, and the top reached to heaven; and* behold, *the angels of God afcending and defcending upon it; and* behold, *the Lord flood above it;* fo here are three *beholds* in a very few lines.   Was there any thing very extraordinary in that? perhaps the Deifts would fay, your patriarch was tired, and dreamed among other things of a ladder; yes, he did, but this dream was of God, and how kind was he to meet him at the end of the firft day's journey, to ftrengthen and animate him to go forward in this lonefome pilgrimage !

This ladder is reckoned by fome to denote the providence of God: it was let down as it were from heaven, particularly at this time to poor Jacob, that he might know that however he was become a pilgrim, and left his all, all for God's glory, that God would take care for his comfort, and give his angels charge over him to keep him in all his ways, which was denoted by the angels afcending and defcending upon the ladder.   Some think that particular faints and countries have particular guardian

F f f 2   angels,

angels, and therefore that the angels that afcended were thofe that had the particular charge of that place, fo far as Jacob had come; that the angels that defcended were another fet of angels, fent down from heaven to guard him in his future journey; perhaps, this is more a fancy than the word of God. However, I very much like the obfervation of good Mr. Burket, " Why fhould we difpute whether " every individual believer has got a particu- " lar angel, when there is not one believer " but has got guards of angels to attend him," which are a great deal better than a great many fervants, that prove our plagues, and inftead of waiting upon us make us wait upon them.

But, my dear hearers, I don't know one fpiritual commentator, but agrees that this ladder was a type of the Lord Jefus Chrift; and that as Jacob was now banifhed from his father's houfe, and while fleeping upon a hard, cold ftone, God was pleafed not only to give him an affurance that he would be with him in the way, but gave him a bleffed fight of Jefus Chrift, in whom Jacob believed.

A ladder you know is fomething by which we climb from one place to another; hence,

in

in condefcenfion to our weak capacities, God
ordered a ladder to be let down, to fhew us
that Chrift is the way to heaven: *I am the*
way, the truth, and the life; *I am the door*,
fays he; neither is there falvation in any other,
for there is no other name given under heaven
whereby we muft be faved. The Deifts,
who own a God but deny his Son, dare go
to a God out of Chrift; but Jacob is here
taught better: how foon does God reveal the
gofpel unto him; here is a ladder, by which
God preaches to us; if you have a mind to
climb from earth to heaven, you muft get up
by the Son of God; no one ever pointed out
a proper way to heaven for us but himfelf.
When Adam and Eve fell from God, a flaming
fword turned every way to keep them from
the tree of life; but Jefus alone is a new and
living way, not only to the Holy of Holies
below, but into the immediate prefence of
God; and that we might know that he was
a proper Saviour, the top of it reached to
heaven; if it had ftopped fhort Jacob might
have faid, ah! the ladder is within a little way
of heaven, but does not quite reach it; if I
climb up to the top I fhall not get there after
all; but the top reached to heaven, to point
out

out the divinity and exaltation of the Son of God; such a Saviour became us who was God, God over all, blessed for evermore: and therefore the Arian scheme is most uncomfortable and destructive; to talk of Christ as a Saviour that is not God, is no Christ at all. I would turn Deist to-morrow if I did not know that Christ was God; *but curfed is the man that builds his faith upon an arm of flesh.* If Christ is God, the Arians and Socinians, by their own principles, are undone for ever; but Jesus Christ is very God and very man, begotten (and not made) of the Father: God, of his infinite mercy, write his divinity deep in our hearts!

The bottom of the ladder reached to the earth; this points out to us the humiliation of the blessed Lord; for us men he came down from heaven; we pray to and for a descending God. All the sufferings which our Lord voluntarily expofed himself to, were that he might become a ladder for you and I to climb up to heaven by. Come down from the crofs, fay they, and we will believe thee; if he had, what would have become of us? did they believe on him when he was dead, buried, and rifen again? no. Some people fay,

if

if Chrift was here, O dear we fhould love him; juft as much as they did when they turned him out of doors, when he came down before. If he had come down from the crofs, they would have hung him up again : O that you and I might make his crofs a ftep to glory !

As the top of the ladder pointed out his ex-altation, the bottom his humiliation, the two fides of the ladder being joined together, point out the union of the Deity and manhood in the perfon of Chrift; and that as this ladder had fteps to it, fo, blefled be God, Jefus Chrift has found out a way whereby we may go, ftep after ftep, to glory. The firft ftep is the righteoufnefs of Chrift, the active and paffive obedience of the Redeemer; no fetting one foot upon this ladder without coming out of ourfelves, and relying wholly upon a better righteoufnefs than our own. Again, all the other fteps are the graces of the blefled Spirit; therefore, you need not be afraid of our de-ftroying inward holinefs, by preaching the doctrine of the imputation of Chrift's righte-oufnefs, that one is the foundation, the other the fuperftructure; to talk of my having the righteoufnefs of Chrift imputed to my foul,

without

without my having the holiness of Chrift imparted to it, and bringing forth the fruits of
the Spirit as an evidence of it, is only deceiving
ourfelves. I would never preach upon imputed righteoufnefs, without fpeaking of inward holinefs, for if you don't take a great deal
of care, you will unawares, under a pretence
of exalting Chrift, run into Antinomianifm,
depths that Calvin never went into ; probably,
you will imbitter others fpirits that don't agree
with you, and at the fame time hurt the
fruits of the Spirit: may God give you clear
heads, and at the fame time warm hearts.

On the ladder Jacob faw the angels of God
afcending and defcending ; what is that for ?
to fhow that they are miniftring fpirits, fent
forth to minifter to them that fhall be heirs of
falvation ; therefore we find them attending
upon Chrift. We do not hear much of them
after the canon of fcripture was clofed, but as
foon as ever Chrift was born, the angels fang,
till then we never hear of their finging below,
as far as I can judge, fince the creation ; then
the fons of God fhouted for joy ; but when
Eve reached out her hand to pluck the fatal
apple, and gave to Adam, earth groaned, and
the angels hung, as it were, their harps upon
the

the willows; but when Chrift, the fecond Adam, was born, the angels fang at midnight, *Glory to God in the higheft.* I pray to God we may all die finging that anthem, and fing it to all eternity. After his temptations, they came and miniftred to him, as fome think, food for his body, and wifhed him joy and comfort in his foul; and in his agonies in the garden, an angel ftrengthned him. After his refurrection two appeared again, one at the head and another at the foot of his fepulchre, to let thofe that looked into the fepulchre know, that they would not only wait upon the head but the foot; and the angels are glad to wait upon the meaneft of the children of God. When our Lord departed, a cloud received him out of their fight, which probably was a cloud of angels: having led his difciples out of the city, he bleffed them, and then away he went to heaven: may that bleffing reft upon you and your children! This intimates that God makes ufe of angels to attend his people, efpecially when they are departing into eternity: perhaps, part of our entertainment in heaven will be, to hear the angels declare how many millions of times they have affifted and helped us. Our Lord fays, an-

gels

gels do there behold the face of the Father of
his little ones; and therefore I love to talk
to the lambs of the flock, and why should I
not talk to them whom angels think it their
honour to guard; and if it was not for this,
how would any children escape the dangers
they are expofed to in their tender age? it is
owing to the particular providence of God,
that any one child is brought to manhood;
therefore I can't help admiring that part of the
Litany, in which we pray, that God would
take care not only of the grown people, but of
children alfo: God take care of yours both in
body and foul.

But what gave the greateſt comfort to Jacob was, that the Lord was on the top of
the ladder, which I do not know whether it
would have been fo, if Jacob had not feen
God there. It comforts me, I aſſure you, to
think, that whenever God ſhall call for me, I
ſhall be carried by angels into Abraham's bofom; and I have often thought that whenever
that time comes, that bleſſed, long longed-for
moment comes, as foon as ever they have
called upon me, my firſt queſtion will be to
them, where is my dear maſter? where is
Jefus? where is that dear Emanuel, who has
                                          loved

loved me with an everlafting love, and has
called me by his grace, and have fent you to
fetch me home to fee his face? But I believe
you and I fhall have no occafion to afk where
he is, for he will come to meet us, he will
ftand at the top of his ladder to take his pil-
grims in; fo God was at the top of the ladder,
pray mind that. He appears not fitting, as
he is often reprefented in heaven, but ftanding;
as much as to fay, here, here, Jacob, thy brother wants to kill thee; here thou art come
out without a fervant, art lying upon a hard
bed, but here I am ready in order to preferve
thee; I ftand above, and I fee thy wearinefs,
I fee the fatigue and hardfhips thou haft yet
to undergo, though thou doft not fee it thyfelf; thou haft thrown thyfelf upon my providence and protection, and I will give thee
the word of a God that I will ftand by thee;
the Lord ftood above; if he had faid nothing,
that would have been enough to have fhewn
his readinefs to help.

But God fpeaks, *behold :* well might this
be ufhered in with the word *behold*; a ladder
fet on the earth, and *behold* the angels of God
afcending and defcending on it; and, above
all, *behold* God fpeaking from it! what doth

he fay? *I am the Lord God of Abraham thy
father.*   Oh! happy they that can fay, the
Lord God of my father ; happy you that have
got fathers and mothers in heaven.   I remember, about twenty-five years ago as I was travelling from Briftol, I met with a man on the
road, and being defirous to know whether he
was ferious or not, I began to put in a word
for Chrift, (and God forbid I fhould travel
with any body a quarter of an hour without
fpeaking of Chrift to them) he told me what
a wicked creature he had been ; but, fir, fays
he, in the midft of my wickednefs people
ufed to tell me, you have got a good many
prayers upon the file for you, your godly father and mother have prayed very often for
you; and it was the pleafure of God he was
wrought upon, and brought to Chrift.   Lay
in a good ftock for your children, get a good
many prayers in for them, they may be anfwered when you are dead and gone.   *I am
the God of Abraham thy father,* not thy grand-
father; to put him in mind what an honour
God would put upon him, to make him as it
were the father of the church.   Though you
have many inftructors, fays Paul, you have
but one Father : *and the God of Ifaac, the land*
                                        whereon

whereon thou lieſt, to thee will I give it, and to thy ſeed. Amazing! amazing! you know very well when perſons buy or come to an eſtate, they uſually take poſſeſſion of it by ſome ceremony, ſuch as receiving or taking up a piece of dirt, or twig, in their hand, as a ſign of their title. Now, ſays God, poor Jacob, thou doſt little think that this very ſpot of ground that thou lieſt on to-night, cold and ſtiff, I intend to give to thee, and thy poſterity, for an inheritance. O my brethren, live all to God, and God will give all to you : who would have thought of this, probably Jacob did not: it is as if God took a pleaſure in ſeeing his dear children lie on ſuch hard ground ; if he had been on a feather-bed, he might not have had ſuch a viſit : thou ſhalt have now a God to lean upon, *to thee will I give it, and to thy ſeed, which ſhall be as the duſt of the earth, and thou ſhalt ſpread abroad to the weſt, and to the eaſt, and to the north, and to the ſouth ; and in thee, and in thy ſeed, ſhall all the families of the earth be bleſſed.* Thus did heaven balance the loſs of the comforts of his father's houſe, by the diſcovery of his and his offspring's proſperity, by an intereſt in the promiſed ſeed.

My

My particular circumftances call me to obferve, and I believe God has done it on purpofe to encourage me, that faith, refting on
the promife, is eafily refigned to the lofs of
prefent good, whereas worldly hearts confider
profperity as a portion, they don't care if the
devil takes them hereafter, fo they have it
now; and that makes carnal people wonder
how we can give up things in this world, for
the fake of thofe not yet born; but it is to
glorify God, and lay a foundation for others
happinefs. Here God gives Jacob to know,
that hereafter his feed fhould fpread on the
eaft, weft, north, and fouth, his branches
fhould multiply, and at laft from his loins
fhould Jefus Chrift come; what for? *in whom
all the families of the earth fhould be bleffed:*
God Almighty grant we may be bleffed in
him.

Then if Jacob fhould fay in his heart, haft
thou no promife for me? here is another
behold comes in; *Behold, I am with thee, and
will keep thee in all places whither thou goeft.*
What a word is this! thou haft nobody with
thee, nothing but a ftaff, (he could not carry
much upon his back, like a poor foldier with
a napfack behind, and a little bread in his
pocket)

pocket) well, faith God, I do not defpife
thee becaufe thou art deftitute, but I love
thee the better for it; thy brother Efau longs
to kill thee, but if Efau ftabs thee he fhall ftab
thy God firft; I will not only be with thee
now, but I will watch every ftep thou takeft,
*I will be with thee in all places whither thou
goeft:* as much as to fay, Jacob, thou art a
pilgrim, thy life is to be a moving life, I
don't intend thou fhalt fettle and keep in one
place; thy life is to be a life of changes, thou
art to move from place to place, but *I will
be with thee in all places whither thou goeft,*
and thereby it fhall be known that I am Jacob's God, and alfo by my bringing thee again
into this land. He not only affures him of a
fuccefsful journey, whither he was now going, but promifes to bring him back once
more to fee his dear father and mother, and
relations again; *I will bring thee back to this
land*; and to confirm his faith and hope, the
great God adds, *I will not leave thee till I have
done that I have fpoken to thee of*; that is, all
the good he had juft now promifed. Some
people promife, but they cannot do it to-day,
and they will not do it to-morrow. I have
known the world, and have rung the changes
of

of it ever fince I have been here ; but, bleffed be God, an unchangeable Chrift having loved his own, he loved them to the end; *I will not leave you till I have performed all things I have promifed you:* may this promife come upon you and your children, and all that God fhall call.

Thus fpake the great Jehovah to poor Jacob, juft fetting out to a ftrange land, knowing not whither he went; but now God fpeaks not only to Jacob, but he fpeaks to you ; and, bleffed be the living God, he fpeaks to me alfo, lefs than the leaft of all ; and as my defign is (though I cannot tell but this may be the laft opportunity) to fpeak fomething to you about my departure; yet, brethren, my grand defign in preaching to you is, to recommend the Lord Jefus Chrift to your fouls; and, before I go, to make a particular, perfonal application. Give me leave, therefore, to afk you, it may be the laft time I may afk many of you, whether you have ever fet your foot upon this bleffed ladder, the Son of God ? I afk you in the name of the Lord Jefus Chrift, in the name of the Father, Son, and Holy Ghoft, did you ever fet your foot, I fay, upon this ladder? that is, did you ever

yet

yet believe on Jefus Chrift, and come to him
as poor loft finners, relying upon no other
righteoufnefs than that of the Son of God?
perhaps, if you was to fpeak, fome of you
would fay, away with your ladder; and what
will you do then? why, fay you, I will climb
to heaven without it; what ladder will you
climb upon? O, I think to go to heaven becaufe I have been baptized, that ladder will
break under you; what, a ladder made of
water, what are you dreaming of? no; O, I
think I fhall go to heaven becaufe I have done
nobody any harm; what, a ladder made of
negative goodnefs, no; I think to go, you'll
fay, by good works; a ladder made of good
works, that has not Chrift for its bottom,
what is that? I think, fay you, to go to heaven by my prayers and faftings; all thefe are
good in their place: but, my brethren, don't
think to climb to heaven by thefe ropes of
fand. If you never before fet your foot on
Chrift, this bleffed ladder, God grant this may
be the happy time.

I have been praying before moft of you
were up I believe, that God would give me a
parting bleffing. I remember, foon after I
left England laft, that a dear Chriftian friend

told me, that there was one woman, who came only out of curiosity, that dated her conversion from hearing my last sermon; and, I bless God, I never once left England, but some poor soul has dated their conversion from my last sermon. When I put on my surplice, to come out to read the second service, I thought it was just like a person's being decently dressed to go out to be executed; I would rather, was it the will of God, it should be so, than to feel what I do in parting from you, then death would put an end to all; but I am to be executed again and again, and nothing will support me under the torture, but the consideration of God's blessing me to some poor souls. Do pray for me, ye children of God, that God would give us a parting blessing. God help you, young people, to put your foot on this ladder; don't climb wrong: the devil has got a ladder, but it reaches down to hell; all the devil's children go down, not up; the bottom of the devil's ladder reaches to the depths of the damned, the top of it reaches to the earth; and when death comes, then up comes the devil's ladder to let you down; for God's sake come away from the devil's ladder; climb, climb, dear young men.

O it

O it delighted me on Friday night at the Tabernacle, when we had a melting parting facrament; and it delighted me this morning to fee fo many young men at the table; God add to the bleffed number! Young women, put your feet upon this ladder; God lets one ladder down from heaven, and the devil brings another up from hell. O, fay you, I would climb up God's ladder, I think it is right, but I fhall be laughed at; do you think to go to heaven without being laughed at? the Lord Jefus Chrift help you to climb to heaven; come, climb till you get out of the hearing of their laughter. O truft not to your own righteoufnefs, your vows, and good refolutions.

Some of you, bleffed be God, have climbed up this ladder, at leaft are climbing; well, I wifh you joy, God be praifed for fetting your feet on this ladder, God be praifed for letting down this ladder: I have only one word to fay to you, for Jefus Chrift's fake, and your own too, climb a little fafter; take care the world does not get hold of your heels. It is a fhame the children of God don't climb fafter; you may talk what you pleafe, but God's people's lukewarmnefs is more provoking to him than all the fins of the nation. We cry

H h h 2   out

out againſt the ſins of the land, would to God
we did cry out more of the ſins of the ſaints;
*I will ſpue you out of my mouth, becauſe you
are lukewarm,* ſays Chriſt; and if any of you
ſay you cannot climb becauſe you are lame-
footed, look to Jeſus Chriſt, my dear friends,
and your affliction ſhall make you climb;
and if any of you are coming down the ladder
again, the Lord Jeſus Chriſt bleſs the fooliſh-
neſs of preaching to help you up again. O,
ſay you, I am giddy, I ſhall fall; here, I will
give you a rope, be ſure lay hold of it; juſt
as the ſailors do when you go aboard a ſhip,
they let down a rope, ſo God lets down a
promiſe: climb, climb, then, till you have
got higher into a better climate, and God ſhall
put his hand out by and by when you get to
the top of the ladder to receive you to himſelf.
Bleſſed be the living God, I hope and believe
I ſhall meet many of you by and by.

· And now, my brethren, it is time for me
to preach my own funeral ſermon; and I
would humbly hope that, as a poor ſinner, I
may put in my claim for what God promiſed
Jacob; and I do put in, with full aſſurance
of faith that God will be with me. I am now
going, for the thirteenth time, to croſs the

1769

Atlantic :

Atlantic: when I came from America laft, I took my leave of all the Continent, from the one end of the provinces to the other, except fome places which we had not then taken; I took my leave for life, without the leaft defign of returning there again, my health was fo bad ; and the profpect of getting the orphan-houfe into other hands made me fay when I firft came over, I have no other river to go over than the river Jordan. I thought then of retiring, for I did not chufe to appear when my nerves were fo relaxed that I could not ferve God as I could wifh to do ; but as it hath pleafed God to reftore my health much, and has fo ordered it by his providence, that I intend to give up the orphan-houfe, and all the land adjoining, for a public college. I wifhed to have had a public fanction, but his grace the late archbifhop of Canterbury put a ftop to it; they would give me a charter, which was all I defired, but they infifted upon, at leaft his grace and another did, that I fhould confine it totally to the Church of England, and that no extempore prayer fhould be ufed in a public way in that houfe, though Diffen-ters, and all forts of people, had contributed to it: I would fooner cut my head off than

betray

betray my truft, by confining it to a narrow
bottom; I always meant it fhould be kept upon
a broad bottom, for people of all denomina-
tions, that their children might be brought up
in the fear of God: by this means the orphan-
houfe reverted into my hands; I have once
more, as my health was reftored, determined
to purfue the plan I had fixed on; and, thro'
the tender mercies of God, Georgia, (which
about thirty-two years ago was a total defolate
place; and when the land, as it was given
me by the Houfe of Commons, would have
been totally deferted, and the colony have quite
ceafed, had it not been for the money I have
laid out for the orphan-houfe, to keep the poor
people together) that colony is rifing to a moft
amazing height, by the fchemes now going
on, public buildings are erecting. I had news
laft week of the great profperity of the negroes;
and I hope by the twenty-fifth of March,
which is the day, the anniverfary day, I laid
the firft brick, in the year 1739; I fay, I hope
by that time all things will be finifhed, and a
bleffed provifion will be made for orphans and
poor ftudents that will be brought up there; it
will be a bleff.d fource of provifion for the
children of God in another part of the world.
                                        This

This is the grand defign I am going upon ;
this is my vifible caufe ; but I never yet went
to them, but God has been pleafed to blefs
my miniftration among them ; and therefore
after I have finifhed the orphan-houfe affair, I
intend to go all along the Continent by land,
(which will keep me all the winter and
fpring) and when I come to the end of it,
which will be Canada and New-England, then
I hope to return again to this place; for, let
people fay what they will, I have not fo
much as a fingle thought of fettling abroad on
this fide eternity ; and I am going in no public capacity, I fhall fet out like a poor pilgrim,
at my own expence, trufting upon God to take
care of me, and to bear my charges ; and I
call God to witnefs, and I muft be a curfed
devil and hypocrite, to ftand here in the pulpit and provoke God to ftrike me dead for
lying, I never had the love of the world, nor
never felt it one quarter of an hour in my heart,
fince I was twenty years old. I might have
been rich : but though the Chapel is built, and
I have a comfortable room to lie in, I affure
you I built it at my own expence, it coft nobody but myfelf any thing. I have a watch-
coat made me, and in that I fhall lie every
night

night on the ground, and may Jacob's God
blefs me. I will not fay much of myfelf, but
when I have been preaching, I have read and
thought of thofe words with pleafure, *Surely
this is the houfe of God. And I will bring thee
again to this land.* Whether that will be my
experience or not, bleffed be God, I have a
better land in view; and, my dear brethren, I
do not look upon myfelf at home till I land in
my Father's kingdom; and if I am to die in
the way, if I am to die in the fhip, it comforts me that I know I am as clear as the fun,
that I go by the will of God; and though
people may fay, will you leave the world?
will you leave the Chapel? O, I am aftonifhed
that we cannot leave every thing for Chrift;
my greateft trial is, to part with thofe who are
as dear to me as my own foul; and however
others may forget me, as thoufands have, and
do forget me, yet I cannot forget them: and
now may Jacob's God be with you; O keep
clofe to God, my dear London friends; I do
not bid you keep clofe to Chapel, you have
done fo always: I fhall endeavour to keep up
the word of God among you in my abfence;
I fhall have the fame perfons that managed
for me when I was out laft, and they fent

me

me word again and again, by letter, that it
was remarkable, that the Tottenham-court
people were always prefent when ordinances
were there.

You fee I went upon a fair bottom; I
might have had a thoufand a year out of this
place if I had chofe it; when I am gone to
heaven you will fee what I have got on earth *;
I do not like to fpeak now, becaufe it may be
thought boafting; but I am fure there are
numbers of people here, if they knew what I
have, would love me as much as they now
hate me. When we come before the great
Judge of quick and dead, while I ftand before
him, God grant you may not part with me
then, it will be a dreadful parting then, it
will be worfe then to go into the fire, to be
among the devil and his angels; God forbid
it! God forbid it! God forbid it! O remember that my laft words were, come, come to
Chrift; the Lord help you to come to Chrift;
come to Chrift, come to Jacob's God; God
give you faith like Jacob's faith.

You that have been kind to me, that have
helped me when I was fick, fome of whom

I i i   are

---

* The greateft part of the fubftance this man of God left
behind him, which was not much, was bequeathed to him by
deceafed friends.

are here that have been very kind to me; may God reward you, my friends, and God forgive my enemies; God, of his infinite mercy, blefs you all; you will be amply provided for, I believe, here; may God fpread the gofpel every where; and may God never leave you, nor forfake you. Even fo, Lord Jefus. Amen and Amen.

SERMON

✧✧✧✧✧✧✧✧✧✧✧✧✧✧✧✧✧✧✧✧✧✧✧✧✧✧

S E R M O N   XVIII.

The Good Shepherd.

A F A R E W E L S E R M O N.

JOHN x. ver. 27, 28.

My sheep hear my voice, and I know them, and
they follow me.   And I give unto them eter-
nal life, and they shall never perish, neither
shall any pluck them out of my hand.

IT is a common, and, I believe, generally
speaking, my dear hearers, a true saying,
that bad manners beget good laws. Whether this will hold good in every particular, in
respect to the affairs of this world, I am persuaded the observation is very pertinent in respect to the things of another; I mean bad
manners, bad treatment, bad words, have been
over-ruled by the sovereign grace of God, to
produce and to be the cause of the best sermons that were ever delivered from the mouth
of the God-man, Christ Jesus.

One

One would have imagined, that as he came cloathed with divine efficience, as he came with divine credentials, as he fpake as never man fpake, that no one fhould have been able to have refifted the wifdom with which he fpake; one would imagine they fhould have been fo ftruck with the demonftration of the Spirit, that with one confent they fhould all own, that he was *that prophet that was to be raifed up like unto Mofes.* But you feldom find our Lord preaching a fermon, but fomething or other that he faid was cavilled at; nay, their enmity frequently broke through all good manners; they often, therefore, interrupted him whilft he was preaching, which fhows the enmity of their hearts long before God permitted it to be in their power to fhed his innocent blood. If we look no farther than this chapter, where he reprefents himfelf as a good fhepherd, one that laid down his life for his fheep; we fee the beft return he had, was to be looked upon as poffeffed or diftracted; for we are told that there was a divifion therefore again among the Jews for thefe fayings, and many of them faid, *he hath a devil and is mad, why hear ye him?* If the mafter of the houfe was ferved fo, pray what are the

fer-

fervants to expect? Others, a little more fober-
minded, faid, *thefe are not the words of him
that hath a devil*; the devil never ufed to
preach or act in this way. *Can a devil open
the eyes of the blind?* So he had fome friends
among thefe rabble. This did not difcourage
our Lord, he goes on in his work; and we
fhall never, never go on with the work of
God, till, like our mafter, we are willing to
go through good and through evil report; and
let the devil fee we are not fo complaifant as
to ftop one moment for his barking at us as
we go along.

We are told, that our Lord was at Jerufalem at the feaft of the dedication, and it was
winter; the feaft of dedication held, I think,
feven or eight days for the commemoration of
the reftoration of the Temple and Altar after
its profanation by Antiochus: now this was
certainly a mere human inftitution, and had
no divine image, had no divine fuperfcription
upon it; and yet I don't find that our bleffed
Lord and Mafter preached againft it; I don't
find that he fpent his time about this; his
heart was too big with fuperior things; and
I believe when we, like him, are filled with
the Holy Ghoft, we fhall not entertain our
audi-

audiences with difputes about rites and ceremonies, but fhall treat upon the effentials of
the gofpel, and then rites and ceremonies will
appear with more indifference. Our Lord does
not fay, that he would not go up to the feaft,
for, on the contrary, he did go there, not fo
much to keep the feaft, as to have an opportunity to fpread the gofpel-net, and that fhould
be our method not to follow difputing; and
it is the glory of the Methodifts, that we have
been now forty years, and, I thank God,
there has not been one fingle pamphlet wrote
by any of our preachers about the non-effen-
tials of religion.

Our Lord always made the beft of every
opportunity; and we are told, *he walked in
the temple in Solomon's porch.* One would
have thought the Scribes and Pharifees would
have put him in one of their ftalls, and have
complimented him with defiring him to preach,
no, they let him walk in Solomon's porch;
fome think he walked by himfelf, nobody
choofing to keep company with him. Methinks, I fee him walking and looking at the
temple, and forefeeing within himfelf how
foon it would be deftroyed; he walked pen-
five, to fee the dreadful calamities that would
come

come upon the land, for not knowing the day
of its vifitation; and it was to let the world
fee he was not afraid to appear in public: he
walked, as much as to fay, have any of you
any thing to fay to me? and he put himfelf
in their way, that if they had any thing to
afk him, he was ready to refolve them; and
to fhew them, that though they had treated
him fo ill, yet he was ready to preach falvation to them.

In the twenty-fourth verfe we are told,
*Then came the Jews round about him, and faid
unto him, how long doft thou make us to doubt?*
They came round about him when they faw
him walking in Solomon's porch; now, fay
they, we will have him, now we will attack
him. And now was fulfilled that paffage in
the Pfalms, *they compaffed me about like bees
to fting me,* or rather like wafps. Now, fay
they, we will get him in the middle of us,
and fee what fort of a man he is; we will fee
whether we can't conquer him; they came to
him and they fay, *how long doft thou make us
to doubt?* Now this feems a plaufible queftion,
how long doft thou make us to doubt? Pray how
long, fir, do you intend to keep us in fufpenfe? Some think the words will bear this

inter-

interpretation; pray, fir, how long do you intend thus to fteal away our hearts? they would reprefent him to be a defigning man, like Abfalom, to get the people on his fide, and then fet up himfelf for the Meffiah; thus carnal minds always interpret good mens actions. But the meaning feems to be this, they were doubting concerning Chrift; doubting Chriftians may think it is God's fault that they doubt, but God knows it is all their own. *How long doft thou make us to doubt?* I wifh you would fpeak a little plainer, fir, and not let us have any more of your parables; pray let us know who you are, let us have it from your own mouth; *if thou be the Chrift tell us plainly*; and I don't doubt but they put on a very fanctified face and looked very demure; *if thou be the Chrift tell us plainly,* intending to catch him: if he does not fay he is the Chrift, we will fay he is afhamed of his own caufe; if he does tell us plainly that he is the Chrift, then we will impeach him to the governor, we will go and tell the governor that this man fays he is the Meffiah; now we know of no Meffiah but what is to joftle Cæfar out of his throne. The devil always wants to make it believed that God's

feople,

people, who are the moſt loyal people in the world, are rebels to the government under which they live ; *if thou be the Chriſt tell us plainly.* "Our Lord does not let them wait long for an anſwer ; honeſty can ſoon ſpeak : *I told you and ye believed not : the works that I do in my Father's name, they bear witneſs of me.* Had our Lord ſaid, I am the Meſſiah, they would have taken him up ; he knew that, and therefore he joined *the wiſdom of the ſer-pent* with *the innocence of the dove* ; ſays he, I appeal to my works and doctrine, and if you will not infer from them that I am the Meſſiah, I have no further argument. *But,* he adds, *ye believe not, becauſe ye are not of my ſheep.* He complains twice ; for their un-belief was the greateſt grief of heart to Chriſt : then he goes on in the words of our text, *My ſheep hear my voice, and I know them, and they follow me. And I give unto them eternal life, and they ſhall never periſh, neither ſhall any pluck them out of my hand.* My ſheep hear my voice ; you think to puzzle me, you think to chagrin me with this kind of conduct, but you are miſtaken ; you don't believe on me, becauſe you are not of my ſheep. The great Mr. Stodart, of New-Eng-

land,

land, (and no place under heaven produces greater divines than New England) preached once from thefe words, *but ye believe not, becaufe ye are not of my. fheep*; a very ftrange text to preach upon to convince a congregation, yet God fo bleffed it, that two or three hundred fouls were awakened by that fermon : God grant fuch fuccefs to attend the labours of all his faithful minifters.

My fheep hear my voice, and they follow me. It is very remarkable, there are but two forts of people mentioned in fcripture; it does not fay the Baptifts and Independents, nor the Methodifts and Prefbyterians ; no, Jefus Chrift divides the whole world into but two claffes, fheep and goats: the Lord give us to fee this morning to which of thefe claffes we belong.

But it is obfervable, believers are always compared to fomething that is good and profitable, and unbelievers are always defcribed by fomething that is bad, and good for little or nothing.

If you afk me why Chrift's people are called fheep? as God fhall enable me, I will give you a fhort, and I hope it will be to you an anfwer of peace. Sheep, you know, generally love to be together; we fay a flock of
fheep,

fheep, we don't fay a herd of fheep ; fheep
are little creatures, and Chrift's people may be
called fheep, becaufe they are little in the
eyes of the world, and they are yet lefs in their
own eyes. O fome people think if the great
men were on our fide, if we had king, lords,
and commons on our fide, I mean if they
were all true believers, O if we had all the
kings upon the earth on our fide, fuppofe you
had; alas! alas! do you think the church
would go on the better ? why, if it was fafhionable to be a Methodift at court, if it was
fafhionable to be a Methodift abroad, they
would go with a bible or a hymn-book inftead of a novel; but religion never thrives
under too much fun-fhine. *Not many mighty,*
not many noble are called, but God hath chofen
the foolifh things of the world to confound the
wife, and God hath chofen the weak things of
the world to confound the things which are
mighty. Dr. Watts fays, here and there I fee
a king, and here and there a great man in
heaven, but their number is but fmall.

Sheep are looked upon to be the moft
harmlefs, quiet creatures that God hath made :
O may God, of his infinite mercy, give us
to know that we are his fheep, by our having

this bleſſed temper infuſed into our hearts by the Holy Ghoſt. *Learn of me,* ſaith our bleſſed Lord; what to do, to work miracles? no; *Learn of me, for I am meek and lowly in heart.* A very good man, now living, ſaid once, if there is any one particular temper I deſire more than another, it is the grace of *meekneſs,* quietly to bear bad treatment, to forget and to forgive; and at the ſame time that I am ſenſible I am injured, not to be overcome of evil, but to have grace given me to overcome evil with good. To the honour of Moſes it is declared, that he was the meekeſt man upon earth. Meekneſs is neceſſary for people in power; a man that is paſſionate is dangerous; every governor ſhould have a warm temper, but a man of an unrelenting, unforgiving temper, is no more fit for government than Phaeton to drive the chariot of the ſun, he only ſets the world on fire.

You all know, that ſheep of all creatures in the world are the moſt apt to ſtray and be loſt; Chriſt's people may juſtly, in that reſpect, be compared to ſheep; therefore, in the introduction to our morning ſervice, we ſay, *We have erred and ſtrayed from thy ways like loſt ſheep.* Turn out a horſe, or a dog, and

and they will find their way home, but a fheep wanders about, he bleats here and there, as much as to fay, dear ftranger, fhew me my way home again : thus Chrift's fheep are too apt to wander from the fold; having their eye off the great fhepherd, they go into this field, and that field, over this hedge and that, and often return home with the lofs of their wool.

But at the fame time fheep are the moft ufeful creatures in the world; they manure the land, and thereby prepare it for the feed; they clothe our bodies with wool, and there is not the leaft part of a fheep but is ufeful to man: O my brethren, God grant that you and I may, in this refpect, anfwer the character of fheep. The world fays, becaufe we preach faith we deny good works; this is the ufual objection againft the doctrine of imputed righteoufnefs, but it is a flander, an impudent flander. It was a maxim in the firft reformers time, that tho' the *Arminians* preached up good works, you muft go to the *Calvinifts* for them. Chrift's fheep ftudy to be ufeful, and to clothe all they can; we fhould labour with our hands, that we may have to give to all thofe that need.

Believers

Believers confider Chrift's property in them; he fays, *My fheep:* O bleffed be God for that little, dear, great word *My*. We are his by eternal election: *the fheep which thou haft given me*, fays Chrift. They were given by God the Father to Chrift Jefus, in the covenant made between the Father and the Son from all eternity. They that are not led to fee this, I wifh them better heads; though, I believe, numbers that are againft it have got better hearts: the Lord help us to bear with one another where there is an honeft heart.

He calls them my fheep, they are his by purchafe. O finner, finner, you are come this morning to hear a poor creature take *his laft farewel*; but I want you to forget the creature that is preaching, I want to lead you farther than the Tabernacle; where do you want to lead us? why, to Mount Calvary, there to fee at what an expence of blood Chrift purchafed thofe whom he calls his own; he redeemed them with his own blood, fo that they are not only his by eternal election, but alfo by actual redemption in time; and they were given to him by the Father, upon condition that he fhould redeem them by his heart's blood. It was a hard bargain, but

Chrift

Chrift was willing to ftrike the bargain, that you and I might not be damned for ever.

They are his, becaufe they are enabled in a day of God's power voluntarily to give themfelves up unto him ; Chrift fays of thefe fheep efpecially, that *they hear his voice, and that they follow him.* Will you be fo good as to mind that ? here is an allufion to a fhepherd : now in fome places in fcripture, the fhepherd is reprefented as going after his fheep * ; that is our way in England) but in the Eaftern nations, the fhepherds generally went before ; they held up their crook, and they had a particular call that the fheep underftood. Now, fays Chrift, *My fheep hear my voice. This is my beloved Son,* faith God, *hear ye him.* And again, *the dead fhall hear the voice of the Son of God, and live :* now the queftion is, what do we underftand by hearing Chrift's voice ?

Firft, we hear Mofes' voice, we hear the voice of the law ; there is no going to Mount Zion but by the way of Mount Sinai, that is the right ftraight road. I know fome fay, they don't know when they were converted ; thofe are, I believe, very few : generally, nay I may fay almoft always, God deals otherwife.

Some

* 2 Sam. vii. 8. Pfal. lxxviii. 71.

Some are, indeed, called fooner by the Lord than others, but before they are made to fee the glory of God, they muft hear the voice of the law; fo you muft hear the voice of the law, before ever you will be favingly called unto God. You never throw off your cloak in a ftorm but you hug it the clofer, fo the law makes a man hug clofe his corruptions *; but when the gofpel of the Son of God fhines into their fouls, then they throw off the corruptions which they have hugged fo clofely; they hear his voice faying, Son, daughter, be of good cheer, thy fins, which are many, are all forgiven thee. *They hear his voice;* that befpeaks the habitual temper of their minds: the wicked hear the voice of the devil, the lufts of the flefh, the lufts of the eye, and the pride of life; and Chrift's fheep themfelves attended to them before converfion; but when called afterwards by God, they hear the voice of a Redeemer's blood fpeaking peace unto them, they hear the voice of his word and of his Spirit.

The confequence of hearing his voice, and the proof that we do hear his voice, will be to follow him. Jefus faid unto his difciples,

If

* Rom. vii. 7, 8, 9.

If any man will come after me, let him deny himself, and take up his crofs and follow me. And it is faid of the faints in glory, that *they followed the Lamb whitherfoever he went.* Wherever the fhepherd turns his crook, and the fheep hear his voice, they follow him; they often tread upon one another, and hurt one another, they are in fuch hafte in their way to heaven. Following Chrift, means following him through life, following him in every word and gefture, following him out of one clime into another. *Bid me come to thee upon the water,* faid Peter: and if we are commanded to go over the water for Chrift, God, of his infinite mercy, follow us! We muft firft be fure that the Great Shepherd points his crook for us: but this is the character of a true fervant of Chrift, that he endeavours to follow Chrift in thought, word, and work.

Now, my brethren, before we go farther, as this is the laft opportunity I fhall have of fpeaking to you for fome months if we live; fome of you, I fuppofe, don't chufe in general to rife fo foon as you have this morning; now I hope the world did not get into your hearts before you left your beds; now you are here, do let me intreat you to enquire

L l l   whether

whether you belong to Chrift's fheep or no. Man, woman, finner, put thy hand to thy heart and anfwer me, didft thou ever hear Chrift's voice fo as to follow him, to give up thyfelf without referve to him? I verily do believe from my inmoft foul, and that is my comfort now I am about to take my leave of you, that I am preaching to a vaft body, a multitude of dear, precious fouls, who, if it was proper for you to fpeak, would fay, Thanks be unto God, that we can follow Jefus in the character of fheep, though we are afhamed to think how often we wander from thee, and what little fruit we bring unto thee; if that is the language of your hearts, I wifh you joy; welcome, welcome, dear foul, to Chrift. O bleffed be God for his rich grace, his diftinguifhing, fovereign, electing love, by which he has diftinguifhed you and me. And if he has been pleafed to let you hear his voice, through the miniftration of a poor, miferable finner; a poor, but happy pilgrim, may the Lord Jefus Chrift have all the glory.

If you belong to Jefus Chrift, he is fpeaking of you; for, fays he, *I know my fheep.* I know them, what does that mean? why, he knows their number, he knows their names,

he

he knows every one for whom he died; and if there was to be one miffing for whom Chrift died, God the Father would fend him down again from heaven to fetch him. *Of all,* faith he, *that thou haft given me, have I loft none.* Chrift knows his fheep; he not only knows their number, but the words fpeak the peculiar knowledge and notice he takes of them; he takes as much care of each of them, as if there was but that one fingle fheep in the world. To the hypocrite he faith, *Verily, I know you not*; but he knows his faints, he is acquainted with all their forrows, their trials and temptations; he bottles up all their tears, he knows their domeftic trials, he knows their inward corruptions, he knows all their wanderings, and he takes care to fetch them back again. I remember I heard good Dr. Marryat, who was a good market-language preacher, once fay at Pinner's-hall, (I hope that pulpit will be always filled with fuch preachers) *God has got a great dog to fetch his fheep back,* fays he. Don't you know that when the fheep wander, the fhepherd fends his dog after them to fetch them back again? fo when Chrift's fheep wander, he lets the devil go after them, and fuffers him to bark at them,

who,

who, inftead of driving them farther off, is made a means to bring them back again to Chrift's fold.

There is a precious word I would have you take notice of, *I know them*; that may comfort you under all your trials. We fometimes think that Chrift does not hear our prayers, that he does not know us; we are ready to fufpect that he has forgotten to be gracious; but what a mercy it is that he does know us. We accufe one another, we turn devils to one another, are accufers of the brethren, and what will fupport two of God's people when judged by one another but this, Lord, thou knoweft my integrity, thou knoweft how matters are with me?

But, my brethren, here is fomething better, here is good news for you; what is that? fay you; why, *I give unto them eternal life, and they fhall never perifh, neither fhall any pluck them out of my hand.* O that the words may come to your hearts with as much warmth and power as they did to mine thirty-five years ago. I never prayed againft any corruption I had in my life, fo much as I did againft going into holy orders, fo foon as my friends were for having me go; and bifhop Benfon was

pleafed

pleafed to honour me with peculiar friendfhip, fo as to offer me preferment, or do any thing for me: my friends wanted me to mount the church betimes, they wanted me to knock my head againft the pulpit too young; but how fome young men ftand up here and there and preach, I don't know how it may be to them; but God knows how deep a concern entering into the miniftry and preaching was to me; I have prayed a thoufand times till the fweat has dropped from my face like rain, that God, of his infinite mercy, would not let me enter the church before he called me to, and thruft me forth in his work. I remember once in Gloucefter, I know the room, I look up at the window when I am there and walk along the ftreet; I know the window, the bedfide, and the floor upon which I have laid proftrate: I faid, Lord, I cannot go, I fhall be puffed up with pride, and fall into the condemnation of the devil; Lord, don't let me go yet; I pleaded to be at Oxford two or three years more; I intended to make an hundred and fifty fermons, and thought I would fet up with a good ftock in trade however; but I remember praying, wreftling, and ftri-ving with God; I faid, I am undone, I am

unfit

unfit to preach in thy great name, fend me not, pray, Lord, fend me not yet. I wrote to all my friends in town and country, to pray againft the bifhop's folicitation, but they infifted I fhould go into orders before I was twenty-two. After all their folicitation thefe words came into my mind, *nothing fhall pluck you out of my hand.* O may the words be blefled to you, my dear friends, that I am parting with, as they were to me when they came warm upon my heart; then, and not till then, I faid, Lord, I will go, fend me when thou wilt. I remember when I was in a place called Dover-Ifland, near Georgia, we put in with bad winds; I had an hundred and fifty in family to maintain, and not a fingle farthing to do it with, in the deareft part of the king's dominions; I remember, I told a minifter of Chrift now in heaven, I had thefe words once, fir, *Nothing fhall pluck you out of my hand.* O, fays he, take comfort from them, you may be fure God will be as good as his word, if he never tells you fo again. And our Lord knew his poor fheep would be always doubting they fhould never reach heaven, therefore, fays he, *I give to them eternal life, and they fhall never perifh.*

Here

Here are in our text three bleſſed declarations, or promiſſes:

Firſt. *I know them.*

Second. *They ſhall never periſh;* though
they often think they ſhall periſh by the hand
of their luſts and corruptions ; they think they
ſhall periſh by the deceitfulneſs of their hearts ;
but Chriſt ſays, *they ſhall never periſh.* I have
brought them out of the world to myſelf, and
do you think I will let them go to hell after
that. *I give to them eternal life;* pray mind
that; not I will, but I do. Some talk of being juſtified at the day of judgment, that is
nonſenſe; if we are not juſtified here, we ſhall
not be juſtified there. He gives them eternal
life, that is, the earneſt, the pledge, and aſſurance of it; the indwelling of the Spirit of
God here, is the earneſt of glory hereafter.

Third. *Neither ſhall any pluck them out of
my hand.* He holds them in his hand, that is,
he holds them by his power, none ſhall pluck
them thence ; there is always ſomething pluck-
ing at Chriſt's ſheep, the devil, the luſts of
the fleſh, the luſts of the eye, and the pride
of life, all try to pluck them out of Chriſt's
hand. O my brethren, they need not pluck
us, for we help all three to pluck ourſelves

out of the hand of Jefus; but *none fhall pluck them out of my hand*, fays Chrift. *I give to them eternal life. I am going to heaven to prepare a place for them, and there they fhall be.* O my brethren, if it was not for keeping you too long, and too much exhaufting my own fpirits, I could call upon you to leap for joy; there is not a more bleffed text to fupport the final perfeverance of the faints; and I am aftonifhed any poor foul, and good people I hope too, can fight againft the doctrine of the perfeverance of the faints; what if a perfon fay they fhould perfevere in wickednefs? ah! that is an abufe of the doctrine; what, becaufe fome people fpoil good food, are we never to eat it? But, my brethren, upon this text I can leave my cares, all my friends, and all Chrift's fheep to the protection of Chrift Jefus's never-failing love.

I thought this morning, when I came here riding from the other end of the town, it was to me like coming to be executed publicly; and when the carriage turned juft at the end of the walk, and I faw you running here, O thinks I, it is like a perfon now coming juft to the place where he is to be executed: when I went up to put on my gown, I thought it

was

was juft like dreffing myfelf to be made a public fpectacle to fhed my blood for Chrift; and
I take all heaven and earth to witnefs, and
God and the holy angels to witnefs, that tho'
I had preferment enough offered me, that tho'
the bifhop took me in his arms, and offered
me two parifhes when I was but twenty-two
years old, and always took me to his table;
though I had preferment enough offered me
when I was ordained, thou, O God, knoweft,
that when the bifhop put his hand upon my
head, I looked for no other preferment than
publickly to fuffer for the Lamb of God: in
this fpirit I came out, in this fpirit I came
up to this metropolis. I was thinking when
I read of Jacob's going over the brook with a
ftaff, that I would not fay fo much, but I
came up without a friend, I went to Oxford
without a friend, I had not a fervant, I had
not any one to introduce me; but God, by
his Holy Spirit, was pleafed to raife me up
to preach for his great name's fake: through
his Divine Spirit I continue to this day, and
feel my affections are as ftrong as ever towards
the work, and the people of the living God.
The congregations at both ends of the town
are dear to me: God has honoured me to

M m m

build

build this and the other place; and, bleſſed be his name, as he called me to Georgia at firſt, and I left all London affairs to God's care, when I had moſt of the churches in London open for me, and had twelve or fourteen con-ftables to keep the doors, that people might not crowd too much; I had offers of hundreds then to fettle in London, yet I gave it up for God, to go into a foreign clime; and I hope with that fame fingle intention I am going now.

When I came from America laſt, I thought I had no other river to paſs over but the ri-ver Jordan, I remember I told you ſo; and as the orphan-houfe was then to be given, I thought, out of my hands, I then intended to retire into fome little corner, and pray when I could not preach, my ſpirits were ſo low, and my nerves and animal frame ſo weak, but God, of his infinite mercy, has renewed my ftrength, and is pleafed to raife my ſpirits, ſo that I find my heart is willing to go here or there, wherever God fhall call.

The orphan-houfe being turned into a col-lege is a matter of great confequence; you that have not been in America can't tell, but I heartily wifh, I am neither a prophet, nor
the

the fon of a prophet, and I hope none of us
will ever be driven to America for an afylum,
where God's people were driven from this land
an hundred years ago: clouds are growing
thick, and if a fpirit of moderation does not
prevail among governors and governed, what
but confufion muft happen to perfons who
ftrive one with another, and are making fport
for the devil by deftroying one another ? may
the great and gracious God avert every im-
pending ftorm; and by diffufing a fpirit of
moderation and of a found mind, and by
keeping his people clofe to himfelf, avert
thofe ftorms, thofe terrible judgments, that
we have reafon to expect from our repeated
provocations. I am going now to fettle the
orphan-houfe upon a proper bafis; I go now
in the fall, that I may be in Georgia in the
winter, which is fine weather there. The
twenty-fifth of March is the anniverfary of the
day on which I laid the firft brick of the
orphan-houfe; by that time, I hope, all the
buildings will be finifhed, and the plantation
fettled; and then I hope to go and preach
along the continent to New-England, and
from thence I intend, if God permit me, to

return

return to my dear London and Englifh friends again.

I have blefled news from the orphan-houfe; one writes me word, Would to God you could fend a thoufand fuch as you have fent, Mr. Dixon, and his wife, that have been old fervants there; Mr. Wright, Mr. Crayne, and Mr. Wright's brother, and thofe that have been employed with them to carry on the work of the Lord; and I cannot think but God intends to lay a foundation for a blefled feminary for Chrift: Lord Jefus, hear our prayers upon that account.

Now I muft come to the hardeft part I have to act: I was afraid when I came out from home, that I could not bear the fhock, but I hope the Lord Jefus Chrift will help me to bear it, and help you to give me up to the blefled God, let him do with me what he will. This is the thirteenth time of my crofling the mighty waters; it is a little difficult at this time of life; and though my fpirits are improved in fome degree, yet weaknefs is the beft of my ftrength: but I delight in the caufe, and God fills me with a peace that is unutterable, which nobody knows, and a ftranger intermeddles not with: into

his

his hands I commend my fpirit; and I beg that this may be the language of your hearts, Lord, keep him, let nothing pluck him out of thy hands. I expect many a trial while I am on board, fatan always meets me there; but that God which has kept me, I believe will keep me. I thank God, I have the ho-nour of leaving every thing quite well and eafy at both ends of the town; and, my dear hearers, my prayers to God fhall be, that no-thing may pluck you out of Chrift's hands. Witnefs againft me, if I ever fet up a party for myfelf; did ever any minifter, or could any minifter in the world fay, that I ever fpoke againft any one going to any dear mi-nifter? I thank God, that he has enabled me to be always ftrengthning the hands of all, though fome have afterwards been afhamed to own me. I declare to you, that I believe God will be with me, and will ftrengthen me; and I believe it is in anfwer to your prayers, that God is pleafed to revive my fpirits: may the Lord help you to pray on. If I am drowned in the waves I will fay, Lord, take care of my London, take care of my Englifh friends, let nothing pluck them out of thy hands.

And

And as Chrift has given us eternal life, O my brethren, fome of you, I doubt not, will be gone to him before my return; but, my dear brethren, my dear hearers, never mind that; we fhall part, but it will be to meet again forever. I dare not meet you now, I can't bear your coming to me to part from me, it cuts me to the heart and quite overcomes me, but by and by all parting will be over, and all tears fhall be wiped away from our eyes. God grant that none that weep now at my parting, may weep at our meeting at the day of judgment; and if you never were among Chrift's fheep before, may Chrift Jefus bring you now. O come, come, fee what it is to have eternal life; don't refufe it; hafte, finner, hafte away: may the great, the good fhepherd, draw your fouls. Oh! if you never heard his voice before, God grant you may hear it now; that I may have this comfort when I am gone that I had laft, that fome fouls are awakened at the parting fermon. O that it may be a farewel fermon to you; that it may be a means of your taking a farewel of the world, the lufts of the flefh, the lufts of the eye, and the pride of life.

O come,

O come, come, come, to the Lord Jesus Christ; to him I leave you.

And you, dear sheep, that are already in his hands, O may God keep you from wandering; God keep you near Christ's feet; I don't care what shepherds keep you, so as you are kept near the great shepherd and bishop of souls. The Lord God keep you, lift up the light of his countenance upon you, and give you peace. Amen.

F I N I S.

☞ Thefe SERMONS being entered in the Hall-Book of the Company of Stationers, whoever prefumes to pirate them will be profecuted.

CPSIA information can be obtained
at www.ICGtesting.com
Printed in the USA
LVHW01s0026210118
563312LV00001B/86/P